THE AMERICAN NEGRO

HIS HISTORY AND LITERATURE

THE
FREEDMEN'S BOOK

L. Maria Child

ARNO PRESS and THE NEW YORK TIMES

NEW YORK 1968

General Editor
WILLIAM LOREN KATZ

THE CIVIL WAR PRODUCED ONE OF THE greatest social revolutions in American history. Four million slaves were liberated; two hundred thousand black men from Southern plantations and Northern cities fought for Union and freedom; civil and political equality for all Americans, regardless of color, were guaranteed by the constitutional amendments that followed the war. Unfortunately, the post-Civil War generation saw the recrudescence of a quasislavery in the South that betrayed the promise of freedom and whose unhappy consequences are still with us today. But in one area—education—the Civil War generation made a lasting contribution to racial progress. During and after the war, abolitionists, philanthropists, and churches in the North, aided by the Freedmen's Bureaus, established dozens of freedmen's education societies, founded hundreds of schools for the ex-slaves, and sent thousands of teachers South to bring literacy to the black masses. The freedmen's schools represented the real beginning of Negro education in this country. They trained the black leaders of subsequent generations, and out of these early schools grew such important institutions as Howard, Fisk, and Atlanta Universities, Morehouse and Spelman Colleges, Meharray Medical School, Hampton Institute, and many other Negro colleges and universities.

Lydia Maria Child, a white abolitionist who in 1833 had given up a promising career as a novelist and writer of children's stories to cast her lot with the persecuted advocates of black freedom, published *The Freedmen's Book* in 1865 as a textbook for the freedmen's schools. This interesting volume contains a miscellany of essays, short biographies, poems, anecdotes, and household hints, many of them written by Mrs. Child herself. There are stories about Toussaint L'Ouverture, Benjamin Banneker, Phillis Wheatley, Frederick Douglass and other black heroes whose careers were a source of pride and inspiration for young freedmen. Essays and anecdotes about slavery and the abolition movement were included to acquaint students with events in American history directly relevant to their present situation. Because many of the pupils in freedmen's schools were adults whose experiences in slavery had provided little training for the responsibilities of freedom, Mrs. Child sprinkled the book with advice on home economics, the raising of children, rules of good health, habits of industry and morality, and the like. *The Freedmen's Book* is of value to the modern reader not only for the intrinsic interest of its contents, but also for its portrayal of the reading material used in advanced classes of freedmen's schools. It was a part of the beginnings of Negro education, and helps us understand the nature of that great social movement.

James M. McPherson
DEPARTMENT OF HISTORY
PRINCETON UNIVERSITY

THE

FREEDMEN'S BOOK.

By L. MARIA CHILD.

O dark, sad millions, — patiently and dumb
Waiting for God, — your hour, at last, has come,
    And Freedom's song
Breaks the long silence of your night of wrong.
                    JOHN G. WHITTIER.

BOSTON:
TICKNOR AND FIELDS.
1865.

UNIVERSITY PRESS : WELCH, BIGELOW, & CO.,
CAMBRIDGE.

TO THE FREEDMEN.

I HAVE prepared this book expressly for you, with the hope that those of you who can read will read it aloud to others, and that all of you will derive fresh strength and courage from this true record of what colored men have accomplished, under great disadvantages.

I have written all the biographies over again, in order to give you as much information as possible in the fewest words. I take nothing for my services; and the book is sold to you at the cost of paper, printing, and binding. Whatever money you pay for any of the volumes will be immediately invested in other volumes to be sent to freedmen in various parts of the country, on the same terms; and whatever money remains in my hands, when the book ceases to sell, will be given to the Freedmen's Aid Association, to be expended in schools for you and your children.

Your old friend,

L. MARIA CHILD.

CONTENTS.

——◆——

* The names of the colored authors are marked with an asterisk.

THE FREEDMEN'S BOOK.

IGNATIUS SANCHO.

BY L. MARIA CHILD.

THIS was the name of a remarkable African, who excited a good deal of interest in his day. His father and mother were stolen from Africa and put on board a slave-ship in 1729, which was one hundred and thirty-six years ago. He was born during the passage, and when the vessel arrived at Carthagena, in South America, he was baptized by the name of Ignatius. His mother died soon after, and his father, seeing no means of escape from slavery, killed himself in a fit of despair. The man who took possession of the little orphan, and claimed to be his master, carried him to England, and gave him to three unmarried sisters who lived at Greenwich. He was then about two years old, a bright, lively, funny little creature. As he grew older, he showed such an inquisitive mind, said so many droll things, and was so full of mischief, that the ladies named him Sancho, after a very comical character in a famous old Spanish novel. He was very eager in the pursuit of knowledge; but this commendable disposition was not approved by the ladies. They thought that all a black servant had occasion to know was how to obey orders, and that it was not necessary or proper for him to learn to read and write. But nature had given Ignatius a very lively

1

mind, and a very susceptible heart, and neither of them could be kept quiet. He early plunged into love affairs, and was always overrunning with fun and frolic. Doubtless he was a great trial to the respectable maiden ladies, who were training him for a servant; and·he, on his part, thought them very sour, severe, and disagreeable. Sometimes, when they were angry with him, they reminded him that he had been a slave, and threatened to send him into slavery again. This excited uneasiness in his mind, and kindled resentment.

The Duke of Montagu lived in the neighborhood, and his attention was attracted by the bright, frank countenance of the black boy. He entered into conversation with him occasionally, and was so much struck by his intelligence and wit, that he told the ladies their servant was a remarkable lad, and that his earnest desire to improve his mind ought to be gratified. They persisted in their opinion that knowledge was a very improper and dangerous thing for a black servant. But the Duke introduced him to the Duchess, and they both encouraged him to learn to read and write. They lent him books, and were greatly entertained by his bright remarks concerning what he read.

It was a great grief to Ignatius when the friendly Duke died. He besought the Duchess to receive him into her service, and she consented. He remained in her household as long as she lived. At her death, she left him an annuity of about one hundred and fifty dollars a year; and he had three hundred and fifty dollars, which he had laid up from his wages. He might have made this sum the foundation of a comfortable little property. But nature had made him very full of fun and frolic. He had such lively manners, and uttered so many pleasant jokes, that his company was much sought for. This proved a temptation too strong for him. He accepted invitations to go to taverns, where he gambled away his earnings. He had a great passion for going to the theatre; and his conduct with regard to women was far from being correct.

But he soon saw the error of his ways, and resolved to reform. He went to the Chaplain of Montagu House, and begged to be taken into his service, where he remained several months. The descendants of his old friend, the Duke, encouraged him to persevere in his good resolutions; and when the young Duke saw that he continued sober and industrious, he took him into his employ. By the blessing of the Heavenly Father, another saving influence came to help him into the paths of virtue. He formed a serious attachment for a very worthy young woman from the West Indies, to whom he was soon after married. He remained in the employ of the Duke of Montagu until he was about forty-four years old. Frequent attacks of the gout, and clumsiness resulting from an hereditary tendency to corpulence, rendered him unfit to continue in the service to which he had so long been accustomed. His good friend and patron the Duke assisted him to establish a small shop for groceries. By economy and industry, he and his good wife managed to rear and educate well a numerous family of children.

He always retained his love of learning, and was such a diligent reader, that he was well acquainted with the current literature of that time. He was treated with respect and attention by many intelligent and educated people. Though not so full of fun as he was in his younger days, his conversation was entertaining. The letters he wrote to various persons abound with good sense, and show that he was very affectionate and devoted as a husband and father. He evidently regarded his wife as the best blessing of his life. In one of his letters to a friend he says: "The hot weather does not befriend Mrs. Sancho, but time will, I hope. If true worth could plead exemption from pain and sickness, she would, by right divine, enjoy the best of health." On another occasion he writes: "I can compare her to nothing so properly as a diamond in the dirt. But, my friend, that is Fortune's fault, not mine; for had I the power, I would case her in gold." Years later, he writes: "Dame Sancho would be better in health, if she cared less. I am her barometer. If a sigh escapes me, it is answered by a tear in her eye. I often assume gayety to illume her dear sensibility with a smile, which twenty years ago almost bewitched me, and which still constitutes my highest pleasure. May such be your lot, my friend. What more can friendship wish you than to glide down the stream of time with a partner of congenial principles and fine feelings, whose very looks speak tenderness and sentiment."

After a severe illness he wrote to a friend: "I had excruciating pains and great lack of patience. Mrs. Sancho had a week of it. Gout did not sweeten my temper. It was washing week, and she had to attend the shop. God bless her, and reward her. She is good; good in heart, good in principle, good by habit."

The children appear to have been the delight of his heart. He called them "Sanchonettas," which would be the Italian way of saying Little Sanchos. He was never tired of describing their little winning ways. At the end of a letter to one of his friends he wrote: "Lydia trots about amazingly; and Kitty imitates her, with this addition, that she is as mischievous as a monkey." But little William, his youngest, was evidently his pet. To another of his friends he wrote: "You cannot imagine what hold little Billy gets of me. He grows, he prattles, every day he learns something new. The rogue is fond of me to excess. By his good-will he would be always in the shop with me. The little monkey! He clings round my legs; and if I chide him, or look sour, he holds up his little mouth to kiss me."

Ignatius Sancho had a very kind heart. It hurt his feelings very much to see any animal tormented. He tried to get some laws passed to prevent cruel market-men from abusing their donkeys; and he always tried to be a friend to everybody that was in distress. In one of his letters he says: "The joy of giving and of making happy is almost the attribute of a god. There is as much sweetness conveyed to the senses by doing a right good-natured deed as our frame can consistently bear."

Such a disposition is better than a remarkable intellect. But he had a quick intellect also, and generally took sensible views of things. Writing to a young colored friend, who had been somewhat wild, he says: —

"Look round upon the miserable fate of almost all of our unfortunate color. See slavery added to ignorance. See the contempt of the very wretches who roll in affluence from our labors. Hear the ill-bred, heart-racking abuse of the ignorant vulgar. If you tread as cautiously as the strictest rectitude can guide you, you must suffer from this. But if you are armed with truth and conscious integrity, you will be sure of the plaudits and countenance of the good.

"You are a happy lad. You have kind benefactors,

to whom you ought to look up with reverence, and humbly beg the Almighty to give you strength to imitate them in doing good. Your parts are as quick as most men's. If you urge your speed in the race of virtue with the same zeal you have exhibited in error, you will recover, to the satisfaction of your noble patrons, and to the glory of yourself.

"Some philosopher, whose name I forget, wished for a window in his breast, that the world might see his heart. I recommend him to your imitation. Vice is a coward. To be truly brave, a man must be truly good. You hate the name of cowardice; then detest a lie and shun liars. Be above revenge. If others have taken advantage either of your guilt or your distress, punish them only with forgiveness ; and if you can serve them at any future time, do it.

"I sincerely congratulate thee upon thy repentance. It is thy birthday to real happiness."

To one of the white gentlemen who liked to correspond with him, he wrote : —

"There is something so amazingly grand and affecting in contemplating the works of the Divine Architect, either in the moral or the intellectual world, that I think one may rightly call it the cordial of the soul, the best antidote against pride and discontent. The friendly warmth of that glorious planet the sun, the leniency of the air, the cheerful glow of the atmosphere, make me involuntarily cry, 'Lord, what is man, that thou, in thy mercy, art so mindful of him? or what is the son of man, that thou so parentally carest for him?'

"Sometimes, when I endeavor to turn my thoughts inward, to review the powers or properties the indulgent all-wise Father has endowed me with, I am struck with wonder and with awe; poor, insignificant worm as I am, in comparison with superior beings, mortal like myself. At the head of our riches I reckon the power of reflection. Where doth it lie? Search every member, from the toe to the nose, — they are all ready for action, but they are all dead to thought. It is that breath of life which the Sacred Architect breathed into the nostrils of the first man. We feel and acknowledge it, but it is quite past the power of definition. Then to think of the promise of never-ending existence! To rise, perhaps, by regular progression from planet to planet, to behold the wonders of immensity, to pass from good to better, increasing in goodness, in knowledge, in love. To glory in our Redeemer, to joy in ourselves, to be acquainted with prophets, sages, heroes, and poets of old times, and to join in the symphony with angels."

To a white young friend, who had obtained a situation in India, he wrote : —

"It is with sincere pleasure I hear you have a lucrative establishment. Your good sense will naturally lead you to a proper economy, as distant from frigid parsimony as from heedless extravagance. As you may have some time for recreation, give me leave to obtrude my poor advice. I have heard it more than once observed of fortunate adventurers, that they come home rich in purse, but wretchedly barren in intellect. My dear Jack, the mind wants food as well as the stomach. Why, then, should not one wish to increase in knowledge as well as in money? The poet Young says, —

'Books are fair Virtue's advocates and friends.'

My advice to you is, to lay by something every year to buy a little library. You have to thank God for strong natural parts; you have a feeling, humane heart; you write with sense and discernment. Improve yourself, my dear Jack. Then if it should please God to return you to your friends with a fortune, the embellishments of your mind may be ever considered as greatly superior to your riches, and only inferior to the goodness of your heart. This is a good old adage : 'A few books and a few friends, and those well chosen.'"

The same young friend wrote a letter to his father, from Bombay, in India, in which he wrote : "The inhabitants here, who are chiefly blacks, are a set of canting, deceitful people, of whom one must have great caution."

Ignatius Sancho was always ready to defend the despised and the oppressed, and his sympathy was all the more lively if they were of his own color. He at once wrote to his young friend : —

"In one of your letters to your father, you speak with honest indignation of the treachery and chicanery of the natives of India. My good friend, you should remember from whom they learned those vices. The first visitors from Christian countries found them a simple, harmless people. But the cursed avidity for wealth urged those first visitors, and all the succeeding ones, to such acts of deception and wanton cruelty, that the poor, ignorant natives soon learned their knavish arts, and turned them upon their teachers. As a resident of your country, Old England, I love it. I love it for its freedom. For the many blessings I enjoy in it England shall ever have my warmest wishes, prayers, and blessings. But I must observe, and I say it with reluctance, that the conduct of your country has been uniformly wicked in the East Indies, in the West Indies, and on the coast of Guinea. The grand object of English navigators, and indeed of all the navigators of Christian nations, has been money, money,

money. Commerce was meant by the goodness of Deity to diffuse the various goods of the earth into every part; to unite mankind with the blessed bonds of brotherly love and mutual dependence. Enlightened Christians should diffuse the riches of the Gospel of Peace together with the commodities of their respective lands. If commerce were attended with strict honesty and religion for companions, it would be a blessing to every shore it touched at.

"The poor wretched Africans are blessed with a most fertile and luxuriant soil; but they are rendered miserable by what Providence meant for a blessing. The abominable traffic in slaves, and the horrid cruelty and treachery of the petty kings, is encouraged by their Christian customers. They carry them strong liquors, powder, and bad fire-arms to inflame them to madness, and to furnish them with the hellish means of killing and kidnapping. It is a subject that sours my blood. I mention these things to guard my friend from being too hasty in condemning a people who have been made much worse by their Christian visitors.

"Wherever thou residest, make human nature thy study. Whatever may be the religion or the complexion of men, study their hearts. Let simplicity, kindness, and charity be thy guides; and with these, even savages will respect you, while God will bless you."

The writings of the Rev. Laurence Sterne, who was living in England at that time, were well calculated to inspire humanity toward animals and kindly feelings toward the poor. These writings were very popular, and two of the characters conspicuous in them, called Uncle Toby and Corporal Trim, were great favorites with the public. Ignatius Sancho especially delighted in the writings of Sterne; and in 1776, when he was about

1 *

forty-seven years old, he addressed a letter to him as
follows : —

"REVEREND SIR, — It would perhaps look like an insult upon your humanity to apologize for the liberty I
am taking. I am one of those people whom the vulgar
and illiberal call ' Negurs.' The first part of my life was
rather unlucky, as I was placed in a family who judged
ignorance to be the best and only security for obedience.
By unwearied application I got a little reading and writing. Through God's blessing, the latter part of my life
has been truly fortunate, for I have spent it in the service
of one of the best families in the kingdom. My chief
pleasure has been books. How very much, good sir, am
I, among millions, indebted to you for the character of
your amiable Uncle Toby! I declare I would walk ten
miles, in dog-days, to shake hands with the honest Corporal. Your sermons have touched me to the heart, and I
hope have amended it. In your tenth discourse I find
this very affecting passage : ' Consider how great a part
of our species, in all ages, down to this, have been trodden under the feet of cruel and capricious tyrants, who
would neither hear their cries nor pity their distresses.
Consider Slavery, what a bitter draught it is, and how
many millions are made to drink of it.'

"I am sure you will forgive me if I beseech you to
give some attention to Slavery, as it is practised at this
day in the West Indies. That subject, handled in your
striking manner, would perhaps ease the yoke of many ;
but if only of one, what a feast for a benevolent heart !
and sure I am, you are an Epicurean * in acts of charity.

* Epicureans were the followers of a philosopher in ancient Greece
who taught that pleasure was the great object in life, — an excellent
doctrine, if confined to the highest kind of pleasure, which consists in
doing good.

You, who are universally read and as universally admired, could not fail. Dear sir, think that in me you behold the uplifted hands of thousands of my brother Moors. You pathetically observe that grief is eloquent. Figure to yourself their attitudes, hear their supplications, and you cannot refuse."

Mr. Sterne wrote the following reply : —

"July 27th, 1766.

"There is a strange coincidence, Sancho, in the little events of this world, as well as the great ones. I had been writing a tender tale of the sorrows of a poor, friendless negro girl, and my eyes had scarce done smarting with it, when your letter, in behalf of so many of her brethren and sisters, came to me. But why *her* brethren or *your* brethren, Sancho, any more than *mine*? It is by the finest tints, and the most insensible gradations, that nature descends from the fairest face to the sootiest complexion. At which of these tints are the ties of blood to cease? and how many shades lower in the scale must we descend, ere mercy is to vanish with them?

" It is no uncommon thing, my good Sancho, for one half of the world to *use* the other half like brutes, and then endeavor to *make* them so. For my part, I never look Westward, when I am in a pensive mood, without thinking of the burdens our brothers and sisters are there carrying. If I could ease their shoulders from one ounce of them, I declare I would this hour set out upon a pilgrimage to Mecca for their sakes. It casts a sad shade upon the world, that so great a part of it are, and have so long been, bound in chains of darkness and chains of misery. I cannot but respect you and felicitate you, that by so much laudable diligence you have broken the

chains of darkness, and that by falling into the hands of
so good and merciful a family, you have been rescued by
Providence from the chains of misery.

"And so, good-hearted Sancho, adieu. Believe me, I
will not forget your letter.

"Yours,
"LAURENCE STERNE."

The last sickness of Ignatius Sancho was very painful, but he was tenderly cared for by his good wife. He
was fifty-two years old when he died. After his death,
a small volume was published, containing a number of his
letters, some articles he had written for newspapers, and
an engraved likeness of him, which looks very bright and
good-natured. The book was published by subscription,
in which a large number of the English nobility and
some distinguished literary men joined.

EXTRACT FROM THE TENTH PSALM.

"THE wicked in his pride doth persecute the poor. He
hath said in his heart, God hath forgotten; He hideth his
face; He will never see it. Thou *hast* seen it; for thou
beholdest mischief and spite, to requite it with thy hand.
The poor committeth himself unto thee; thou art the
helper of the fatherless. Lord, thou hast heard the desire
of the humble. Thou wilt cause thine ear to hear; thou
wilt prepare their heart to judge the fatherless and the
oppressed, that the man of the earth may no more oppress."

PREJUDICE REPROVED.

BY LYDIA H. SIGOURNEY.

GOD gave to Afric's sons
  A brow of sable dye;
And spread the country of their birth
  Beneath a burning sky.

With a cheek of olive He made
  The little Hindoo child;
And darkly stained the forest tribes,
  That roam our Western wild.

To me He gave a form
  Of fairer, whiter clay;
But am I, therefore, in his sight,
  Respected more than they?

No; — 't is the hue of *deeds* and *thoughts*
  He traces in his book;
'T is the complexion of the *heart*
  On which He deigns to look.

Not by the tinted cheek,
  That fades away so fast,
But by the color of the *soul*,
  We shall be judged at last.

BENJAMIN BANNEKER.

BY L. MARIA CHILD.

THIS remarkable man was born near the village of Ellicott's Mills, Baltimore County, Maryland, in 1732. That was one hundred and thirty-three years ago, when there were very few schools and very few books in this country, and when it was not as easy as it now is for even white people to obtain a tolerably good education. His parents were both black, and though they were free, they were too poor to do much for their bright boy. They sent him to a school in the neighborhood, where he learned reading and writing and a little of arithmetic.

His father was a slave at the time of his marriage, but his wife was a free woman; and she was so energetic and industrious, that she soon earned money enough to buy his freedom. Then they worked together, and earned enough to buy a few acres of land, and build a small cabin.

Benjamin was obliged to labor diligently when he was at home from school, but every spare moment he could catch he was ciphering, and planning how to make things. As his parents grew old, he had to work early and late, to support himself and help them. His mother always continued active enough to do the in-door work. When she was seventy years old, if she wanted to catch a chicken she would run it down without appearing to be tired. The place was thinly peopled, and the few neighbors they had took no particular notice of Benjamin, though he had the name of being a bright, industrious lad. His hands worked hard, but his brain was always busy. He was particularly fond of arithmetic, and was always working out sums in his head. He took notice of everything around him, observed how everything was made, and never forgot one word of what he had learned at school. In this way, he came to have more knowledge than most of his white neighbors; and they began to say to one another, "That black Ben is a smart fellow. He can make anything he sets out to; and how much he knows! I wonder where he picked it all up."

At thirty years old, he made a clock, which proved an excellent timepiece. He had never seen a clock, for nobody in that region had such an article; but he had seen a watch, and it occupied his thoughts very much. It seemed to him such a curious little machine, that he was very desirous to make something like it. The watch was made of gold and silver and steel; but Benjamin Banneker had only wood for material, and the rudest kind of tools to work with. It was a long while before he could make the hand that marked the hours, and the hand that marked the minutes, and the hand that marked the seconds, correspond exactly in their motions; but by perseverance he succeeded at last. He was then about thirty years old. This was the first clock ever made in this country. It kept time exactly, and people began to talk about it as a wonderful thing for a man to do without instruction. After a while, the Ellicott family, who owned the Mills, heard of it, and went to see it. Mr. Elias Ellicott, a merchant in Baltimore, became very much interested in the self-taught machinist. He lent him a number of books, among which were some on astronomy, — a science which treats of the sun, moon, and stars. Banneker was so interested in this new knowledge that he could think of nothing else. He sat up all night to watch the planets, and to make calculations about their motions. Mr. Ellicott went to see him to explain to him how to use some of the tables for calculations contained in the books he had lent him; but he found, to his great surprise, that the earnest student had studied them all out himself, and had no need of help. It was not long before he could calculate when the sun or the moon would be eclipsed, and at what time every star would rise and set. He was never known to make a mistake in any of his astronomical calculations; and he became so exact, that he pointed out two mistakes made by celebrated astronomers in Europe.

In order to pursue his favorite studies without interruption, he sold the land which his parents had left him, and bought an annuity with the money, on which he lived in the little cabin where he was born. He was so temperate and frugal, that he needed very little to support him; and when it was necessary to have more than his annuity, he could always earn something by going out to work. But, as he was no longer seen in the fields late and early, his ignorant white neighbors began to talk against him. They peeped into his cabin and saw him asleep in the daytime. They did not know that he had been awake all night watching the stars, and ciphering out his calculations. In fact, they did not know that the planets moved at all; and if he had told them that he could calculate their movements exactly, they would only have laughed at him. I suppose they felt some ill-will toward him because he was black, and yet knew so much more than they did; and perhaps it excited their envy that the Ellicott family and other educated gentlemen liked to go to his cabin and talk with him about his studies and observations.

But Banneker was wise enough not to enter into any quarrels because they called him a lazy, good-for-nothing fellow. He endeavored to live in such a way that they could not help respecting him. He was always kind and generous, ready to oblige everybody, and not at all inclined to boast of his superiority.

When he was fifty-nine years old, he made an Almanac. It is a very difficult job to calculate all about the changes of the moon, and the rising and ebbing of the tides, and at what time the sun will rise and set every day, all the year round; and it was a much more difficult task then than it is now; because now there is a great improvement in astronomical books and instruments. But notwithstanding Banneker's limited means and scanty education, he made an excellent Almanac. It was published by Goddard and Angell of Baltimore. In a Preface, they say: "We feel gratified to have an opportunity of presenting to the public, through our press, what must be considered an extraordinary effort of genius, — a complete and accurate Ephemeris* for the year 1792, calculated by a sable son of Africa. It has met the approbation of several of the most distinguished astronomers of America; and we hope a philanthropic public will give their support to the work, not only on account of its intrinsic merit, but from a desire to controvert the long-established illiberal prejudice against the blacks."

This was the first Almanac ever made in this country. It contained much useful information of a general nature, and interesting selections in prose and verse. Before it

_____
* A daily journal of the state of the planets.

was printed, Banneker sent a manuscript copy, in his
own handwriting, to Thomas Jefferson, then Secretary
of State, and afterward President of the United States.
After apologizing for the liberty he took in addressing a
person whose station was so far above his own, he says: —

"Those of my complexion have long been considered
rather brutish than human, — scarcely capable of mental
endowments.   But, in consequence of the reports that
have reached me, I hope I may safely admit that you
are measurably friendly and well-disposed toward us.
I trust that you agree with me in thinking that one
Universal Father hath given being to us all; that He
has not only made us all of one flesh, but has also, without partiality, afforded us all the same sensations, and
endowed us all with the same faculties; and that, however various we may be in society or religion, however
diversified in situation or color, we are all of the same
family, and all stand in the same relation to Him.   Now,
sir, if this is founded in truth, I apprehend you will
readily embrace every opportunity to eradicate the absurd and false ideas and opinions which so generally
prevail with respect to us.

"Suffer me, sir, to recall to your mind, that when the
tyranny of the British crown was exerted to reduce you
to servitude, your abhorrence thereof was so excited, that
you publicly held forth this true and invaluable doctrine,
worthy to be recorded and remembered in all succeeding
ages: 'We hold these truths to be self-evident, that all
men are created equal, and that they are endowed by
their Creator with certain inalienable rights; that among
these are life, liberty, and the pursuit of happiness.'

"Your tender feelings for yourselves engaged you thus
to declare.   You were then impressed with proper ideas

of the great value of Liberty, and the free possession of those blessings to which you were entitled by nature. But, sir, how pitiable it is to reflect that, although you were so fully convinced of the benevolence of the Father of mankind, and of his equal and impartial distribution of those rights and privileges which He had conferred upon them, that you should at the same time counteract his mercies in detaining, by fraud and violence, so numerous a part of my brethren under groaning captivity and cruel oppression; that you should at the same time be found guilty of that most criminal act which you detested in others with respect to yourselves.

"Sir, I freely and most cheerfully acknowledge that I am of the African race; and in that color which is natural to them I am of the deepest dye. But, with a sense of most profound gratitude to the Supreme Ruler of the universe, I confess that I am not under that state of tyrannical thraldom and inhuman captivity to which so many of my brethren are doomed. I have abundantly tasted of those blessings which proceed from that free and unequalled liberty with which you are favored.

"Sir, I suppose your knowledge of the situation of my brethren is too extensive for it to need a recital here. Neither shall I presume to prescribe methods by which they may be relieved, otherwise than by recommending to you and others to wean yourselves from those narrow prejudices you have imbibed with respect to them, and to do as Job proposed to his friends, — 'Put *your* souls in *their* souls' stead.' Thus shall your hearts be enlarged with kindness and benevolence toward them, and you will need neither the direction of myself nor others in what manner to proceed.

"I took up my pen to direct to you, as a present, a

copy of an Almanac I have calculated for the succeeding
year. I ardently hope that your candor and generosity
will plead with you in my behalf. Sympathy and affection for my brethren has caused my enlargement thus far;
it was not originally my design.

"The Almanac is the production of my arduous study.
I have long had unbounded desires to become acquainted
with the secrets of Nature, and I have had to gratify my
curiosity herein through my own assiduous application to
astronomical study; in which I need not recount to you
the many difficulties and disadvantages I have had to en-
counter. I conclude by subscribing myself, with the most
profound respect, your most humble servant,

"B. BANNEKER."

To this letter Jefferson made the following reply : —

"SIR, — I thank you sincerely for your letter, and for
the Almanac it contained. Nobody wishes more than I
do to see such proofs as you exhibit that Nature has given
to our black brethren talents equal to those of the other
colors of men, and that the appearance of a want of them
is owing only to the degraded condition of their existence,
both in Africa and America. I can add, with truth, that
no one wishes more ardently to see a good system com-
menced for raising the condition, both of their body and
mind, to what it ought to be, as fast as the imbecility of
their present existence, and other circumstances which
cannot be neglected, will admit. I have taken the liberty
of sending your Almanac to Monsieur Condorcet, Secretary of the Academy of Sciences at Paris, and to members of the Philanthropic Society, because I considered
it a document to which your whole color had a right, for
their justification against the doubts which have been

entertained of them. I am, with great esteem, sir, your most obedient servant,

"THOMAS JEFFERSON."

In 1803, Mr. Jefferson invited the astronomer to visit him at Monticello, but the increasing infirmities of age made it imprudent to undertake the journey. His Almanacs sold well for ten years, and the income, added to his annuity, gave him a very comfortable support; and what was a still greater satisfaction to him was the consciousness of doing something to help the cause of his oppressed people, by proving to the world that Nature had endowed them with good capacities.

After 1802 he found himself too old to calculate any more Almanacs, but as long as he lived he continued to be deeply interested in his various studies.

He was well informed on many other subjects besides arithmetic and astronomy. He was a great reader of history; and he kept a Journal, which shows that he was a close observer of the vegetable world, of the habits of insects, and of the operations of Nature in general. That his busy mind drew inferences from what he observed is evident from the following entry in his Journal: —

"Standing at my door to-day, I heard the discharge of a gun, and in four or five seconds of time the small shots came rattling about me, which plainly demonstrates that the velocity of sound is greater than that of a common bullet."

After the Constitution of the United States was adopted, in 1789, commissioners were appointed to determine the boundaries of the District of Columbia. They invited Banneker to be present and assist them in running the lines; and he was treated by them with as much respect as if he had been of their own color. His Almanacs were much praised by scientific men, and they often visited him in his humble little cabin. But these attentions never made him pert and vain. He rejoiced in his abilities and acquisitions, because he thought they might help to raise the condition of his oppressed brethren; but he always remained modest and unobtrusive in his manners.

He died in 1804, in the seventy-second year of his age. His friend, Mr. Benjamin H. Ellicott, collected various facts concerning him, which have been published. In a letter on this subject, Mr. Ellicott says: "During the whole of his long life he lived respectably, and was much esteemed by all who became acquainted with him; more especially by those who could fully appreciate his genius and the extent of his acquirements. His mode of life was extremely regular and retired. Having never married, he lived alone, cooking his own victuals and washing his own clothes. He was scarcely ever absent from home, yet there was nothing misanthropic in his character. A gentleman who knew him speaks of him thus: 'I recollect him well. He was a brave-looking, pleasant man, with something very noble in his appearance. His mind was evidently much engrossed in his calculations, but he was glad to receive the visits we often paid him.' Another writes: 'When I was a boy, I became very much interested in him. His manners were those of a perfect gentleman. He was kind, generous, hospitable, humane, dignified, and pleasing. He abounded in information on all the various subjects and incidents of the day, was very modest and unassuming, and delighted in society at his own house. Go there when you would, by day or night, there was constantly in the middle of the floor a large table covered with books and papers. As he was an eminent mathematician, he was constantly in correspondence with other mathematicians in this country, with whom there was an interchange of questions of difficult solution. His head was covered with thick white hair, which gave him a venerable appearance. His dress was uniformly of superfine drab broadcloth, made in the old style of a plain coat with strait collar, a long waistcoat, and a broad-brimmed hat. His color was not jet black, but decidedly negro. In size and personal appearance he bore a strong resemblance to the statue of Benjamin Franklin, at the Library in Philadelphia.'"

The good which Banneker did to the cause of his colored brethren did not cease with his life. When the Abbe Gregoire pleaded for emancipation in France, and when Wilberforce afterward labored for the same cause in England, the abilities and character of the black astronomer were brought forward as an argument against the enslavement of his race; and, from·that day to this, the friends of freedom have quoted him everywhere as a proof of the mental capacity of Africans.

"THEY *found* them slaves! but who that title *gave*?
The God of Nature never formed a slave!
Though fraud or force acquire a master's name,
Nature and justice must remain the same; —
Nature imprints upon whate'er we see,
That has a heart and life in it, BE FREE!"

COWPER.

ETHIOPIA.

BY FRANCES E. W. HARPER.

YES, Ethiopia yet shall stretch
　　Her bleeding hands abroad;
Her cry of agony shall reach
　　Up to the throne of God.

The tyrant's yoke from off her neck,
　　His fetters from her soul,
The mighty hand of God shall break,
　　And spurn the base control.

Redeemed from dust and freed from chains,
　　Her sons shall lift their eyes;
From cloud-capt hills and verdant plains
　　Shall shouts of triumph rise.

Upon her dark, despairing brow
　　Shall play a smile of peace;
For God shall bend unto her woe,
　　And bid her sorrows cease.

'Neath sheltering vines and stately palms
　　Shall laughing children play,
And aged sires with joyous psalms
　　Shall gladden every day.

Secure by night, and blest by day,
　　Shall pass her happy hours ;
Nor human tigers hunt for prey
　　Within her peaceful bowers.

Then, Ethiopia, stretch, O stretch
　　Thy bleeding hands abroad !
Thy cry of agony shall reach
　　And find redress from God.

THE HOUR OF FREEDOM. *

BY WILLIAM LLOYD GARRISON.

THE hour of freedom ! come it must.
　　O hasten it, in mercy, Heaven !
When all who grovel in the dust
　　Shall stand erect, their fetters riven ;

When glorious freedom shall be won
　　By every caste, complexion, clime ;
When tyranny shall be o'erthrown,
　　And *color* cease to be a *crime*.

* Written in 1832.

2

WILLIAM BOEN.

BY L. MARIA CHILD.

WILLIAM BOEN was born in 1735, one hundred and thirty years ago. He was the slave of a man who lived near Mount Holly, in New Jersey. His master and most of the neighbors belonged to the Society of Friends, commonly called Quakers. That Society made it a rule that none of their members should hold a slave, long before the people of any other sect were convinced that slavery was wrong. But at the time William Boen was born some of the Quakers did hold slaves, though many of their members were preaching against it.

They were a very friendly and conscientious people, and as William grew up among them he naturally imbibed many of their ideas. However, like most boys, he did not think very seriously about religion, until the importance of it was impressed upon his mind by the following circumstance. In the time of the old French war, when he was a mere lad, his master sent him into the woods to cut down trees. The Indians were fighting on the side of the French, and they often killed the Americans. Some of them came into the neighborhood of Mount Holly; and when he went home at night, after his day's work in the woods, he would often hear that Indians had been lurking about in the neighborhood, and that somebody had been shot by their sharp arrows. This made him very much afraid to work alone in the woods.

He was always thinking that Indians might be hidden among the bushes; and if a bird flew off her nest it sounded to him like the whizzing of an arrow. It was very still in the forest, and it seemed very solemn to look up at the sky through the tall trees. William thought to himself, "What if the Indians should kill me before I have any time to think about it? Am I fit to die?" He thought he was not fit to die, and he longed earnestly to know what he ought to do to become fit to die. He had heard the Quakers talk about a light which God had placed in the soul, to show men what was wrong. And he said it went through his mind "like a flaming sword," that if he would be fit to die he must follow this inward light in every particular, even in the most trifling things. So he began to be very thoughtful about every action of his life; and if he felt uneasy about anything he was tempted to do, he said to himself, "This is the inward light, showing me that the thing is wrong. I will not do it." Pursuing this course, he became careful not to do anything which did not bring peace to his soul; and as the soul can never be peaceful when it disobeys God, he was continually travelling toward Zion while he strove to follow this inward light in his soul; and the more humbly he tried to follow it, the clearer the light became. He did not always keep in the straight path. Sometimes he did or said something wrong; then peace went away from his mind. But he confessed his sin before God, and prayed for strength not to do wrong any more. By humility and obedience he again found the path of peace. Religion comes in many different ways to human souls. This was the way it came to William Boen.

All who knew him saw that his religious feeling was deep and sincere, for it brought forth fruit in his daily life. He never made others unhappy by indulging freaks of temper. He was extremely temperate, scrupulously honest, and very careful never to say anything but the exact truth. His character was so excellent that all the neighbors respected and trusted him. Many said it was a shame to keep him in slavery, and his master became uneasy about it. People said to him, from time to time, "William, thy master talks of letting thee be free." He heard it so often, that it became an old story, and he thought nothing would ever come of it. But one day his master was walking with him as he went to his work in the fields, and suddenly he inquired whether he would like to be free. William was silent for a while, and then began to talk about the work he was to do. But the question dwelt on his mind and excited his hopes. He told one of his friends about it, and when he was asked, "What didst thou say, William?" he replied, "I did not say anything; for I thought he might *know* I would like to be free."

When he was nearly twenty-eight years old his master offered to make a contract with him by which he could obtain his freedom. He was soon after married to a worthy young woman, and by industry and strict economy they were able in a few years to buy a few acres of land, and build a comfortable house. He led a peaceful and diligent life, doing good to others whenever he could, and harming no one. His conscience was extremely tender. He would never eat anything made of sugar manufactured by slaves, and he never would wear any garments made of cotton raised by slave labor. He thought Slavery was so wrong, that he did not feel easy to connect himself with it, even in the remotest degree.

He was equally scrupulous about telling the truth.

One of his neighbors, a rich white man, was very much in the habit of borrowing his tools. One day, when he had been using his grindstone, he thanked him for it, and William answered, in the customary way, "Thou art welcome." But soon he began to ask himself, "Was that the exact truth?" His mind was troubled by doubts about it, and finally he went to his neighbor, and said, "When I told thee thou wert welcome, I spoke mere complimentary words, according to custom; for the truth is, I do honestly think thou art better able to have a grindstone of thy own, than I am."

He had also a very nice sense of justice with regard to the rights of property. Nothing would induce him to use what belonged to another person without first obtaining leave. One day, when he was mowing in the meadows, he accidentally killed a fat partridge with his scythe. The other workmen advised him to take it home for his wife to roast. But he replied, "Nay, the partridge does not belong to me, it belongs to the owner of the meadow." Accordingly he carried it to his employer. Another time, when he was working with others in the woods, they found an empty cabin, wherein they stowed their provisions, and lodged for a fortnight, till they had finished cutting the timber. After William returned home he took an early opportunity to tell the owner of the cabin what he had done, and to offer payment for the accommodation.

He constantly attended Quaker meetings, and followed their peculiar customs in dress and language; but he was not admitted into full membership with that religious society till he was nearly eighty years old, though he had made application to join it thirty years before.

He was scrupulously neat in his person. His linen

was always very white, and his light drab-colored clothes showed no speck of dirt. He wore his beard long, and as he grew old it became very white; his curly hair also was white as snow. His dark face was very conspicuous in the midst of all this whiteness, and gave him an odd appearance. But he had such a friendly, pleasant expression of countenance, and there was so much modest dignity in his manners, that he inspired respect. A stranger once said to one of his wealthy neighbors, "I wonder that boys and giddy young folks don't ridicule that old black man, his dress and appearance are so very peculiar." The neighbor replied, "William Boen is a religious man, and everybody respects him. The light-minded are so much impressed by his well-known character, that they are restrained from making fun of his singular appearance."

He died in his ninetieth year; not from any disease, but the mere weakness of old age. His faculties were clear, and his mind serene and cheerful to the last. He spoke of his approaching death with the greatest composure; saying that he had no wish about the manner of his exit from this life, that he was resigned to the Divine will in all things.

One of the last things he said was, "I am glad to see that the feeling against slavery is growing among the Society of Friends. Once I felt as if I was alone in my testimony against that wicked system."

After his death, the Society of Friends at Mount Holly wrote a Memorial concerning his character, which was read in their Yearly Meeting. It concluded thus: "In early life, he was concerned 'to do justly, love mercy, and walk humbly with his God.' By close attention to the light of Christ within, he was enabled, not only to bear many precious testimonies faithfully to the end of his days, but also to bring forth those fruits of the spirit which redound to the glory of God and the salvation of the soul. As he lived, so he died, — a rare pattern of a self-denying follower of Christ. 'Mark the perfect man, and behold the upright; for the end of that man is peace.'"

ANECDOTE OF GENERAL WASHINGTON.

DURING the war of the Revolution, Primus Hall was the colored servant of Colonel Pickering, with whom General Washington often held long consultations. One night, finding they must be engaged till late, he proposed to sleep in the Colonel's tent, provided there was a spare blanket and straw. Primus, who was always eager to oblige the Commander-in-Chief, said, "Plenty of straw and blankets."

When the long conference was ended, the two officers lay down to rest on the beds he had prepared. When he saw they were asleep, he seated himself on a box, and, leaning his head on his hand, tried to take as comfortable a nap as he could. General Washington woke in the night, and seeing him nodding there, called out, "Primus!" The servant started to his feet, and exclaimed, "What do you wish for, General?"

"You told me you had plenty of straw and blankets," replied Washington; "but I see you are sitting up all night for the sake of giving me your bed."

"It is no matter about me," rejoined Primus.

"Yes, it is," replied General Washington. "If one of us must sit up, I will take my turn. But there is no need of that. The blanket is wide enough for two. Come and lie down with me."

Primus, who reverenced the Commander-in-Chief as he did no other mortal, protested against it. But Washington threw open the blanket, and said, "Come and lie down, I tell you! There is room enough for both, and I insist upon it."

The tone was too resolute to admit of further parley, and the General and his colored friend slept comfortably under the same blanket till morning.

PRAYER OF THE SLAVE.

BY BERNARD BARTON.

O FATHER of the human race!
    The white, the black, the bond, the free,
Thanks for thy gift of heavenly grace,
    Vouchsafed through Jesus Christ to me.

This, 'mid oppression's every wrong,
    Has borne my sinking spirits up;
Made sorrow joyful, weakness strong,
    And sweetened Slavery's bitter cup.

Hath not a Saviour's dying hour
    Made e'en the yoke of thraldom light?
Hath not thy Holy Spirit's power
    Made bondage freedom? darkness bright?

Thanks then, O Father! for the gift
    Which through thy Gospel thou hast given,
Which thus from bonds and earth can lift
    The soul to liberty and heaven.

But not the less I mourn their shame,
    Who, mindless of thy gracious will,
Call on the holy Father's name,
    Yet keep their brethren bondmen still.

Forgive them, Lord! for Jesus' sake;
    And when the slave thou hast unbound,
The chains which bind the oppressor break!
    Thus be thy love's last triumph crowned.

TOUSSAINT L'OUVERTURE.

> " Everywhere thy name shall be
> Redeemed from color's infamy;
> And men shall learn to speak of thee
> As one of earth's great spirits, born
> In servitude and nursed in scorn,
> Casting aside the weary weight
> And fetters of its low estate,
> In that strong majesty of soul
> Which knows no color, tongue, or clime,
> Which still hath spurned the base control
> Of tyrants, through all time."
>   JOHN G. WHITTIER.

ON the western coast of Africa, a tribe called the Arradas are said to be superior to most of the other tribes in intelligence and strength of will.   The son of their chief, named Gaou-Guinou, was seized by a prowling band of slave-traders, one day when he was out hunting.   He was packed in the hold of a European ship, with a multitude of other unfortunate victims, and carried to the island of Hayti to be sold.   This is one of the largest of the West India Islands, and lies between Cuba and Porto Rico.   It was first discovered by Spaniards, who found it inhabited by mild-tempered Indians, leading a very simple and happy life.   These natives called their island Hayti, which in their language signified a Land of Mountains.   A lofty ridge of mountains runs across it, and gives it a solemn, dreary appearance, when seen in the distance.   But it is a very beautiful and fertile island. The high, rocky precipices, piled one above another, look down on broad flowery plains, flowing with water, and

2 *   c

loaded with tropical fruits. When the Spaniards established a colony there, they introduced the cultivation of
sugar, cotton, and coffee, to supply the markets of Europe. They compelled the native Indians to work so
hard, and treated them so badly, that the poor creatures
died off very fast. Then they sent men in ships to
Africa to steal negroes to work for them. They founded
a city in the eastern part of the island, and named it
St. Domingo; and the whole island came to be called by
that name by European nations.

The French afterward took possession of the western
part of the island. Their principal city was named
Cap Francois, which means French Cape. The African
prince Gaou-Guinou was sold in the market of that city.
He was more fortunate than slaves generally are. He
was bought by the manager of a sugar plantation belonging to a French nobleman, named the Count de Breda.
He was kind-hearted, and was very careful to employ
none but humane men to take charge of his laborers.
The condition of the young African was also less desolate than it would have been, by reason of his finding on
the Breda estate several members of the Arradas tribe,
who, like him, had been stolen from their homes. They
at once recognized him as the son of their king, and
treated him with the utmost respect. In process of time
he married a black slave, who is said to have been handsome and virtuous. They joined the Roman Catholic
Church, which was the established religion of France and
the French islands. Of their eight children, the oldest,
born in 1743, one hundred and twenty-two years ago,
was named Toussaint. The day of his birth is not certainly known. It has been said to have been on the
20th of May. But, from his name, it seems more likely

that it was on the 1st of November. In Catholic countries, almost every day of the year is set apart to the
worship of some saint; and a child born on the day of
any particular saint is very apt to receive his name from
that day. The first of November is a festival of the
church, called All Saints' Day; and Toussaint, in the
French language, means All Saints.

In the neighborhood of Gaou-Guinou lived a very honest, religious old black man, named Pierre Baptiste. He
had been in the service of Jesuit missionaries, and had
there learned to read and write, also a little of geometry.
By help of the Catholic Prayer-Book he learned some
prayers in Latin, and found out their meaning in French.
This man stood godfather for Toussaint at his baptism,
and as the boy grew older it was his pleasure to teach
him what little he himself knew. The language of the
Arradas tribe was always spoken in the family of Gaou-
Guinou, but from his godfather Toussaint learned to
speak tolerably good French, which was the language of
the whites in the western part of St. Domingo. It is
said that Gaou-Guinou was allowed to cultivate a little
patch of ground for his family, and that some of his
fellow-slaves were permitted to assist him occasionally.
This indulgence indicates that he stood well in his master's opinion. But, in common with other slaves, it is
probable that he and his wife toiled early and late in the
fields or the sugar-house, and that their family were huddled together in a hut too small to allow of their observ-
ing the laws of cleanliness or modesty.

For several years Toussaint was so feeble and slender
that his parents called him by a name which signified
"The Little Lath." But he gained strength as he grew
older; and by the time he was twelve years old he could
beat all the boys in running, jumping, and leaping.

It was the business of young slaves to tend the flocks and herds. They generally neglected and abused the creatures under their care, because they themselves were accustomed to hard treatment. But Toussaint was of a kindly disposition, and there was less violence on his master's plantation than elsewhere. It was remarked in the neighborhood that he differed from other boys in his careful and gentle treatment of the animals under his care. He was naturally a silent and thoughtful child, and probably this tendency was increased by being much alone, watching the browsing cattle in the stillness of the great valleys. Perhaps also the presence of the mountains and the sky made him feel serious and solemn. His pious godfather told him legends of Catholic saints, which he had heard among the missionaries. All these things combined to give him a religious turn of mind, even in his boyhood. From his own father he learned a great deal about Africa and the customs that prevailed in the tribe of his grandfather, King of the Arradas; also the medicinal qualities of many plants, which afterward proved very useful to him. Nothing is recorded of the moral and intellectual character of his father; but Toussaint always respected him highly, and when he was himself an old man he spoke of him as a good parent, who had trained him well by lessons of honor and virtue.

Toussaint Breda, as he was called, from the name of the estate on which he worked, early acquired a reputation for intelligence, sobriety, and industry. The Manager of the estate, M. Bayou de Libertas, was so much pleased with his conduct and manners that he made him his coachman, a situation much coveted by the slaves, as being more easy and pleasant than most of their tasks. His kindness to animals fitted him for the care of horses, and he was found as faithful in this new business as he had been while he was herds-boy. He was afterward promoted to an office of greater trust, being made steward of the sugar-house.

Having arrived at manhood, he began to want a home of his own. Most of the slaves took up together without any form of marriage, that being one of the bad customs which grows out of Slavery. But Toussaint was religious, and it would have troubled his conscience to live in that bad way. He had become attached to a widow named Suzan, who had one little son called Placide. She was not handsome, but he loved her for her good sense, good temper, and modest manners. They were married according to the ceremonies of the Catholic Church. He adopted her little boy, and brought him up as tenderly as he did his own children. The Manager allowed him a small patch of ground for vegetables, and all the hours they could snatch from plantation labors he and his wife devoted to the cultivation of their little garden. M. Bayou de Libertas was such a humane and considerate man that life in his service seems to have been as happy as the condition of slaves can be. Long afterward, Toussaint, speaking of this period of his life, said: "My wife and I went hand in hand to labor in the fields. We were scarcely conscious of the fatigues of the day. Heaven always blessed our toil. We had abundance for ourselves, and the pleasure of giving to other blacks who needed it. On Sundays and festival days my wife, my parents, and myself went to church. Returning to our cottage we had a pleasant meal, passed the remainder of the day in family intercourse, and closed it by prayer, in which all took part."

Thus contented in his humble station, and faithfully

performing its duties, he gained the respect and confidence of both blacks and whites. Many of the slaves in the French colonies were cruelly treated, as is always the case wherever Slavery exists. Toussaint could not avoid seeing a great deal of wrong and suffering inflicted on people of his color, and he was doubtless grateful to God that his lot was so much better than theirs. But he was too intelligent and thoughtful not to question in his own mind why either he or they should be held in bondage merely on account of the complexion which it had pleased God to give them. He was fond of reading, and M. Bayou de Libertas, contrary to the usual custom, allowed him the use of his books. He read one volume at a time, and tried to understand it thoroughly. He devoted every spare moment to it, and while he was at work he was busily thinking over what he had read. It took complete possession of his soul for the time, and he would repeat extracts from it to his companions for weeks after. In this earnest way he read several books of ancient history, biography, and morals, and a number of military books. There was a French author, called the Abbé Raynal, who was much opposed to Slavery. In some way or other, one of his books fell into the hands of Toussaint Breda, and made a deep impression on him. It contained the following sentence: "What shall be done to overthrow Slavery? Self-interest alone governs kings and nations. We must look elsewhere. A courageous chief is all the negroes need. Where is he? Where is that great man whom Nature owes to her vexed, oppressed, and tormented children? He will doubtless appear. He will come forth and raise the sacred standard of Liberty. This venerable signal will gather round him his companions in misfortune. More impetuous than the torrents, they will everywhere leave the indelible traces of their just resentment. Everywhere people will bless the name of the hero who shall have re-established the rights of the human race."

When the Abbé Raynal wrote those prophetic words, he did not foresee that they would meet the eye of the very man he called for ; and the humble slave, when he read them, did not hear in them the voice of his own destiny.

While he was diligently toiling for his humane masters, and seizing every opportunity to increase his small stock of knowledge, the island of St. Domingo was growing very rich by agriculture and commerce. The planters acquired enormous wealth, built splendid houses, and lived in luxury, laziness, and dissipation, upon the toil of the poor unpaid negroes. Twenty thousand slaves were imported from Africa every year, to make up the deficiency of those who were killed by excessive toil and cruel treatment. These new victims, men and women, had the name of their purchaser branded on their breastbones with red-hot iron.

But men never violate the laws of God without suffering the consequences, sooner or later. Slavery was producing its natural fruits of tyranny and hatred, cruelty and despair. The reports of barbarity on one side and suffering on the other attracted attention in Europe ; and benevolent and just men began to speak and write against Slavery as a wicked and dangerous institution. The Abbé Gregoire, a humane Bishop of the Catholic Church, introduced the agitating question into the French Assembly, a body similar to our Congress. He also formed a society called *Les Amis de Noirs*, which means " The Friends of the Blacks." Of course, this was very vexatious to slaveholders in the French colonies. They knew very well that if the facts of Slavery were made known, every good man would cry out against it. Political parties were formed in St. Domingo. Some of the planters wanted to secede from France, and set up an independent government. Others wanted to increase their political power by having a Colonial Assembly established in the island, by means of which they could mainly manage their own concerns as they chose. For this purpose they sent deputies to France. But their request gave rise to the question who should have the right to be members of such an Assembly; and, for the following reasons, that question was very annoying to the haughty slaveholders of St. Domingo.

In the United States of America, slaveholders made a law that "the child shall follow the condition of the *mother*"; consequently, every child of a slave-woman was born a slave, however light its complexion might be. This was a very convenient arrangement for white fathers, who wanted to sell their own children. In the French colonies, the law was, "the child shall follow the condition of its *father*." The consequence was, that all the children the planters of St. Domingo had by their slaves were born free. This was, of course, a numerous class. In fact, their numbers were two thirds as great as those of the whites. There were at that time in St. Domingo thirty thousand whites, twenty thousand free mulattoes, and five hundred thousand black slaves. Not unfrequently the white planters sent their mulatto children to France to be educated like gentlemen. Many of them acquired great wealth and held numerous slaves. But they were a class by themselves. However rich and educated they might be, they were kept trampled down

in a degraded and irritating position, merely on account
of their color. They despised the negro slaves, from
whom they had descended on the mother's side; and
they in their turn were despised by the whites, whose
children they were, because their color connected them
with the enslaved race. They were not allowed to be
doctors, lawyers, or priests; they could hold no public
office; they could not inherit the name or the property
of their fathers; they could not attend school with white
boys, or sit at a white man's table, or occupy the same
portion of a church with him, or be buried in the same
graveyard. They were continually insulted by whites,
but if they dared to give a blow in return, the penalty
was to have the right hand cut off. This class of free
mulattoes claimed that, being numerous and wealthy, and
the payers of taxes, they had a right to send representatives to the Colonial Assembly to look after their interests. They had the more hopes of gaining this point,
because a great Revolution was then going on in France,
and the friends of liberty and equality were daily growing stronger there. When the white planters sent deputies to France, the mulattoes sent deputies also, with a
present of more than a million of dollars, and an offer to
mortgage a fifth part of all their property toward the
payment of the French national debt. All they asked in
return was that the law should put them on an equality
with white men. Being slaveholders, they manifested
the same selfishness that white slaveholders did. They
declared that they asked redress of grievances only for
oppressed *freemen;* that they had no wish to change the
condition of the negroes, who were slaves.

This petition was drawn up in 1790, and sent to Paris
by a wealthy colored man named Ogé. It excited lively

discussion in the National Assembly of France. One of the members, named Lamoth, who owned large estates in St. Domingo, said: "I am one of the largest proprietors in that island; but I would lose all that I possess there rather than disown principles which justice and humanity have consecrated. I am not only in favor of admitting men of color into the Colonial Assemblies, but I also go for the emancipation of the negro slaves." After animated discussion, the reply received by the mulatto deputies from the President of the Assembly was: "No portion of the French nation shall in vain claim its rights from the representatives of the French people."

When the white planters of St. Domingo heard of this, they were filled with wrath. In one place, a mulatto named Lacombe, whose only crime was that he had signed the petition, was seized and hung. In another place, the mob seized a highly respected old white magistrate and cut off his head, because he had drafted for the mulattoes a very moderate petition, begging to be released from some of the hardships under which they had so long suffered. When the colored deputy Ogé returned from France and demanded that mulattoes should have the rights of citizenship, which had been decreed to them by the French Assembly, soldiers were sent to seize him, and he was sentenced to have all his limbs broken on a wheel, and then to have his head cut off.

Besides the classes of which I have spoken there was another class in St. Domingo called *petit blancs*, which means small whites. They were so called to distinguish them from the large landed proprietors. They occupied a position not unlike that of the class known as "poor whites" in the slaveholding portion of the United States.

They were ready instruments to carry out the vengeance of the infuriated planters. They seized every opportunity to insult the free mulattoes, and to inflict cruelty and outrage on the negro slaves. They went about as patrols, traversing the plantations, and bursting into negro huts at all times of night, under the pretence that they were plotting insurrection. The poor ignorant slaves did not understand what all this mobbing and murdering was for; but finding themselves so much suspected and abused without cause, they became weary of their lives. Many committed suicide, others tried to poison their tormentors. At Port au Prince an attempt was made to get up an insurrection. Fifty slaves, suspected of being connected with it, were beheaded, and their heads, stuck on poles, were set up by the hedges in a row.

While the fire was thus kindling under their feet the white planters came out in open defiance of the French government, and refused to take the oath of allegiance. They called on the English for aid, and offered to make the island over to Great Britain. The mulattoes were filled with dismay, for the French government was their only hope. They had hitherto kept aloof from the negroes; but now, seeing the necessity of curbing the power of the white planters, at all hazards, they instigated the already exasperated slaves to seize this favorable moment of commotion and rise against their masters. They did rise, on the 22d of August, 1791. All at once the sky was red with the reflection of burning houses and canefields. The cruelties which they had witnessed or suffered, they now, in their turn, inflicted on white men, women, and children. It was a horrible scene.

Toussaint was working as usual on the Breda estate, when he heard that the planters had called in the aid

of the English, and that four thousand negroes had risen
in insurrection. He exerted his great influence with his
fellow-slaves to prevent the destruction of houses and
cane-fields on the Breda estate. For a month, he kept
the insurgents at bay, while he helped M. Bayou de
Libertas to convey a cargo of sugar on board a Baltimore
ship, for the support of his family, and aided his mistress
to collect such articles of value as could conveniently be
carried away. Then he secretly conveyed them to the
same ship; and it was an inexpressible relief to his heart
when he saw them sailing away, bound for the shores of
the United States.

The armed negroes increased in numbers, and mar-
shalled themselves under an intelligent leader named
Jean François. When the French governor in St. Domingo called upon them to lay down their arms, their
leaders replied for them: "We have never thought of
failing in the respect and duty we owe to the representatives of the King of France. The king has bewailed our
lot and broken our chains. But those who should have
proved fathers to us have been tyrants, monsters, unwor-
thy the fruits of our labors. Do you ask the sheep to
throw themselves into the jaws of the wolf? To prove
to you, excellent sir, that we are not so cruel as you may
think, we assure you that we wish for peace with all
our souls; but on condition that all the whites, without
a single exception, leave the Cape. Let them carry with
them their gold and their jewels. All we seek is our
liberty. God grant that we may obtain it without shedding of blood. Believe us, it has cost our feelings very
much to have taken this course. But victory, or death
for freedom, is our profession of faith; and we will main-
tain it to the last drop of our blood."

The negroes were mistaken in supposing that Louis XVI., king of France, had broken their chains, or that the king's party, called Royalists, were trying to do anything for their freedom. It was the revolutionary party in France, called Republicans, who had declared themselves in favor of emancipating the negro slaves, and giving the free mulattoes their civil rights. The main body of the negroes had been kept in the lowest ignorance, and of course could not understand the state of political parties. The world was ringing with French doctrines of liberty and equality, to be applied to men of all colors; and they could not help hearing something of what was so universally talked of. · The Spaniards ·in the eastern part of St. Domingo were allies of the French king, and they wa.·'ed the negroes to help them fight the French planters, who were in rebellion against the king. In order to give them a strong motive for doing so, they told them that Louis XVI. had been cast into prison in France, and that they were going to kill him, because he wanted to emancipate the slaves in his colonies. They readily believed that it was so, because they saw their masters in arms against the king. Therefore they called their regiments "The King's Own," and carried flags on which were inscribed, "Long live the King," "The Ancient System of Government."

The slaveholders mounted the English cockade, and entered into alliance with Great Britain, while their revolted slaves joined the Spanish. The war raged horribly on both sides. Jean François was of a gentle disposition, and disposed to be merciful; but the two other leaders of the negroes, named Jeannot and Biassou, were monsters of revenge and cruelty. The bleeding heads of white men surrounded their camps, and the bodies of black men hung on trees round the camps of the planters.

This state of things shocked the soul of Toussaint Breda. Much as he desired the freedom of his own race, he was reluctant to join an enterprise marked by so many cruelties. Conscience forbade him to enlist on the side of the slaveholders, and he would gladly have remained neutral; but he found that men of his own color were suspicious of him, because he had adhered so faithfully to M. Bayou de Libertas. He joined the black insurgents; but, resolved not to take part in their barbarities, he occupied himself with healing the wounded, — an office for which he was well qualified by his tender disposition and knowledge of medicinal plants.

After a while, however, the negroes were compelled to retreat before the superior discipline of the white troops; and feeling greatly the need of intelligent officers, they insisted upon making Toussaint aide-de-camp to Biassou, under the title of Brigadier. He desired, above all things, that hostilities should cease, that the negroes should return to their work, and that the planters should consent to cease from oppressing them. A very little justice and kindness would have pacified the revolted slaves; but the slaveholders were so full of rage and pride, that if a slave attempted to return to his master, however sincere he might be, he was instantly put to death. Three commissioners came from France to try to negotiate a peace between the contending parties. The blacks sent deputies to the Colonial Assembly to help the French commissioners in this good work; but the planters treated their overtures with haughtiness and contempt.

It is said that Toussaint wept when he saw the hopes

of peace vanish.   It was plain that his people must resist their tyrants, or be forever hopelessly crushed.   He
was then fifty years old, in the prime of his bodily and
mental strength.   By becoming a leader he felt that he
might protect the ignorant masses, and restrain those who
were disposed to cruelty.   Perhaps he remembered the
prediction of the Abbé Raynal, and thought that he was
the appointed deliverer, — a second Moses, sent by God
to bring his people out of bondage.   From that time
henceforth he made it the business of his life to conquer
freedom for his race; but never in a bloodthirsty spirit.

Biassou was so enraged by the contemptuous manner
in which their deputies had been treated, that he gave
orders to put to death all the white prisoners in their
camps.   But Toussaint remonstrated, and succeeded in
saving their lives.   His superior intelligence gave him
great influence, and he always exerted it on the side of
humanity.   He also manifested extraordinary courage
and sagacity in the very difficult position in which he
was placed.   He was surrounded by conflicting parties,
fighting against each other, agreeing only in one thing,
and that was hostility to the negroes; all of them ready
to make the fairest promises, and to break them as soon
as they had gained their object.   France was in a state
of revolutionary confusion, and rumors were very contra-
dictory.   One thing was certain, — their former masters
were fighting against the king of France; and instinct
led them to take the other side.   Toussaint deemed it
wisest to keep under the protection of their Spanish allies, and fight with them for the king's party.   By a succession of battles, he gained possession of several districts
in the mountains, where he entrenched his forces strongly,
and tried to bring them under regular military discipline.

He was very strict, and allowed no disobedience of orders. He forbade his soldiers to go about plundering, or revenging past injuries. His motto was, "No Retaliation," —a noble, Christian motto, totally disregarded by men whose opportunities for enlightened education were a thousand times greater than his. When he felt himself secure in the mountain districts, he invited the white planters of that region to return and cultivate the estates which they had abandoned in their terror. He promised them that their persons and property should be protected; and he faithfully kept his word. In his language and in his actions he was always saying to the whites, "Why will you force us to fight? I cherish no revenge against you. All I want is the freedom of my race." His energy and ingenuity in availing himself of every resource and supplying every deficiency were truly wonderful. On one occasion a map was greatly needed, in order to plan some important campaign, and no map could be procured. Toussaint, having made diligent inquiries of various persons well acquainted with the portion of country to be traversed, employed himself in making a map. By help of the little geometry taught him by his godfather, he projected a map, and marked down the important towns, mountains, and rivers, with the distances between them.

No trait in the character of Toussaint Breda was stronger than his domestic affections. He was devotedly attached to his wife and children, and he had not seen them for seven months. At last an interval of quiet enabled him to visit the Spanish part of the island, whither he had sent them for security. The Spanish authorities, in acknowledgment of his services, received him with the greatest distinction. Toussaint thanked them, but humbly ascribed his successes to a superintending Providence.

Always strict in religious observances, he went to the church to offer prayers. His general, the Spanish Marquis Hermona, seeing him kneel to partake of the communion, said: "In this lower world God visits no purer soul than his."

But the Spaniards had no regard for the rights and welfare of the negroes. They used them while they had need of their help, and were ready to oppress them when it served their own interests. News came from France that the Republican party were triumphant, and that the king had been beheaded. The Spanish had nothing further to gain by adhering to the defeated Royalist party. Accordingly, Spain and Great Britain entered into a league to divide the island of St. Domingo between them, and restore Slavery. On the contrary, the Republican party in France, assembled in convention at Paris, February, 1794, proclaimed freedom to the slaves in all the French colonies; and as the government was now in their hands, there was no doubt of their having power to protect those they had emancipated. Under these circumstances, there was but one course for Toussaint to take. He left the Spanish and joined the French forces, by whom he was received with acclamation. His rude bands of untaught negroes had now become a well-disciplined army. They were proud of their commander, and almost worshipped him. Under his guidance, they performed wonders, proving themselves equal to any troops in the world. Toussaint was on horseback night and day. It seemed as if he never slept. Wherever he was needed, he suddenly appeared; and as he seemed to be wanted in twenty places at once, his followers thought he had some powers of witchcraft to help him. But the witchcraft consisted in his superior intelligence,

3   D

his remarkable activity, his iron constitution, and his iron
will.   His heart was never of iron.   In the midst of constant warfare he paid careful attention to the raising of
crops ; and if women and children, black or white, were
suffering with hunger, he caused them to be supplied
with food.   He and his brave officers and troops everywhere drove the English before them.   The French
general Laveaux appointed him second to himself in
command ; and, in his proclamation to that effect, he
declared : " This is the man whom the Abbé Raynal
foretold would rise to be the liberator of his oppressed
race."

One day, when he had gained some important advantage, a white officer exclaimed, " General Toussaint
makes an opening everywhere."   His black troops heard
the words, and feeling that he had made an opening for
them, from the dungeon of Slavery to the sunlight of
Freedom, they shouted, " *L' Ouverture*," " *L' Ouverture* " ;
which, being translated into English, means The Opening.   From that day henceforth he was called Toussaint
l'Ouverture.

The English general Maitland, finding him so formida-
ble, wished to have a conference with him to negotiate
terms of accommodation.   The request was granted ; and
such was his confidence in the black chieftain that he
went to his camp with only three attendants, through
miles of country full of armed negroes.   One of the
French officers wrote to General Toussaint that it would
be an excellent opportunity to take the English commander prisoner.   General Maitland was informed of
this while he was on his way ; but he said, " I will
trust General Toussaint.   He never breaks his promise."   When he arrived, General Toussaint handed him

two letters, saying, "There is a letter I have received, advising me to detain you as prisoner ; and there is my reply. I wish you to read them before we proceed to business, that you may know I am incapable of such a base action." The answer he had written was, " I have promised this Englishman my protection, and he shall have it."

The English, seeing little prospect of conquering him by force, or outwitting him by stratagem, tried to bribe him to their interest. They offered to make him king of St. Domingo, to establish him with a sufficient naval force, and give freedom to the blacks, if he would come over to their side. But the English still held slaves in the neighboring islands, while the French had proclaimed emancipation in all their colonies. He felt grateful to the Republican government of France, and he resolved to stand by it. The only crown he coveted was the freedom of his race. He pursued the English vigorously, till he drove them from the island. Yet he had no desire to harm them, any further than was inevitable for the protection of his people. An English naval officer, named Rainsford, being driven on the coast of St. Domingo by a violent storm, was arrested as a spy. A court-martial was held, at which General Christophe presided, in the absence of General Toussaint. Rainsford was convicted, and sentenced to die. He was put into a dungeon to wait till the sentence was signed by General Toussaint. The women of the island pitied the stranger, and often sent him fruit and sweetmeats. When Toussaint returned, he examined into the case, and said : " The trial appears to have been fair, and the sentence just, according to the rules of war. But why should we execute this stranger ? He is alone, and can do us no harm. His death would break his mother's heart. Let us have compassion on her. Let us send him home, that he may tell the English what sort of people we are, and advise them not to attempt to reduce us to Slavery."

Having cleared the island of foreign enemies, Toussaint exerted all his abilities to restore prosperity. He discharged the greater part of the regular troops, and sent them to till the soil. At that time, men were afraid to trust to immediate, unconditional emancipation; they had not then learned by experiment that it is the wisest policy, as well as the truest justice. Toussaint feared that when the former slaves were disbanded from the army they would sink into laziness and vice, and thus cause the name of freedom to be evil spoken of. Therefore, with the view of guarding public morals, he instituted a kind of apprenticeship. He ordained that they should work five years for their masters, on condition of receiving one fourth of the produce, out of which the cost of their subsistence was to be defrayed. Regulations were made by which the laborers became a sort of proprietors of the soil; but I do not know what were the terms. He did everything to encourage agriculture, and tried to impress on the minds of the blacks that the permanence of their freedom depended in a great measure upon their becoming owners and cultivators of land. He proclaimed a general amnesty to men of all colors and all parties, even to those who had fought with the English against their own country. He invited the return of all fugitives who were willing to become good citizens, and by public discourses and proclamations promised them pardon for the past and protection for the future. Before any important measure was carried into execution, he summoned all the people to church, where, after prayers were offered, he discoursed to them upon the prospects of the republic, and what he considered essential to its future peace and prosperity. He ordered prayers to be said night and morning at the head of the regiments. The discipline of the army was so strict, that some accused him of severity. But the soldiers almost idolized him, which I think they would not have done, if he had not proved to them that he was just as well as strict. After such a long period of foreign and civil war, it required a very firm and judicious hand to restore order and security. His troops, once lawless and savage, had become perfectly orderly under his regulations. They committed no thefts on the plantations and no pillage in the cities. He opened to all nations an unrestricted commerce with St. Domingo; and he has the honor of being the first ruler in the world who introduced a system of free trade. In the distribution of offices, he sought out the men that were best fitted, without regard to complexion. In many things he seemed to favor the whites more than the blacks; probably from his extreme fear of not being impartial; perhaps also because he knew the whites distrusted him and needed to be conciliated, while people of his own color had entire confidence in him. But the most obstinate prejudices gradually gave way before the wisdom and uprightness of his government. White planters, who had been accustomed to talk of him as a revolted slave and a lawless brigand, began to acknowledge that he was a conscientious man and a wise legislator. A general feeling of security prevailed, activity in business was restored, and wealth began to flow in through its former channels.

But, with all his prudence and efforts at universal conciliation, he could not at once heal the old animosities that had so long rankled in the breasts of men. Some of the returned French planters resumed their old habits of haughtiness and contempt toward the negroes. Some of the proprietors, both white and black, in their haste to grow rich, overworked their laborers; and, in addition to these causes of irritation, it was whispered round that the whites were influencing the French government to restore Slavery. In one of the northern districts a proposition was made to disband the black troops. This excited suspicion, and they rose in rebellion. Buildings were fired, and three hundred whites slaughtered. Toussaint hastened to the scene of action, and by assurances and threats quelled the tumult. The command of that district was in the hands of General Moyse, the son of Toussaint's brother Paul. He disliked the system of conciliation pursued toward the whites, and had expressed his opinions in terms less respectful than was proper toward a man of his uncle's age and character. The agricultural returns from his district had been smaller than from other portions of the island; and when Toussaint remonstrated with him for neglecting that department, he replied: "Whatever my old uncle may see fit to do, I cannot consent to be the executioner of my race, by causing them to be worked to death. All your orders are given in the name of France. But to serve France is to serve the interests of the whites; and I shall never love the whites till they give me back the eye I lost in battle." When the insurrection broke out in his district, the relatives of the slaughtered whites complained to General Toussaint that his nephew had not taken any efficient measures to put down the riot; and the black insurgents excused themselves by saying General Moyse approved of their rising. A court-martial was held, and

General Moyse and several of the ringleaders were condemned to be shot. The execution of this sentence excited a good deal of ill-feeling toward Toussaint. He was loudly accused of favoring the whites more than he did his own color; and to this day it is remembered against him in the island. It certainly is the harshest action recorded of Toussaint l'Ouverture. But it must be remembered that he had invited the whites to come back, and had given them promises of protection, because he thought the peace and prosperity of the island could best be promoted in that way; and having done so, it was his duty to see that their lives and property were protected. Moreover, he knew that the freedom of his race depended upon their good behavior after they were emancipated, and that insurrections would furnish the French government with a pretext for reducing them to Slavery again. If he punished any of the ringleaders with death, he could not, without partiality, pardon his own nephew, who had been condemned by the same court-martial. In this matter it is fair to judge Toussaint by his general character, and that leaves no room to doubt that severity was painful to him, and that when he resorted to it he was actuated by motives for the public good.

That he could forgive offences against himself was shown by his treatment of the mulattoes, who made trouble in the island about the same time. They had never been pleased to see one of the black slaves, whom they had always despised, placed in a situation which made him so much superior to any of themselves. They manifested their dissatisfaction in a variety of ways. They did their utmost to increase the feeling that he showed partiality to the whites. In several instances attempts were made to take his life. At one time, the plume in his military cap was shot away. On another occasion, balls passed through his carriage, and his coachman was killed; but he happened to be riding off on horseback in another direction. This hostile feeling led the mulattoes into an extensive conspiracy to excite rebellion against his government. Toussaint was forewarned of it, and the attempt was put down. Eleven of the leaders were carried to the Cape and imprisoned. Toussaint called a meeting of the civil and military authorities, and ordered the building to be surrounded by black troops while the mulatto prisoners were brought in under guard. They looked extremely dejected, expecting nothing but death. But he announced to them that, deeming the forgiveness of injuries a Christian duty, he pardoned what they had attempted to do against him. He gave them money to defray their travelling expenses, told them they were at liberty to return to their homes, and gave orders that they should be protected on the way. As he passed out of the building, they showered blessings on his head, and the air was filled with shouts of "Long live Toussaint l'Ouverture."

These outbreakings of old hatreds were local and short-lived. The confidence in Toussaint's goodness and ability was almost universal; and his popularity was so great with all classes, that he might have made himself emperor, if he would. But through all the changes in France he had been faithful to the French government; and now to the habit of loyalty was added gratitude to that government for having proclaimed freedom to his race. Next to the emancipation of his people, he sought to serve the interests of France. Personal ambition never tempted him from the path of duty. When the affairs of the colony seemed to be arranged on a secure basis, he manifested willingness to resign the authority which he had used with so much wisdom and impartiality. He published a proclamation, in which he said: —

"Penetrated with that which is set forth in our Lord's Prayer, 'forgive us our transgressions, as we forgive those who transgress against us,' I have granted a general amnesty. Fellow-citizens, not less generous than myself, endeavor to have the past forgotten. Receive misled brethren with open arms, and let them in the future be on their guard against the snares of bad men. Civil and military authorities, my task is accomplished. It now belongs to you to take care that harmony is no more disturbed. Allow no one to reproach those who went astray, but have now returned to their duty. But, notwithstanding my proclamation of amnesty, watch bad men closely, and do not spare them if they excite disturbance. A sense of honor should guide you all. A true, confiding peace is necessary to the prosperity of the country. It must be your work to establish such a peace. Take no rest until you have accomplished it."

The people refused to accept the resignation of their "friend and benefactor," as they styled him. He replied: "If I undertake the administration of civil affairs, I must have a solid rock to stand on; and that rock must be a constitutional government." Feeling the necessity of laws and regulations suited to the altered state of the country, he called a meeting of deputies from all the districts to draft a constitution. Of these nine deputies eight were white and one a mulatto. They were selected for their learning and ability. Very likely Toussaint's habitual caution led him to choose men from the two classes that had been hostile to him, that there might

3 *

be no pretext for saying he used his popularity with the blacks to carry any measure he wished.

Among other things, this constitution provided that Slavery should never more exist in St. Domingo; that all who were born there were free citizens of the French republic. It also provided that offices were to be distributed according to virtue and ability, without regard to color. The island was to be ruled by one governor, appointed for five years, with a proviso that the term might be prolonged as a reward for good conduct. But "in consideration of the important services rendered to the country by General Toussaint l'Ouverture," he was named governor for life, with power to appoint his successor. This was early in the summer of 1800. The constitution, approved by Toussaint and published, was accepted by the people with solemn formalities and demonstrations of joy. This new colonial government was to go into operation provisionally, until it should receive the sanction of the authorities in France.

General Napoleon Bonaparte was then at the head of the French government, under the title of First Consul. Governor Toussaint wrote to him, that, in the absence of laws, after the revolution in St. Domingo, it had been deemed best to draft a constitution. He added: "I hasten to lay it before you for your approbation, and for the sanction of the government which I serve. All classes of citizens here have welcomed it with joy, which will be renewed when it is sent back with the sanction of the French government."

Some writers have accused Toussaint of personal ambition because he consented to be governor for life. He himself said it was because circumstances had given him influence, which he could exert to unite a divided people;

and that he deemed changes of administration might be injurious until the new order of things had become more settled.

He assumed all the outward style that had been considered befitting the rank of governor and commander-in-chief. He had an elegant carriage and a number of handsome horses. When he rode out, he was followed by attendants in brilliant military dress, and he himself wore a rich uniform. On stated days, he gave reception-parties, to which magistrates, military officers, distinguished strangers, and influential citizens were invited. There was a good deal of splendor in the dresses on such occasions; but he always appeared in the simple undress uniform of a general officer. At these parties, whites, blacks, and mulattoes mingled together with mutual politeness, and it is said that the style of manners was easy and elegant. All rose when the Governor entered, and none seated themselves until he was seated. This was a strange experience for a black man, who was formerly a slave; and it had been brought about, under the blessing of God, solely by the strength and excellence of his own character. All prejudices gave way before his uncommon intelligence, well-tried virtues, and courteous dignity of manner.

Every evening he gave free audience to all the people who chose to call. His dress was such as the landed proprietors usually wore. However weary he might be, he made the circuit of the rooms, and said something to each one on the subjects most likely to interest them. He talked with mothers about their children, and urged upon them the great importance of giving them religious instruction. Not unfrequently he examined the children in their catechisms, and gave a few words of fatherly advice to the young folks.

He has been accused of vanity for assuming so much pomp in his equipage and gentility in his dress. Doubtless he had some vanity. No human being is free from it. But I believe very few men, of any color, could have passed through such extraordinary changes as he did, and preserved their balance so well. In the style he assumed he was probably somewhat influenced by motives of policy. He was obliged to receive many distinguished French gentlemen, and he knew they attached great importance to dress and equipage. The blacks also were fond of splendor, and it gratified them to see their great chieftain appear in princely style. The free mulattoes, who despised his mean birth, would have spared no ridicule if he had been neglectful of outward appearances; and in his peculiar situation it was important to command respect in every way. His person also needed every borrowed advantage that it could obtain. His figure was short and slim, and his features were homely, though his bright, penetrating eyes gave his face an expression of animation and intelligence. With these disadvantages, and a deficiency of education, betrayed by imperfect grammar, it is wonderful how he swayed assemblies of men whenever he addressed them. The secret lay in his great earnestness. Whatever he said, he said it with his whole soul, and therefore it took possession of the souls of others.

Though he paid so much attention to external show in public, his own personal habits were extremely simple and frugal. There was a large public house at the Cape, called The Hotel of the Republic, frequented by whites and blacks, officers and privates. Toussaint l'Ouverture often took a seat at the table in any chair that happened to be vacant. If any one rose to offer him a higher seat, he would bow courteously, and reply, "Distinctions are to be observed only on public occasions." His food consisted of vegetable preparations, and he drank water only. He had a wonderful capacity of doing without sleep. During the years that so many public cares devolved upon him, it is said he rarely slept more than two hours out of the twenty-four. He thought more than he spoke, and what he said was uttered in few words. Surrounded as he was by inquisitive and treacherous people, this habit of reserve was of great use to him. Enemies accused him of being deceitful. The charge was probably grounded on the fact that he knew how to keep his own secrets; for there are many proofs that he was in reality honest and sincere. It is singular how* he escaped the contagion of impurity which always pollutes society where Slavery exists. But his respect and affection for his wife was very constant, and he was always clean in his manners and his language. A colored lady appeared at one of his reception-parties dressed very low at the neck, according to the prevailing Parisian fashion. When he had greeted her, he placed a handkerchief on her shoulders, and said in a low voice, "Modesty is the greatest ornament of woman."

His ability and energy as a statesman were even more remarkable than his courage and skill as a military leader. He was getting old, and he was covered with the scars of wounds received in many battles; but he travelled about with wonderful rapidity, inspecting everything with his own eyes, and personally examining into the conduct of magistrates and officers. Often, after riding some distance in a carriage, he would mount a swift horse and ride off in another direction, while the coach went on. In this way, he would make his appearance sud-

denly at places where he was not expected, and ascertain
how things went on in his absence. It was a common
practice with him to traverse from one hundred to one
hundred and fifty miles a day. After giving his evening audience to the people, he sat up late into the night
answering letters, of which he received not less than a
hundred daily. He dictated to five secretaries at once,
so long that he tired them all; and he examined every
letter when finished, that he might be sure his dictation
had not been misunderstood.

The eastern part of the island had been ceded to the
French by treaty, but had never been given up by the
Spanish, who still held slaves there. Complaints were
brought to General Toussaint that the Spaniards kidnapped both blacks and mulattoes from the western
part of the island, where all were free, and carried
them off to sell them to slave-traders. Resolved to
destroy Slavery, root and branch, throughout the island,
in January, 1801, he marched into the Spanish territory
at the head of ten thousand soldiers. The Spanish blacks
were desirous to come under French dominion, in order
to secure their freedom, and the whites offered but slight
resistance. Having taken possession of the territory in
the name of the French republic, he issued a proclamation, in which he declared that all past offences should
be forgotten, and that the welfare and happiness of Spaniards and Frenchmen should be equally protected. He
then assembled his troops in the churches and caused
prayers of thanksgiving to be offered for the success of
their enterprise, almost without bloodshed. Most of the
wealthy Spanish slaveholders made arrangements to depart to Cuba and other neighboring islands. But the
main body of the people received General Toussaint

with the greatest distinction. As he passed through the
principal towns, he was everywhere greeted with thunder
of artillery, ringing of bells, and loud acclamations of the
populace.

Under his wise and watchful administration all classes
were protected, and all parts of the country became prosperous.   The desolations occasioned by so many years of
warfare were rapidly repaired.   Churches were rebuilt,
schools established, waste lands brought under cultivation, and distances shortened by new and excellent roads.
The French commissioner Roume was struck with admiration of his plans, and pronounced him to be "a philosopher, a legislator, a general, and a good citizen."   The
Frenchman, Lavoque, who was well acquainted with him
and the condition of the people, said to Bonaparte, "Sire,
let things remain as they are in St. Domingo.   It is the
happiest spot in your dominions."   The historian Lacroix,
though prejudiced against blacks, wrote, "That the island
was preserved to the French government was solely owing to an old negro, who seemed to bear a commission
from Heaven."   Strangers who visited St. Domingo expressed their surprise to see cities rising from their ashes,
fields waving with harvests, and the harbors filled with
ships.   Planters, who had fled with their families to various parts of the world heard such good accounts of the
activity of business, and the security of property, that
many of them so far overcame their repugnance to be
governed by a negro as to ask permission to return.
This was easily obtained, and they were received by the
Governor without anything on his part which they might
deem offensive familiarity, but with a dignified courtesy
which prevented familiarity, or airs of condescension, on
their side.   He had annually sent some token of remem-

brance to M. Bayou de Libertas, then residing in the
United States. He now wrote to invite him to return
to St. Domingo. The invitation was gladly accepted.
When he arrived, he was received with marked kindness, but with dignified reserve. Governor Toussaint
evidently did not wish bystanders to be reminded of the
former relation that existed between them as overseer
and slave. "Return to the plantation," said he, "and
take care of the interests of the good old master. See
that the blacks do their duty. Be firm, but just. You
will thus advance your own prosperity; and at the same
time increase the prosperity of the colony."

This return of the old slaveholders excited some uneasiness among the black laborers. But Toussaint, who
often spoke to them in simple parables, sprinkled a few
grains of rice into a vessel of shot, and shook it. "See,"
said he, "how few grains of white there are among the
black."

At that time General Napoleon Bonaparte had become
very famous by his victories, and had recently been made
ruler of France. There were many points of resemblance
between his career and that of the hero of St. Domingo;
and it was a common thing for people to say, "Napoleon
is the First of the Whites, and Toussaint l'Ouverture
is the First of the Blacks." If General Toussaint had
known the real character of Napoleon, he would not have
felt flattered by being compared with such a selfish, tyrannical, and treacherous man. But, like the rest of the
world, he was dazzled by his brilliant reputation, and felt
that it was a great honor to him to be called the "The
Black Napoleon." The vainest thing that is recorded
of him is that on one of his official letters to Bonaparte
he wrote, "To the First of the Whites, from the First

of the Blacks." It was a departure from his usual habits of dignity, and was also poor policy; for Bonaparte had been rendered vain by his great success, and he was under the influence of aristocratic planters from St. Domingo, who would have regarded it as a great insult to couple their names with a negro. General Toussaint soon had reason to suspect he had been mistaken in the character of the famous man, whom he had so much admired. He wrote several deferential letters to Bonaparte, on official business; but the First Consul never condescended to make any reply. It was soon rumored abroad that proprietors of estates in St. Domingo, residing in France, were urging him to send an army to St. Domingo to reduce the blacks again to Slavery. Governor Toussaint could not believe that the French government would be persuaded to break the solemn promises it had made to the colony. But when he sent General Vincent to Paris to obtain Bonaparte's sanction to the new constitution, the wicked scheme was found to be making rapid progress. In vain General Vincent remonstrated against it as a measure cruel and dangerous. In vain he represented the contented, happy, and prosperous state of the island. In vain did many wise and good men in Paris urge that such a step would be unjust in itself and very disgraceful to France. The First Consul turned a deaf ear to all but the haughty old planters from St. Domingo. The Legislative Assembly in France, though still talking loudly about liberty and the rights of man, were not ashamed to propose the restoration of Slavery and the slave-trade in the colonies; and the wicked measure was carried by a vote of two hundred and twelve against sixty-five. In May, 1801, Bonaparte issued a decree to that effect. But he afterwards considered it prudent to

E

announce that the islands of St. Domingo and Guadaloupe were to be excepted.

When this news reached St. Domingo, the people were excited and alarmed. They asked each other anxiously, "How long shall we be excepted?" On that point no assurances were given, and all suspected that the French government was dealing with them hypocritically and treacherously. The soul of Toussaint was on fire. If the names of the men who voted for the restoration of Slavery were mentioned in his presence, his eyes flashed and his whole frame shook with indignation. He published a proclamation, in which he counselled obedience to the mother country, unless circumstances should make it evident that resistance was unavoidable. In private, he said to his friends: "I took up arms for the freedom of my color. France proclaimed it, and she has no right to nullify it. Our liberty is no longer in her hands; it is in our own. We will defend it, or perish."

General Toussaint had sent his two eldest sons to Paris to be educated. As a part of the plan of deception, General Bonaparte invited the young men to visit him. He spoke of their father as a great man, who had rendered very important services to France. He told them he was going to send his brother-in-law, General Le Clerc, with troops to St. Domingo; but he assured them it was not for any hostile purpose; it was merely to add to the defence of the island. He wished them to go with General Le Clerc and tell their father that he intended him all protection, glory, and honor. The next day Bonaparte's Minister of Marine invited the young men to a sumptuous dinner, and at parting presented each with a splendid military uniform. The inexperienced youths were completely dazzled and deceived.

In January, 1802, General Le Clerc sailed with sixty ships and thirty thousand of Bonaparte's experienced troops. When Governor Toussaint received tidings that a French fleet was in sight, he galloped to the coast they were approaching, to take a view of them. He was dismayed, and for a moment discouraged. He exclaimed, " All France has come to enslave St. Domingo. We must perish." He had no vessels, and not more than sixteen thousand men under arms. But his native energy soon returned. The people manifested a determination to die rather than be enslaved again. He resolved to attempt no attack on the French, but to act wholly on the defensive. Le Clerc's army attacked Fort Liberty, killed half the garrison, and forced a landing on the island. Toussaint entrenched himself in a position where he could harass the invaders; and the peaceful, prosperous island again smoked with fire and blood. LeClerc, still aiming to accomplish Bonaparte's designs by hypocrisy, scattered proclamations among the blacks of St. Domingo, representing that Toussaint kept them in a kind of Slavery on the plantations, but that the French had come to set them wholly free. This did not excite the rebellion which he intended to provoke, but it sowed the seeds of doubt and discontent in the minds of some. At the same time that he was playing this treacherous game, he sent Toussaint's two sons to their father, accompanied by their French tutor, to deliver a letter from the First Consul, which ought to have been sent three months before. The letter was very complimentary to General Toussaint; but it objected to the constitution that had been formed, and spoke in a very general way about the liberty which France granted to all nations under her control. It counselled submission to General Le Clerc, and threatened punishment for disobedience. The tone of the letter, though apparently peaceful and friendly, excited distrust in the mind of General Toussaint, which was increased by the fact that the letter had been so long kept from him. Knowing the strength of his domestic affections, orders had been given that if he surrendered, his sons should remain with him, but if he refused they were to return to the French camp as hostages. Though his heart yearned toward his children, from whom he had been so long separated, he said to their tutor: "Three months after date you bring me a letter which promises peace, while the action of General Le Clerc is war. I had established order and justice here; now all is confusion and misery. Take back my sons. I cannot receive them as the price of my surrender. Tell General Le Clerc hostilities will cease on our part when he stops the progress of his invading army." His sons told him how kindly they had been treated by Bonaparte, and what promises he had made concerning St. Domingo, — promises which had been repeated in the proclamation brought by General Le Clerc. Toussaint had had too severe an experience to be easily deceived by fair words. He replied: "My sons, you are no longer children. You are old enough to decide for yourselves. If you wish to be on the side of France, you are free to do so. Stay with me, or return to General Le Clerc, whichever you choose. Either way, I shall love you always." Isaac, his oldest son, had been so deceived by flattery and promises, that he declared his wish to return to the French camp, feeling very sure that his father would be convinced that Bonaparte was their best friend. But Placide, his stepson, said: "My father, I will remain with you. I dread the restoration of Slavery, and I am fearful about the

future of St. Domingo." Who can tell what a pang went
through the father's heart when he embraced Isaac and
bade him farewell?

General Le Clerc was very angry when he found that
his overtures were distrusted. He swore that he would
seize Toussaint before he took his boots off. He forth-
with issued a proclamation declaring him to be an outlaw.
When General Toussaint read it to his soldiers, they cried
out with one accord, "We will die with you." He said
to his officers: "When the rainy season comes, sickness
will rid us of our enemies. Till then there is nothing
before us but flame and slaughter." Orders were given
to fire the towns as the French army approached, and to
deal destruction upon them in every way. He gathered
his army together at the entrance of the mountains, and,
aided by his brave generals Christophe and Dessalines,
kept up active skirmishing with the enemy. Horrible
things were done on both sides. The Bay of Mancenille
was red with the blood of negro prisoners slaughtered
by the French. The blacks, infuriated by revenge and
dread of Slavery, killed white men, women, and children
without mercy. General Dessalines was of a savage
temper, and incited his troops to the most ferocious
deeds.

But the natural kindliness of the negro character was
manifested on many occasions, even in the midst of this
horrible excitement. In many cases they guided their
old masters to hiding-places in the mountains or forests,
and secretly conveyed them food.

Toussaint, with only a plank to sleep on and a cloak
to cover him, was constantly occupied with planning attacks and ambuscades, and preaching on Sundays, exhorting the people, with fiery eloquence, to remember that

the cause of Liberty was the cause of God. General
Le Clerc, meanwhile, was disappointed to find so many
difficulties in the way of his wicked project. His troops
wilted under the increasing heat of the climate, and began
to murmur. He issued proclamations, promising, in the
most solemn manner, that the freedom of all classes in
St. Domingo should be respected. These assurances induced several black regiments to go over to the French.
Toussaint's brother Paul, and two of his ablest generals,
Bellair and Maurepas, did the same. Still the Commander-in-Chief, aided by Christophe and Dessalines,
kept up a stout resistance. But news came that fresh
troops were coming from France, and Christophe and
Dessalines had an interview with General Le Clerc, in
which, by fair promises, he succeeded in gaining them
over to the French side. A messenger was then sent to
ask for a conference with General Toussaint. Solemn
assurances were repeated that the freedom of the blacks
should be protected; and a proposition was made that he
should be colleague with General Le Clerc in the government of the island, and that his officers should retain
their rank in the army. With reinforcements coming
from France, and with his best generals gained over,
Toussaint had no longer hopes of defeating the invaders, though he might send out skirmishers to annoy
them. He had too little faith in the promises of General Le Clerc to consent to take an oath of office under
him. He therefore replied: "I might remain a brigand
in the mountains, and harass you with perpetual warfare,
so far as your power to prevent it is concerned. But I
disdain fighting for mere bloodshed; and, in obedience
to the orders of the First Consul, I yield to you. For
myself, I wish to live in retirement; but I accept your
favorable terms for the people and the army."

With four hundred armed horsemen he set out for the Cape, to hold the proposed conference with General Le Clerc. On the way, the people, thinking peace was secured without the sacrifice of their freedom, hailed him as their benefactor. Girls strewed flowers in his path, and mothers held up their children to bless him. General Le Clerc received him with a salute of artillery, and made a speech in which he highly complimented his bravery, magnanimity, and good faith, and expressed a hope that, though he chose to live in retirement, he would continue to assist the government of the island by his wise counsels. In the presence of the troops on both sides, he took an oath on the cross to protect the freedom of St. Domingo. With the same solemn formalities, General Toussaint promised that the treaty of peace should be faithfully observed.

The next day, he explained fully to his officers and soldiers what were the terms of the treaty, and impressed upon their minds that such a promise could not be violated without committing the sin of perjury. He thanked them all for the courage and devotedness they had shown under his command, embraced his officers, and bade them an affectionate farewell. They shed tears, and expressed the greatest reluctance to part with him; but he told them that such a course would best conduce to public tranquillity. The soldiers were inconsolable. They followed him, calling out in the saddest tones, "Have you deserted us?" He replied: "No, my children. Do not be uneasy. Your officers are all under arms, and at their posts."

Twelve years had passed since he was working on the Breda estate, and seeing houses and cane-fields on fire in every direction, had said to his wife, "The slaves have

risen." Since that time, his life had been one scene of
excitement, danger, ceaseless exertion, and overwhelming
responsibility. He had been commander-in-chief of the
armies of St. Domingo during five years, and governor
of the island about one year. Now, with a heart full
of anxiety for his people, but cheered by hopes of domestic happiness, he retired, far from the scene of his official
splendor, to Ennery, a beautiful valley among the mountains. Surrounded by his family, he busied himself with
clearing up the land and cultivating oranges, bananas,
and coffee. The people round about often came to him
for advice, and he freely assisted his neighbors in making
repairs and improvements. Strangers often visited him,
and when he rode abroad he was greeted with every
demonstration of respect.

General Le Clerc, meanwhile, was attacked by a new
and terrible enemy. His troops, unused to the climate,
were cut down by yellow fever, as a mower cuts grass.
In this situation, had Toussaint excited the blacks against
them, they might have been exterminated; but he had
sworn to observe the treaty, and he was never known
to break his word. The kind-hearted negroes, in many
cases, took pity on the suffering French soldiers; they
carried them many little comforts, and even took them
into their houses, and nursed them tenderly.

Meanwhile, General Le Clerc's difficulties increased.
His troops were dying fast under the influence of the
hot season; provisions were getting scarce; he wanted
to disband the negro troops that had joined him, but they
were wide awake and suspicious on the subject of Slavery,
and he dared not propose to disarm them. He was so
treacherous himself that he could not believe in the sincerity of others. He was always suspecting that Tous-

saint would again take command of the blacks and attack the remnant of his army while it was enfeebled by disease.   Bonaparte also felt that the popularity of Toussaint stood much in the way of his accomplishing the design of restoring Slavery.   It was desirable to get him out of the way upon some pretext.   The French officers made him the object of a series of petty insults, and wantonly destroyed the fruit on his grounds.   By these means they hoped to provoke him to excite an insurrection, that they might have an excuse for arresting him. His friends warned him that these continual insults and depredations foreboded mischief, and that he ought not to submit to them.   He replied, "It is a sacred duty to expose life when the freedom of one's country is in peril; but to rouse the people to save one's own life is inglorious."

Finding private remonstrances of no use, he reported to the French head-quarters that he and his neighbors were much annoyed by the conduct of the French troops, and that the people in the valley were made very uneasy by their rude manners and their depredations on property. He received a very polite answer from General Brunet, inviting him to come to his house to confer with him on that and other matters connected with the public tranquillity.   The letter closed with these words: "You will not find all the pleasures I would wish to welcome you with, but you will find the frankness of an honorable man, who desires nothing but the happiness of the colony, and your own happiness.   If Madame Toussaint, with whom it would give me the greatest pleasure to become acquainted, could accompany you, I should be gratified. If she has occasion for horses, I will send her mine. Never, General, will you find a more sincere friend than myself."

Toussaint, who was sincerely desirous to preserve the public peace, and who was too honest to suspect treachery under such a friendly form, went to General Brunet's head-quarters, with a few attendants, on the 10th of June, 1802. He was received with the greatest respect and cordiality. His host consulted with him concerning the interests of the colony; and they examined maps together till toward evening, when General Brunet left the room. An officer with twenty armed men entered, saying : " The Captain-General has ordered me to arrest you. Your attendants are overpowered. If you resist, you are a dead man." Toussaint's first impulse was to defend himself; but seeing it would be useless against such numbers, he resigned himself to his hard fate, saying, " Heaven will avenge my cause."

His papers were seized, his house rifled and burned, his wife and children captured, and at midnight they were all carried on board the French ship Hero, without being allowed to take even a change of clothing. His wrists were chained, he was locked in a cabin guarded by soldiers with fixed bayonets, and not permitted to hold any communication with his family. As the vessel sailed away from St. Domingo, Toussaint, gazing on the outline of its mountains for the last time, said, " They have cut down the tree of Liberty; but the roots are many and deep, and it will sprout again."

Toussaint l'Ouverture was even then incapable of imagining the base designs against him. He supposed that he had been accused of something, and was to be carried to France for trial. Conscious of uniform fidelity to the French government, he felt no uneasiness as to the result, though the treachery and violence with which he had been treated in return for his great services made him very sad. Arrived on the shores of France, he was removed to another vessel, and allowed only a few moments to say farewell to his wife and children. They embraced him with tears, and begged him to remember them, who had always loved him so dearly.

From the vessel, instead of being carried to Paris for trial, as he expected, he was hurried into a carriage, and, followed by a strong guard, was carried to the dismal Castle of Joux, near the borders of Switzerland. That ancient castle stands among the mountains of Jura, on the summit of a solid rock five hundred feet high. He was placed in a deep, dark dungeon, from the walls of which the water dripped continually. This was in August, 1802. But though it was summer elsewhere, it was damp and cold in Toussaint's dreary cell. The keeper was allowed about four shillings a day to provide food for him; and one faithful servant, who had accompanied the family from St. Domingo, was allowed to remain with him.

His spirits were kept up for some time with the daily expectation of being summoned to attend his trial. But time passed on, and he could obtain no tidings from the French government, or from his family. In a letter to General Bonaparte, beseeching him to let him know of what he was accused, and to grant him a trial, he wrote : —

"I have served my country with honor, fidelity, and integrity. All who know me will do me the justice to acknowledge this. At the time of the revolution, I spent all I had in the service of my country. I purchased but one small estate, on which to establish my wife and family. I neglected nothing for the welfare of St. Domingo. I made it my duty and pleasure to develop all the resources

of that beautiful colony. Since I entered the service of
the republic I have not claimed a penny of my salary.
I have taken money from the treasury only for public
use. If I was wrong in forming a constitution, it was
through my great desire to do good, and thinking it
would please the government under which I served. I
have had the misfortune to incur your displeasure; but
I am strong in the consciousness of integrity and fidelity;
and I dare affirm that among all the servants of the state
no one is more honest than myself."

This letter is still in existence, and some of the words
are blotted out by tears that fell while the noble captive
was writing it. Bonaparte paid no attention to this manly
appeal. After weary waiting, Toussaint wrote again: —

"First Consul, it is a misfortune to me that I am not
known to you. If you had thoroughly known me while
I was in St. Domingo, you would have done me more
justice. I am not learned; I am ignorant: but my heart
is good. My father showed me the road to virtue and
honor, and I am very strong in my conscience in that
matter. If I had not been so devoted to the French
government I should not be here. All my life I have
been in active service, and now I am a miserable prisoner,
without power to do anything, sunk in grief, and with
health impaired. I ask you for my freedom, that I may
labor for the support of my family. For my venerable
father, now a hundred and five years old, who is blind,
and needs my assistance; for my dearly loved wife, who,
separated from me, cannot, I fear, endure the afflictions that overwhelm her; and for my cherished family,
who have made the happiness of my life. I call on
your greatness. Let your heart be softened by my mis-
fortunes."

This touching appeal met with the same fate as the first. Bonaparte even had the meanness to forbid the prisoner's wearing an officer's uniform. When he asked for a change of clothing, the cast-off suit of a soldier and a pair of old boots were sent him. There seemed to be a deliberate system of heaping contempt upon him. The daily sum allowed for his food was diminished, and the cold winds of autumn began to howl round his dungeon. They doubtless thought that so old a man, accustomed to tropical warmth, and the devotion of a loving family, would die under the combined influence of solitude, cold, and scanty food. But his iron constitution withstood the severe test. The next step was to deprive him of his faithful servant, Mars Plaisir. Seeing him weep bitterly, Toussaint said to him: "Would I could console thee under this cruel separation. Be assured I shall never forget thy faithful services. Carry my last farewell to my wife and family."

The farewell never reached them. Mars Plaisir was lodged in another prison, lest he should tell of the slow murder that was going on in the Castle of Joux. Toussaint's supply of food was gradually diminished, till he had barely enough to keep him alive, — merely a little meal daily, which he had to prepare for himself in an earthen jug. The walls sparkled with frost, and the floor was slippery with ice, except immediately around his little fire. Thus he passed through a most miserable winter. He was thin as a skeleton; but still he did not die. As a last resort, the governor of the castle went away and took the keys of the dungeon with him. He was gone three days; and when he returned, Toussaint was lying stiff and cold on his heap of straw. Doctors were called in to examine him, and they certified that he

died of apoplexy. This was in April, 1803, after he
had been more than eight months in that horrid dungeon,
and when he was a little more than sixty years old. The
body was buried in the chapel under the castle. It was
given out to the world that the deceased prisoner was
a revolted slave, who had been guilty of every species
of robbery and cruelty; and that he had been thrown into
prison for plotting to deliver the island of St. Domingo
into the hands of the English.

When the family of Toussaint l'Ouverture were informed of his death, they were overwhelmed with grief,
though they had no idea of the horrid circumstances connected with it. The two oldest sons tried to escape from
France, but were seized and imprisoned. The French
government feared the consequences of their returning
to St. Domingo. The youngest son soon after died of
consumption. Madame Toussaint sank under the weight
of her great afflictions. Her health became very feeble,
and at times her mind wandered. When the power of
Bonaparte was overthrown, and a new government introduced into France, a pension was granted for her support,
and her two sons were released from prison. She died
in their arms in 1816.

There was great consternation in St. Domingo when
it was known that Toussaint l'Ouverture had been kidnapped and carried off. There was an attempt at mutiny
among the black soldiers; but the leaders were shot by
the French, and the spirit of insurrection was put down
for a time. No tidings could be obtained from Toussaint,
and after a while he was generally believed to be dead.
But his prediction was fulfilled. The tree of Liberty,
that had been cut down, did sprout again. Bonaparte

sent new troops to St. Domingo to supply the place of those cut off by yellow fever. The French officers frequently subjected black soldiers to the lash, a punishment which had never been inflicted upon them since the days of Slavery. An active slave-trade was carried on with the other French colonies, where Slavery had been restored, and people were frequently smuggled away from St. Domingo and sold. The mulattoes found out that people of their color were sold, as well as blacks. They had formerly acted against their mothers' race, not because they were worse than other men, but because they had the same human nature that other men have. Being free born, and many of them educated and wealthy, and slaveholders also, they despised the blacks, who had always been slaves; but when Slavery touched people of their own color, they were ready to act with the negroes against the whites. Toussaint's generals, though they still held their old rank in the army, grew more and more distrustful of the French. When General Christophe accepted an invitation to dine with General Le Clerc, he ordered his troops to be in readiness for a sudden blow. The French officer who sat next him at table urged him to drink a great deal of wine; but Christophe was on his guard, and kept his wits about him. At last he repulsed the offer of wine with great rudeness, whereupon Le Clerc summoned his guard to be in readiness, and began to accuse Toussaint of treachery to the whites. "Treachery!" exclaimed the indignant Christophe. "Have you not broken oaths and treaties, and violated the sacred rights of hospitality? Those whose blood flows for our liberty are rewarded with prison, banishment, death. Friends, soldiers, heroes of our mountains, are no longer around me. Toussaint, the pride of our race, the terror of our enemies, whose genius led us from Slavery to Liberty, who adorned peace with lovely virtues, whose glory fills the world, was put in irons, like the vilest criminal!"

General Le Clerc deemed it prudent to preserve outward composure, for General Christophe had informed him that troops were in readiness to protect him. But notwithstanding many ominous symptoms of discontent among the blacks and mulattoes, he blindly persevered in carrying out the cruel policy of Bonaparte. Shiploads of slaves were brought into St. Domingo and openly sold. Then came a decree authorizing slaveholders to resume their old authority over the blacks. Bitterly did Toussaint's officers regret having trusted to the promises of the French authorities. The consciousness of having been deceived made the fire of freedom burn all the more fiercely in their souls. The blacks were everywhere ready to die rather than be slaves again. In November, 1803, General Christophe published a document in which he said:—

"The independence of St. Domingo is proclaimed. Toward men who do us justice we will act as brothers. But we have sworn not to listen with clemency to any one who speaks to us of Slavery. We will be inexorable, perhaps even cruel, toward those who come from Europe to bring among us death and servitude. No sacrifice is too costly, and all means are lawful, when men find that freedom, the greatest of all blessings, is to be wrested from them."

The closing scenes of the revolution were too horrible to be described. General Rochambeau, who commanded the French army after the death of General Le Clerc, was a tyrannical and cruel tool of the slaveholders.

Everywhere colored men were seized and executed without forms of law. Maurepas, who had been one of Toussaint's most distinguished generals, was seized on suspicion of favoring insurrection. His epaulets were nailed to his shoulders with spikes, he was suspended from the yard-arm of a vessel, while his wife and children, and four hundred of his black soldiers, were thrown over to the sharks before his eyes. The trees were hung with the corpses of negroes. Some were torn to pieces by bloodhounds trained for the purpose ; some were burnt alive. Sixteen of Toussaint's bravest generals were chained by the neck to the rocks of an uninhabited island, and left there to perish. Most of these victims were firm in the midst of their tortures, and died with the precious word Freedom on their lips. A mother, whose daughters were going to be executed, said to them : " Be thankful. You will not live to be the mothers of slaves."

I am happy to record that all the whites were not destitute of feeling. Some sea-captains, who were ordered to take negroes out to sea and drown them, contrived to aid their escape to the mountains, or landed them on other shores.

The blacks, driven to desperation, became as cruel as their oppressors. They visited upon white men, women, and children all the barbarities they had seen and suffered. The wife of General Paul, brother of Toussaint, was dragged from her peaceful home, and drowned by French soldiers. This murder made him perfectly crazy with revenge. Though naturally of a mild disposition, he thenceforth had no mercy on anybody of white complexion. His old father, Gaou-Guinou, who survived Toussaint about a year, was filled with the same spirit, and the last words he uttered were a malediction on the whites. The spirit of the infernal regions raged throughout all classes, and it was all owing to the wickedness of Slavery.

On the last day of November, 1803, little more than a year after the abduction of Toussaint, the French were driven from the island, never more to return. The colony, which might have been a source of wealth to them, if Toussaint had been allowed to carry out his plans, was lost to France forever. St. Domingo became independent, under its old name of Hayti; and General Christophe, who was as able as Toussaint, but more ambitious, was proclaimed emperor. A law was passed, and still remains in force, that no white man should own a foot of soil on the island. But white Americans and Europeans reside there, and transact various kinds of business under the protection of equal laws.

Perhaps it sometimes seemed to Toussaint, in the loneliness of his dungeon, as if all his great sacrifices and efforts for his oppressed race had been in vain. But they were not in vain. God raised him up to do a great work, which he faithfully performed; and his spirit is still "marching on." Slavery becomes more and more odious in the civilized world, and nation after nation abolishes it. Fifty years after the death of Toussaint all the slaves in the French colonies were emancipated. How his spirit must rejoice to look on the West Indies now!

In 1850 the grave of Toussaint l'Ouverture was discovered by some engineers at work on the Castle of Joux. His skull was placed on a shelf in the dungeon where he died, and is shown to travellers who visit the place.

For a long while great injustice was done to the memory of Toussaint l'Ouverture, and also to the blacks who fought so fiercely in resistance of Slavery; for the histories of St. Domingo were written by prejudiced French writers, or by equally prejudiced mulattoes. But at last the truth is made known. Candid, well-informed persons now acknowledge that the blacks of St. Domingo sinned cruelly because they were cruelly sinned against; and Toussaint l'Ouverture, seen in the light of his own actions, is acknowledged to be one of the greatest and best men the world has ever produced. A very distinguished English poet, named Wordsworth, has written an admirable sonnet to his memory. The celebrated Harriet Martineau, of England, has made him the hero of a beautiful novel. Wendell Phillips, one of the most eloquent speakers in the United States, has eulogized his memory in a noble lecture, delivered in various parts of the country, before thousands and thousands of hearers. And James Redpath has recently published in Boston a biography of Toussaint l'Ouverture, truthfully portraying the pure and great soul of that martyred hero.

Well may the Freedmen of the United States take pride in Toussaint l'Ouverture, as the man who made an opening of freedom for their oppressed race, and by the greatness of his character and achievements proved the capabilities of Black Men.

———————

It is better to be a lean freeman than a fat slave. — *A Proverb in Hayti.*

THE ASPIRATIONS OF MINGO.

A SLAVE in one of our Southern States, named Mingo, was endowed with uncommon abilities. If he had been a white man, his talents would have secured him an honorable position; but being colored, his great intelligence only served to make him an object of suspicion. He was thrown into prison, to be sold. He wrote the following lines on the walls, which were afterward found and copied. A Southern gentleman sent them to a friend in Boston, as a curiosity, and they were published in the Boston Journal, many years ago. The night after Mingo wrote them, he escaped from the slave-prison; but he was tracked and caught by bloodhounds, who tore him in such a shocking manner that he died. By that dreadful process his great soul was released from his enslaved body. His wife lived to be an aged woman, and was said to have many of his poems in her possession. Here are the lines he wrote in his agony while in prison: —

"Good God! and must I leave them now,
  My wife, my children, in their woe?
  'T is mockery to say I 'm sold!
  But I forget these chains so cold,
  Which goad my bleeding limbs; though high
  My reason mounts above the sky.
  Dear wife, they cannot sell the rose
  Of love that in my bosom glows.
  Remember, as your tears may start,
  They cannot sell the immortal part.
  Thou Sun, which lightest bond and free,

Tell me, I pray, is liberty
The lot of those who noblest feel,
And oftest to Jehovah kneel?
Then I may say, but not with pride,
I feel the rushings of the tide
Of reason and of eloquence,
Which strive and yearn for eminence.
I feel high manhood on me now,
A spirit-glory on my brow;
I feel a thrill of music roll,
Like angel-harpings, through my soul;
While poesy, with rustling wings,
Upon my spirit rests and sings.
He sweeps my heart's deep throbbing lyre,
Who touched Isaiah's lips with fire."

May God forgive his oppressors.

BURY ME IN A FREE LAND.

BY FRANCES E. W. HARPER.

MAKE me a grave where'er you will,
  In a lowly plain or a lofty hill;
Make it among earth's humblest graves,
But not in a land where men are slaves.

I ask no monument proud and high,
To arrest the gaze of the passers by;
All that my yearning spirit craves
Is, Bury me not in a Land of Slaves.

PHILLIS WHEATLEY.

BY L. MARIA CHILD.

PHILLIS WHEATLEY was born in Africa, and brought to Boston, Massachusetts, in the year 1761, — a little more than a hundred years ago. At that time the people in Massachusetts held slaves. The wife of Mr. John Wheatley of Boston had several slaves; but they were getting too old to be very active, and she wanted to purchase a young girl, whom she could train up in such a manner as to make her a good domestic. She went to the slave-market for that purpose, and there she saw a little girl with no other clothing than a piece of dirty, ragged carpeting tied round her. She looked as if her health was feeble, — probably owing to her sufferings in the slave-ship, and to the fact of her having no one to care for her after she landed. Mrs. Wheatley was a kind, religious woman; and though she considered the sickly look of the child an objection, there was something so gentle and modest in the expression of her dark countenance, that her heart was drawn toward her, and she bought her in preference to several others who looked more robust. She took her home in her chaise, put her in a bath, and dressed her in clean clothes. They could not at first understand her; for she spoke an African dialect, sprinkled with a few words of broken English; and when she could not make herself understood, she resorted to a variety of gestures and signs. She did not know her own age, but, from her shedding her front teeth at that time, she was supposed to be about seven years old. She could not tell how long it was since the slave-traders tore her from her parents, nor where she had been since that time. The poor little orphan had probably gone through so much suffering and terror, and been so unable to make herself understood by anybody, that her mind had become bewildered concerning the past. She soon learned to speak English; but she could remember nothing about Africa, except that she used to see her mother pour out water before the rising sun. Almost all the ancient nations of the world supposed that a Great Spirit had his dwelling in the sun, and they worshipped that Spirit in various forms. One of the most common modes of worship was to pour out water, or wine, at the rising of the sun, and to utter a brief prayer to the Spirit of that glorious luminary. Probably this ancient custom had been handed down, age after age, in Africa, and in that fashion the untaught mother of little Phillis continued to worship the god of her ancestors. The sight of the great splendid orb, coming she knew not whence, rising apparently out of the hills to make the whole world glorious with light, and the devout reverence with which her mother hailed its return every morning, might naturally impress the child's imagination so deeply, that she remembered it after she had forgotten everything else about her native land.

A wonderful change took place in the little forlorn stranger in the course of a year and a half. She not only learned to speak English correctly, but she was able to read fluently in any part of the Bible. She evidently possessed uncommon intelligence and a great desire for knowledge. She was often found trying to make letters with charcoal on the walls and fences. Mrs. Wheatley's

daughter, perceiving her eagerness to learn, undertook
to teach her to read and write. She found this an easy
task, for her pupil learned with astonishing quickness.
At the same time she showed such an amiable, affectionate disposition, that all members of the family became
much attached to her. Her gratitude to her kind, motherly mistress was unbounded, and her greatest delight
was to do anything to please her.

When she was about fourteen years old, she began to
write poetry; and it was pretty good poetry, too. Owing
to these uncommon manifestations of intelligence, and
to the delicacy of her health, she was never put to hard
household work, as was intended at the time of her purchase. She was kept constantly with Mrs. Wheatley
and her daughter, employed in light and easy services
for them. Her poetry attracted attention, and Mrs.
Wheatley's friends lent her books, which she read with
great eagerness. She soon acquired a good knowledge
of geography, history, and English poetry; of the last
she was particularly fond. After a while, they found
she was trying to learn Latin, which she so far mastered
as to be able to read it understandingly. There was no
law in Massachusetts against slaves learning to read and
write, as there have been in many of the States; and her
mistress, so far from trying to hinder her, did everything
to encourage her love of learning. She always called
her affectionately, "My Phillis," and seemed to be as
proud of her attainments as if she had been her own
daughter. She even allowed her to have a fire and light
in her own chamber in the evening, that she might study
and write down her thoughts whenever they came to her.

Phillis was of a very religious turn of mind, and when
she was about sixteen she joined the Orthodox Church,

that worshipped in the Old-South Meeting-house in Boston. Her character and deportment were such that she was considered an ornament to the church. Clergymen and other literary persons who visited at Mrs. Wheatley's took a good deal of notice of her. Her poems were brought forward to be read to the company, and were often much praised. She was not unfrequently invited to the houses of wealthy and distinguished people, who liked to show her off as a kind of wonder. Most young girls would have had their heads completely turned by so much flattery and attention; but seriousness and humility seemed to be natural to Phillis. She always retained the same gentle, modest deportment that had won Mrs. Wheatley's heart when she first saw her in the slave-market. Sometimes, when she went abroad, she was invited to sit at table with other guests; but she always modestly declined, and requested that a plate might be placed for her on a side-table. Being well aware of the common prejudice against her complexion, she feared that some one might be offended by her company at their meals. By pursuing this course she manifested a natural politeness, which proved her to be more truly refined than any person could be who objected to sit beside her on account of her color.

Although she was tenderly cared for, and not required to do any fatiguing work, her constitution never recovered from the shock it had received in early childhood. When she was about nineteen years old, her health failed so rapidly that physicians said it was necessary for her to take a sea-voyage. A son of Mr. Wheatley's was going to England on commercial business, and his mother proposed that Phillis should go with him.

In England she received even more attention than had

been bestowed upon her at home.   Several of the nobility invited her to their houses; and her poems were published in a volume, with an engraved likeness of the author.   In this picture she looks gentle and thoughtful, and the shape of her head denotes intellect.   One of the engravings was sent to Mrs. Wheatley, who was delighted with it.   When one of her relatives called, she pointed it out to her, and said, "Look at my Phillis!   Does she not seem as if she would speak to me?"

Still the young poetess was not spoiled by flattery. One of the relatives of Mrs. Wheatley informs us, that "not all the attention she received, nor all the honors that were heaped upon her, had the slightest influence upon her temper and deportment.   She was still the same single-hearted, unsophisticated being."

She addressed a poem to the Earl of Dartmouth, who was very kind to her during her visit to England.   Having expressed a hope for the overthrow of tyranny, she says : —

> "Should you, my Lord, while you peruse my song,
> Wonder from whence my love of Freedom sprung, —
> Whence flow these wishes for the common good,
> By feeling hearts alone best understood, —
> I, young in life, by seeming cruel fate,
> Was snatched from Afric's fancied happy state.
> What pangs excruciating must molest,
> What sorrows labor in my parent's breast!
> Steeled was that soul, and by no misery moved,
> That from a father seized his babe beloved.
> Such was my case; and can I then but pray
> Others may never feel tyrannic sway."

The English friends of Phillis wished to present her to their king, George the Third, who was soon expected in London.   But letters from America informed her that her beloved benefactress, Mrs. Wheatley, was in declining health, and greatly desired to see her. No honors could divert her mind from the friend of her childhood. She returned to Boston immediately. The good lady died soon after; Mr. Wheatley soon followed; and the daughter, the kind instructress of her youth, did not long survive. The son married and settled in England. For a short time Phillis stayed with a friend of her deceased benefactress; then she hired a room and lived by herself. It was a sad change for her.

The war of the American Revolution broke out. In the autumn of 1776 General Washington had his headquarters at Cambridge, Massachusetts; and the spirit moved Phillis to address some complimentary verses to him. In reply, he sent her the following courteous note:—

"I thank you most sincerely for your polite notice of me in the elegant lines you enclosed. However undeserving I may be of such encomium, the style and manner exhibit a striking proof of your poetical talents. In honor of which, and as a tribute justly due to you, I would have published the poem, had I not been apprehensive that, while I only meant to give the world this new instance of your genius, I might have incurred the imputation of vanity. This, and nothing else, determined me not to give it a place in the public prints.

"If you should ever come to Cambridge, or near headquarters, I shall be happy to see a person so favored by the Muses,* and to whom Nature had been so liberal and beneficent in her dispensations.

"I am, with great respect,

"Your obedient, humble servant,

"GEORGE WASHINGTON."

* The ancient Greeks supposed that nine goddesses, whom they named Muses, inspired people to write various kinds of poetry.

The early friends of Phillis were dead, or scattered abroad, and she felt alone in the world. She formed an acquaintance with a colored man by the name of Peters, who kept a grocery shop. He was more than commonly intelligent, spoke fluently, wrote easily, dressed well, and was handsome in his person. He offered marriage, and in an evil hour she accepted him. He proved to be lazy, proud, and harsh-tempered. He neglected his business, failed, and became very poor. Though unwilling to do hard work himself, he wanted to make a drudge of his wife. Her constitution was frail, she had been unaccustomed to hardship, and she was the mother of three little children, with no one to help her in her household labors and cares. He had no pity on her, and instead of trying to lighten her load, he made it heavier by his bad temper. The little ones sickened and died, and their gentle mother was completely broken down by toil and sorrow. Some of the descendants of her lamented mistress at last heard of her illness and went to see her. They found her in a forlorn situation, suffering for the common comforts of life. The Revolutionary war was still raging. Everybody was mourning for sons and husbands slain in battle. The country was very poor. The currency was so deranged that a goose cost forty dollars, and other articles in proportion. In such a state of things, people were too anxious and troubled to think about the African poetess, whom they had once delighted to honor; or if they transiently remembered her, they took it for granted that her husband provided for her. And so it happened that the gifted woman who had been patronized by wealthy Bostonians, and who had rolled through London in the splendid carriages of the English nobility, lay dying alone, in a cold, dirty, comfortless room. It was a mournful reverse of fortune; but she was patient and resigned. She made no complaint of her unfeeling husband; but the neighbors said that when a load of wood was sent to her, he felt himself too much of a gentleman to saw it, though his wife was shivering with cold. The descendants of Mrs. Wheatley did what they could to relieve her wants, after they discovered her extremely destitute condition; but, fortunately for her, she soon went "where the wicked cease from troubling, and where the weary are at rest."

Her husband was so generally disliked, that people never called her Mrs. Peters. She was always called Phillis Wheatley, the name bestowed upon her when she first entered the service of her benefactress, and by which she had become known as a poetess.

A PERTINENT QUESTION.

BY FREDERICK DOUGLASS.

IS it not astonishing, that while we are ploughing, planting, and reaping, using all kinds of mechanical tools, erecting houses and constructing bridges, building ships, working in metals of brass, iron, and copper, silver and gold; that while we are reading, writing, and ciphering, acting as clerks, merchants, and secretaries, having among us lawyers, doctors, ministers, poets, authors, editors, orators, and teachers; that while we are engaged in all manner of enterprises common to other men, digging gold in California, capturing the whale in the Pacific, breeding sheep and cattle on the hillside; living, moving, acting, thinking, planning; living in families as husbands, wives, and children; and, above all, confessing and worshipping the Christian's God, and looking hopefully for immortal life beyond the grave; — is it not astonishing, I say, that we are called upon to prove that we àre *men?*"

THE WORKS OF PROVIDENCE.

BY PHILLIS WHEATLEY.

[Written at sixteen years of age.]

ARISE, my soul! on wings enraptured rise,
　　To praise the Monarch of the earth and skies,
Whose goodness and beneficence appear,
As round its centre moves the rolling year;
Or when the morning glows with rosy charms,
Or the sun slumbers in the ocean's arms.
Of light divine be a rich portion lent,
To guide my soul and favor my intent.
Celestial Muse, my arduous flight sustain,
And raise my mind to a seraphic strain!

　　Adored forever be the God unseen,
Who round the sun revolves this vast machine;
Though to his eye its mass a point appears:
Adored the God that whirls surrounding spheres,
Who first ordained that mighty Sol* should reign,
The peerless monarch of th' ethereal train.
Of miles twice forty millions is his height,
And yet his radiance dazzles mortal sight,
So far beneath, — from him th' extended earth
Vigor derives, and every flowery birth.
Vast through her orb she moves, with easy grace,

* *Sol* is the word for sun in Latin, the language spoken by the
ancient Romans.

Around her Phœbus * in unbounded space;
True to her course, the impetuous storm derides,
Triumphant o'er the winds and surging tides.

Almighty! in these wondrous works of thine,
What power, what wisdom, and what goodness shine!
And are thy wonders, Lord, by men explored,
And yet creating glory unadored?

Creation smiles in various beauty gay,
While day to night, and night succeeds to day.
That wisdom which attends Jehovah's ways,
Shines most conspicuous in the solar rays.
Without them, destitute of heat and light,
This world would be the reign of endless night.
In their excess, how would our race complain,
Abhorring life! how hate its lengthened chain!
From air, or dust, what numerous ills would rise!
What dire contagion taint the burning skies!
What pestilential vapor, fraught with death,
Would rise, and overspread the lands beneath!

Hail, smiling Morn, that, from the orient main
Ascending, dost adorn the heavenly plain!
So rich, so various are thy beauteous dyes,
That spread through all the circuit of the skies,
That, full of thee, my soul in rapture soars,
And thy great God, the cause of all, adores!
O'er beings infinite his love extends,
His wisdom rules them, and his power defends.
When tasks diurnal tire the human frame,
The spirits faint, and dim the vital flame,

* Phœbus was the name for the sun, in the language of the ancient
Greeks.

Then, too, that ever-active bounty shines,
Which not infinity of space confines.
The sable veil, that Night in silence draws,
Conceals effects, but shows th' Almighty Cause.
Night seals in sleep the wide creation fair,
And all is peaceful, but the brow of care.
Again gay Phœbus, as the day before,
Wakes every eye but what shall wake no more;
Again the face of Nature is renewed,
Which still appears harmonious, fair, and good.
May grateful strains salute the smiling morn,
Before its beams the eastern hills adorn!

THE DYING CHRISTIAN.

BY FRANCES E. W. HARPER.

THE silver cord was loosened,
      We knew that she must die;
We read the mournful token
      In the dimness of her eye.

Like a child oppressed with slumber,
      She calmly sank to rest,
With her trust in her Redeemer,
      And her head upon his breast.

She faded from our vision,
      Like a thing of love and light;
But we feel she lives forever,
      A spirit pure and bright.

FRAMINGHAM, MASS.

KINDNESS TO ANIMALS.

BY L. MARIA CHILD.

THERE are not many people who are conscientious about being kind in their relations with human beings; and therefore it is not surprising that still fewer should be considerate about humanity to animals. But the Father of all created beings made dumb creatures to enjoy existence in their way, as he made human beings to enjoy life in their way. We do wrong in his sight if we abuse them, or keep them without comfortable food and shelter. The fact that they cannot speak to tell of what they suffer makes the sad expression of their great patient eyes the more touching to any compassionate heart. Fugitive slaves, looking out mournfully and wearily upon a cold, unsympathizing world, have often reminded me of overworked and abused oxen; for though slaves were endowed by their Creator with the gift of speech, their oppressors have made them afraid to use it to complain of their wrongs. In fact, they have been in a more trying situation than abused oxen, for they have been induced by fear to use their gift of speech in professions of contentment with their bondage. Therefore, those who have been slaves know how to sympathize with the dumb creatures of God; and they, more than others, ought to have compassion on them. The great and good Toussaint l'Ouverture was always kind to the animals under his care, and I consider it by no means the smallest of his merits.

It is selfish and cruel thoughtlessness to stand laughing and talking, or to be resting at ease, while horses or oxen are tied where they will be tormented by flies or mosquitos. Last summer I read of a horse that was left fastened in a swamp, where he could not get away from the swarm of venomous insects, which stung him to death, while his careless, hard-hearted driver was going about forgetful of him. It would trouble my conscience ever afterward if I had the death of that poor helpless animal to answer for.

There is a difference in the natural disposition of animals, as there is in the dispositions of men and women; but, generally speaking, if animals are bad-tempered and stubborn, it is owing to their having been badly treated when they were young. When a horse has his mouth hurt by jerking his bridle, it irritates him, as it irritates a man to be violently knocked about; and in both cases such treatment produces an unwillingness to oblige the tormentor. Lashing a horse with a whip, to compel him to draw loads too heavy for his strength, makes him angry and discouraged; and at last, in despair of getting any help for his wrongs, he stands stock still when he finds himself fastened to a heavy load, and no amount of kicking or beating will make him stir. He has apparently come to the conclusion that it is better to be killed at once than to die daily. Slaves, who are under cruel taskmasters, also sometimes sink down in utter discouragement, and do not seem to care for being whipped to death. The best way to cure the disheartened and obstinate laborer is to give him just wages and kind treatment; and the best way to deal with the discouraged and stubborn horse is to give him light loads and humane usage.

It is a very bad custom to whip a horse when he is frightened. It only frightens the poor creature all the more. Habits of running when frightened, or of sheering at the sight of things to which they are not accustomed, is generally produced in horses by mismanagement when they are colts. By gentle and rational treatment better characters are formed, both in animals and human beings. There was a gentleman in the neighborhood of Boston who managed colts so wisely, that all who were acquainted with him wanted a horse of his training. He was very firm with the young animals; he never allowed them to get the better of him; but he was never in a passion with them. He cured them of bad tricks by patient teaching and gentle words; holding them tight all the while, till they did what he wanted them to do. When they became docile, he rubbed their heads, and patted their necks, and talked affectionately to them, and gave them a handful of oats. In that way, he obtained complete control over them. He never kicked them, or jerked their mouths with the bridle; he never whipped them, or allowed a whip to be used; and the result was that they learned to love him, and were always ready to do as he bade them.

I have read of a horse that was so terrified by the sound of a drum, that if he heard it, even from a distance, he would run furiously and smash to pieces any carriage to which he was harnessed. In consequence of this, he was sold very cheap, though he was a strong, handsome animal. The man who sold him said he had whipped and whipped him, to cure him of the trick, but it did no good. People laughed at the man who bought him, and said he had thrown money away upon a useless and dangerous creature; but he replied, " I have some experience in horses, and I think I can cure him."

He resolved to use no violence, but to deal rationally and humanely with the animal, as he would like to be dealt with if he were a horse.

He kept him without food till he had become very hungry, and then he placed a pan of oats before him on the top of a drum. As soon as he began to eat, the man beat upon the drum. The horse reared and plunged and ran furiously round the enclosure. He was led back to the stable without any provender. After a while, oats were again placed before him on the top of a drum. As soon as the drum was beaten, the horse reared and ran away. I suppose he remembered the terrible whippings he had had whenever he heard a drum, and so he thought the thing that made the noise was an enemy to him. The third time the experiment was tried, he had become excessively hungry. He pricked up his ears and snorted when he heard the sound of the drum; but he stood still and looked at the oats wistfully, while the man played a loud, lively tune. Finding the noise did him no harm, he at last ventured to taste of the oats, and his owner continued to play all the while he was eating. When the breakfast was finished, he patted him on the neck and talked gently to him. For several days his food was given to him in the same way. He was never afraid of the sound of a drum afterward. On the contrary, he learned to like it, because it made him think of sweet oats.

The fact is, reasonable and kind treatment will generally produce a great and beneficial change in vicious animals as well as in vicious men.

JAMES FORTEN.

BY L. MARIA CHILD.

JAMES FORTEN was born in 1766, nearly a hundred years ago. His ancestors had lived in Pennsylvania for several generations, and, so far as he could trace them, they had never been slaves. In his boyhood the war of the American Revolution began. The States of this Union were then colonies of Great Britain. Being taxed without being represented in the British Parliament, they remonstrated against it as an act of injustice. The king, George the Third, was a dull, obstinate man, disposed to be despotic. The loyal, respectful petitions of the Colonies were treated with indifference or contempt; and at last they resolved to become independent of England. When James Forten was about fourteen years old he entered into the service of the Colonial navy, in the ship Royal Louis, commanded by Captain Decatur, father of the celebrated commodore. It was captured by the British ship Amphion, commanded by Sir John Beezly. Sir John's son was on board, as midshipman. He was about the same age as James Forten; and when they played games together on the deck, the agility and skill of the brown lad attracted his attention. They became much attached to each other; and the young Englishman offered to provide for the education of his colored companion, and to help him on in the world, if he would go to London with him. But James preferred to remain in the service of his native country. The lads shed tears at parting, and Sir John's son obtained a promise from his father that his friend should not be enlisted in the British army. This was a great relief to the mind of James; for his sympathies were on the side of the American Colonies, and he knew that colored men in his circumstances were often carried to the West Indies and sold into Slavery. He was transferred to the prison-ship Old Jersey, then lying near New York. He remained there, through a raging pestilence on board, until prisoners were exchanged.

After the war was over, he obtained employment in a sail-loft in Philadelphia, where he soon established a good character by his intelligence, honesty, and industry. He invented an improvement in the management of sails, for which he obtained a patent. As it came into general use, it brought him a good deal of money. In process of time, he became owner of the sail-loft, and also of a good house in the city. He married a worthy woman, and they brought up a family of eight children. But though he had served his country faithfully in his youth, though he had earned a hundred thousand dollars by his ingenuity and diligence, and though his character rendered him an ornament to the Episcopal Church, to which he belonged, yet so strong was the mean and cruel prejudice against his color, that his family were excluded from schools where the most ignorant and vicious whites could place their children. He overcame this obstacle, at great expense, by hiring private teachers in various branches of education.

By the unrivalled neatness and durability of his work, and by the uprightness of his character, he obtained extensive business, and for more than fifty years employed many people in his sail-loft. Being near the water, he had opportunities, at twelve different times, to save people from drowning, which he sometimes did at the risk of his own life. The Humane Society of Philadelphia presented him with an engraving, to which was appended a certificate of the number of people he had saved, and the thanks of the Society for his services. He had it framed and hung in his parlor; and when I visited him, in 1835, he pointed it out to me, and told me he would not take a thousand dollars for it. He likewise told me of a vessel engaged in the slave-trade, the owners of which applied to him for rigging. He indignantly refused; declaring that he considered such a request an insult to any honest or humane man. He always had the cause of the oppressed colored people warmly at heart, and was desirous to do everything in his power for their improvement and elevation. He early saw that colonizing free blacks to Africa would never abolish Slavery; but that, on the contrary, it tended to prolong its detestable existence. He presided at the first meeting of colored people in Philadelphia, to remonstrate against the Colonization Society. He was an earnest and liberal friend of the Anti-Slavery Society; and almost the last words he was heard to utter were expressions of love and gratitude to William Lloyd Garrison for his exertions in behalf of his oppressed race. He never drank any intoxicating liquor, and was a steadfast supporter of the Temperance Society. Being of a kindly and humane disposition, he espoused the principles of the Peace Society. His influence and pure example were also given to those who were striving against licentiousness. Indeed, he was always ready to assist in every good word and work.

He died in 1842, at the age of seventy-six years. His funeral procession was one of the largest ever seen in Philadelphia; thousands of people, of all classes and all complexions, having united in this tribute of respect to his character.

THE MEETING IN THE SWAMP.

BY L. MARIA CHILD.

IN 1812 there was war between the United States and Great Britain; and many people thought it likely that a portion of the British army would land in some part of the Southern States and proclaim freedom to the slaves. The more intelligent portion of the slaves were aware of this, and narrowly watched the signs of the times.

Mr. Duncan, of South Carolina, was an easy sort of master, generally thought by his neighbors to be too indulgent to his slaves. One evening, during the year I have mentioned, he received many requests for passes to go to a great Methodist meeting, and in every instance complied with the request. After a while, he rang the bell for a glass of water, but no servant appeared. He rang a second time, but waited in vain for the sound of coming footsteps. Thinking over the passes he had given, he remembered that all the house-servants had gone to Methodist meeting. Then it occurred to him that Methodist meetings had lately been more frequent than usual. He was in the habit of saying that his slaves were perfectly contented, and would not take their freedom if he offered it to them; nevertheless the frequency of Methodist meetings made him a little uneasy, and brought to mind a report he had heard, that the British were somewhere off the coast and about to land.

The next morning, he took a ride on horseback, and

in a careless way asked the slaves on several plantations where was the Methodist meeting last night. Some said it was in one place, and some in another, — a circumstance which made him think still more about the report that the British were going to land. He bought a black mask for his face, and a suit of negro clothes, and waited for another Methodist meeting. In a few days his servants again asked for passes, and he gave them. When the last one had gone, he put on his disguise and followed them over field and meadow, through woods and swamps. The number of dark figures steering toward the same point continually increased. If any spoke to him as they passed, he made a very short answer, in the words and tones common among slaves. At last they arrived at an island in the swamp, surrounded by a belt of deep water, and hidden by forest-trees matted together by a luxuriant entanglement of vines. A large tree had been felled for a bridge, and over this dusky forms were swarming as thickly as ants into a new-made nest. After passing through a rough and difficult path, they came out into a large level space, surrounded by majestic trees, whose boughs interlaced, and formed a roof high overhead, from which hung down long streamers of Spanish moss. Under this canopy were assembled hundreds of black men and women. Some were sitting silent and thoughtful, some eagerly talking together, and some singing and shouting. The blaze of pine torches threw a strong light on some, and made others look like great black shadows.

Mr. Duncan felt a little disturbed by the strange, impressive scene, and was more than half disposed to wish himself at home. For some time he could make nothing out of the confused buzz of voices and chanting of hymns.

5 *

But after a while a tall man mounted a stump and requested silence. "I suppose most all of ye know," said he, "that at our last meeting we concluded to go to the British, if we could get a chance; but we did n't all agree what to do about our masters. Some said we could n't keep our freedom without we killed the whites, but others did n't like the thoughts of that. We 've met again to-night to talk about it. An' now, boys, if the British land here in Caroliny, what shall we do about our masters?"

As he sat down, a tall, fierce-looking mulatto sprang upon the stump, at one leap, and exclaimed: "Scourge *them*, as they have scourged *us*. Shoot *them*, as they have shot *us*. Who talks of mercy to our masters?"

"I do," said an aged black man, who rose up tottering, as he leaned both hands on a wooden staff, — "I do; because the blessed Jesus always talked of mercy. They shot my bright boy Joe, an' sold my pretty little Sally; but, thanks to the blessed Jesus! I feel it in my poor old heart to forgive 'em. I 've been member of a Methodist church these thirty years, an' I 've heard many preachers, white and black; an' they all tell me Jesus said, Do good to them that do evil to you, an' pray for them that spite you. Now I say, Let us love our enemies; let us pray for 'em; an' when our masters flog us, let us sing, —

> ' You may beat upon my body,
> But you cannot harm my soul.
> I shall join the forty thousand by and by.' "

When the tremulous chant ceased, a loud altercation arose. Some cried out for the blood of the whites, while others maintained that the old man's doctrine was right. Louder and louder grew the sound of their excited voices, and the disguised slaveholder hid himself away deeper among the shadows. In the midst of the confusion, a young man of graceful figure sprang on the stump, and, throwing off a coarse cotton frock, showed his back and shoulders deeply gashed by a whip and oozing with blood. He made no speech, but turned round and round slowly, while his comrades held up their torches to show his wounds. He stopped suddenly, and said, with stern brevity, "Blood for blood."

"Would you murder 'em all?" inquired a timid voice. "Dey don't *all* cruelize us."

"Dar's Massa Campbell," pleaded another. "He neber hab his boys flogged. You would n't murder *him*, would you?"

"No, no," shouted several voices; "we would n't murder *him*."

"I would n't murder *my* master," said one of Mr. Duncan's slaves. "I don't want to work for him for nothin'; I 'se done got tired o' that; but he sha'n't be killed, if I can help it; for he 's a good master."

"Call him a good master if ye like," said the youth with the bleeding shoulders. "If the white men don't cut up the backs that bear their burdens, if they don't shoot the limbs that make 'em rich, some are fools enough to call 'em good masters. What right have they to sleep in soft beds, while we, who do all the work, lie on the hard floor? Why should I go in coarse rags, to clothe my master in broadcloth and fine linen, when he knows, and I know, that we are sons of the same father? Ye may get on your knees to be flogged, if ye like; but I 'm not the boy to do it." His high, bold forehead and flashing eye indicated an intellect too active, and a spirit too fiery, for Slavery. The listeners were spell-bound by his superior bearing, and for a while he seemed likely to carry the whole meeting in favor of revenge. But the aged black, leaning on his wooden staff, made use of every pause to repeat the words, "Jesus told us to return good for evil"; and his gentle counsel found response in many hearts.

A short man, with roguish eyes and a laughing mouth, rose up and looked round him with an expression of drollery that made everybody begin to feel good-natured. After rubbing his head a little, he said: "I don't know how to talk like Bob, 'cause I neber had no chance. But I'se *thought* a heap. Many a time I'se axed myself how de white man always git he foot on de black man. Sometimes I tink one ting, and sometimes I tink anoder ting; and dey all git jumbled up in my head, jest like seed in de cotton. At last I finds out how de white man always git he foot on de black man." He took from his old torn hat a bit of crumpled newspaper, and smoothing it out, pointed at it, while he exclaimed: "*Dat's* de way dey do it! Dey got de *knowledge*; and dey don't let poor nigger hab de knowledge. May be de British lan', and may be de British no lan'. But I tell ye, boys, de white man can't keep he foot on de black man, ef de black man git de knowledge. I'se gwine to tell ye how I got de knowledge. I sot my mind on larning to read; but my ole boss he's de most begrudgfullest massa, an' I knows he would n't let me larn. So when I sees leetle massa wid he book, I ax him, 'What you call dat?' He tell me dat's A. So I take ole newspaper, an' ax missis, 'May I hab dis to rub de boots?' She say yes. Den, when I find A, I looks at him till I knows him bery well. Den I ax leetle massa, 'What you call dat?' He say dat's B. I looks at him till I knows him bery well. Den I find C A T, an' I ax leetle massa what dat spell; an' he tell me *cat*. Den, after a great long time, I read de newspaper. An' dar I find out dat de British gwine to lan'. I tells all de boys; and dey say mus' hab Methodist meetin'. An' what you tink dis nigger did todder day? You know Jim, Massa Gubernor's boy? Wal, I wants mighty bad to tell Jim dat de British gwine to lan'; but he lib ten mile off, and ole boss nebber let me go. Wal, Massa Gubernor come to massa's, an' I bring he hoss to de gate. I makes bow, and says, 'How Jim do, Massa Gubernor?' He tells me Jim bery well. Den I tells him Jim and I was leetle boy togeder, an' I wants to sen' Jim someting. He tells me Jim hab 'nuff ob eberyting. I says, 'O yes, Massa Gubernor, I knows you good massa, and Jim hab eberyting he want. But Jim an' I was lee-tle boy togeder, and I wants to sen' Jim some backy.' Massa Gubernor laugh an' say, 'Bery well, Jack.' So I gibs him de backy in de bery bit ob newspaper dat tell de British gwine to lan'. I marks it wid brack coal, so Jim be sure to see it. An' Massa Gubernor hisself carry it! Massa Gubernor hisself carry it! I has to laugh ebery time I tinks on 't."

He clapped his hands, shuffled with his feet, and ended by rolling heels over head, with peals of laughter. The multitude joined loudly in his merriment, and it took some time to restore order. There was a good deal of speaking afterward, and some of it was violent. A large majority were in favor of being merciful to the masters; but all, without exception, agreed to join the British if they landed.

With thankfulness to Heaven, Mr. Duncan again found himself in the open field, alone with the stars. Their glorious beauty seemed to him clothed in new and awful power. Groups of shrubbery took startling forms, and the sound of the wind among the trees was like the un-sheathing of swords. He never forgot the lesson of that night. In his heart he could not blame his bondmen for seeking their liberty, and he felt grateful for the merciful disposition they had manifested toward their oppressors; for alone that night, in the solemn presence of the stars, his conscience told him that Slavery *was* oppression, however mild the humanity of the master might make it. He did not emancipate his slaves; for he had not sufficient courage to come out against the community in which he lived. He felt it a duty to warn his neighbors of impending danger; but he could not bring himself to reveal the secret of the meeting in the swamp, which he knew would cause the death of many helpless creatures, whose only crime was that of wishing to be free. After a painful conflict in his mind, he contented himself with advising the magistrates not to allow any meetings of the colored people for religious purposes until the war was over.

I have called him Mr. Duncan, but I have in fact forgotten his name. Years after he witnessed the meeting in the swamp, he gave an account of it to a gentleman in Boston, and I have stated the substance of it as it was told to me.

A REASONABLE REQUEST.

WE are natives of this country; we ask only to be treated *as well* as foreigners. Not a few of our fathers suffered and bled to purchase its independence; we ask only to be treated *as well* as those who fought against it. We have toiled to cultivate it, and to raise it to its present prosperous condition; we ask only to share *equal* privileges with those who come from distant lands to enjoy the fruits of our labor. — REV. PETER WILLIAMS, *colored Rector of St. Philip's Church, New York*, 1835.

THE SLAVE POET.

MR. JAMES HORTON, of Chatham County, North Carolina, had a slave named George, who early manifested remarkable intelligence. He labored with a few other slaves on his master's farm, and was always honest, faithful, and industrious. He contrived to learn to read, and every moment that was allowed him for his own he devoted to reading. He was especially fond of poetry, which he read and learned by heart, wherever he could find it. After a time, he began to compose verses of his own. He did not know how to write; so when he had arranged his thoughts in rhyme, he spoke them aloud to others, who wrote them down for him.

He was not contented in Slavery, as you will see by the following verses which he wrote : —

"Alas! and am I born for this,
    To wear this slavish chain?
Deprived of all created bliss,
    Through hardship, toil, and pain?

"How long have I in bondage lain,
    And languished to be free!
Alas! and must I still complain,
    Deprived of liberty?

"O Heaven! and is there no relief
    This side the silent grave,
To soothe the pain, to quell the grief
    And anguish of a slave?

" Come, Liberty ! thou cheerful sound,
   Roll through my ravished ears ;
Come, let my grief in joys be drowned,
   And drive away my fears.

" Say unto foul oppression, Cease !
   Ye tyrants, rage no more ;
And let the joyful trump of peace
   Now bid the vassal soar.

" O Liberty ! thou golden prize,
   So often sought by blood,
We crave thy sacred sun to rise,
   The gift of Nature's God.

" Bid Slavery hide her haggard face,
   And barbarism fly ;
I scorn to see the sad disgrace,
   In which enslaved I lie.

" Dear Liberty ! upon thy breast
   I languish to respire ;
And, like the swan unto her nest,
   I'd to thy smiles retire."

George's poems attracted attention, and several were
published in the newspaper called " The Raleigh Register." Some of them found their way into the Boston
newspapers, and were thought remarkable productions
for a slave. His master took no interest in any of his
poems, and knew nothing about them, except what he
heard others say. Dr. Caldwell, who was then President of the University of North Carolina, and several
other gentlemen, became interested for him, and tried to
help him to obtain his freedom. In 1829 a little volume
of his poems, called " The Hope of Liberty," was printed
in Raleigh, by Gales and Son. The pamphlet was sold
to raise money enough for George to buy himself. He
was then thirty-two years old, in the prime of his strength,

both in mind and body. He was to be sent off to Liberia as soon as he was purchased; but he had such a passion for Liberty, that he was willing to follow her to the ends of the earth; though he would doubtless have preferred to have been a freeman at home, among old friends and familiar scenes. He was greatly excited about his prospects, and eagerly set about learning to write. When he first heard the news that influential gentlemen were exerting themselves in his behalf, he wrote: —

> " 'T was like the salutation of the dove,
> Borne on the zephyr through some lonesome grove,
> When spring returns, and winter's chill is past,
> And vegetation smiles above the blast.

> " The silent harp, which on the osiers hung,
> Again was tuned, and manumission sung;
> Away by hope the clouds of fear were driven,
> And music breathed my gratitude to Heaven."

It would have been better for him if his hopes had not been so highly excited. His poems did not sell for enough to raise the sum his master demanded for him, and his friends were not sufficiently benevolent to make up the deficiency. In 1837, when he was forty years old, he was still working as a slave at Chapel Hill, the seat of the University of North Carolina. It was said at that time that he had ceased to write poetry. I suppose the poor fellow was discouraged. If he is still alive, he is sixty-seven years old; and I hope it will comfort his poor, bruised heart to know that some of his verses are preserved, and published for the benefit of those who have been his companions in Slavery, and who, more fortunate than he was, have become freemen before their strength has left them.

H

RATIE:

A TRUE STORY OF A LITTLE HUNCHBACK.

BY MATTIE GRIFFITH.

I WANT to tell you a story of a poor little slave-girl who lived and died away down South.

This little girl's name was Rachel, but they used to call her Ratie. She was a hunchback and a dwarf, with an ugly black face, coarse and irregular features, but a low, pleasant voice, and nice manners. Nobody ever scolded Ratie, for she never deserved it. She always did her work — the little that was assigned her — with a cheerful heart and willing hand. This work was chiefly to gather up little bits of chips in baskets, or collect shavings from the carpenters' shops, and take them to the cabins or the great kitchen, where they were used for kindling fires. She had a sweet, gentle spirit, and a low, cheery laugh that charmed everybody. Even the white folks who lived up at the great house loved her, and somehow felt better when she was near.

Ratie used to go out into the fields on summer days, or in the early spring, and pick the first flowers. Later in the season she caught the butterflies or grasshoppers, but she never hurt them. She would look at the bright spangled wings of the butterflies, or the green coats of the pretty, chirping grasshoppers, with an eye full of admiration; and she always seemed sorry when she gave them up. The lambs used to run to her, and eat from

her hands. If she went into the park, the deer came
to her side lovingly, and the young fawns sported and
played around her. No one harmed Ratie or expected
harm from her.

Poor little hunchback! Many an idle traveller has
paused in his slow wanderings to listen to her song, as
she sat on the wayside stump, knitting stockings for the
work-people, and singing old snatches of songs, and airs
that bring back to the heart glimpses of the paradise of
our lost childhood! No broad-throated robin ever poured
out a wilder, fuller gush of melody than the songs of this
untaught child!

Little Ratie's days were passed in the same even rou-
tine, without thought or chance of change. Up at the
house they loved her; and her young mistresses used to
supply her with cast-off ribbons and shawls and fancy
trappings from their own wardrobes, which she prized
very much, — delighting to deck out her odd little person
with these old fineries.

Once, as she sat singing on an old stile, and knitting
a stocking, a rough sort of gentleman, driving by in his
neat little tilbury, stopped and listened to Ratie's song.
When he looked at the strange child he felt a little
shocked; but he called out in a loud voice, " Halloo,
Dumpey Blackie! here is a fip for your song"; and he
tossed her a small coin. " Take that, and give me
another song."

The child was pleased with the gift, took it up from
where it had rolled on the ground at her feet, and soon
began another of her wild little ditties. As she sang on,
she forgot the exact words, and put in some of her own,
which harmonized just as well with the air. The stranger was so much pleased, that he gave her another fip,

and called for another song, and still another. At length, he asked the child to whom she belonged. She told him that she belonged to her old master.

"And what is your old master's name?" asked the gentleman.

Ratie, who had never been two miles beyond the borders of the plantation, laughed, thinking it a fine joke that anybody should not know the name of her "old master"; for, to her, he was the most important personage in the world. So she only laughed and shook her head derisively in answer.

"Will you not tell me his name?" again asked the stranger.

But the child smiled still more incredulously; so the gentleman deemed it best to follow her home, which he accordingly did, and found that Colonel Williams, a rich old planter, was the owner of this little melodious blackbird.

The stranger alighted and asked to see Colonel Williams. After a little conversation he proposed to buy Ratie from her master. Colonel Williams had never thought of selling the little deformity. He kept her on the place more through charity than aught else. The extent of her musical genius was unappreciated, and even unknown to him; but as she was a happy little creature, much liked by all the family, and was only a trifling expense, he had never thought of parting with her. Now, however, when a handsome price was offered, she assumed something like importance and interest in his eyes. He called her into the house, and she obeyed with great alacrity, coming in neatly dressed, with a fresh white apron, and sundry bits of bright-colored ribbons tied round her head and neck.

"Give us one of your best songs, Ratie," said her master.

The girl broke out in a wild, warbling strain, clear, bird-like, and musical, filling the long room with gushes of melody, until the lofty arches echoed and re-echoed with the wild notes. When she had finished, the enthusiastic stranger exclaimed, "That throat is a mint of gold!"

And so little hunchback Ratie sang song after song, until she exhausted herself; when her master sent her off to the slave-quarters, where she continued her ditties out under the broad, soft light of the low-hanging southern moon.

The gentlemen sat up late that night, talking upon different subjects; but, before they parted, it was arranged that the stranger should buy Ratie at the high price he offered.

The next morning, long before the sun rose, little Ratie was up, walking through the quarter. She stooped down to look at every drop of dew that glittered and sparkled on the green leaves and shrubs; and when the great, round, golden sun began to creep up the eastern sky, and set it all ablaze with red and gold and purple clouds, glorious as the pavilion of the prophet, Ratie's little spirit danced within her, and broke forth in hymns of music such as the wise men long ago — eighteen hundred years past — sang at the foot of a little manger in a stable in Bethlehem of Judæa.

The child was too young and ignorant to know the meaning of the emotions which fluttered and set on fire her own soul, but she was none the less happy for this ignorance. God is very good!

As Ratie wandered on, singing to herself, she grew so happy that the rush of passionate fervor half frightened

her. Tears came to her eyes, and choked the song in
her throat. She paused in her walk, and seated herself
on a little rock that lay in one corner of the quarter. As
she sat there alone, she continued to sing and weep;
wherefore she could not tell. By and by the great, rusty
bell of the quarter rang out from its hoarse, iron tongue
the morning summons for the slaves to assemble. Ragged, tattered, unshorn and unshaven, dirty, ill and angry-
looking, the negroes — men, women, and children, in large
numbers — collected in the quarter-yard, where the overseer, an ugly, harsh white man, with a pistol in his belt,
knife at his side, and whip in hand, stood to call the roll.
At the mention of each name, a slave came forward, saying with a bow, " Here I am, massa."

Ratie, who had no particular work to do, went limping
on past the place of the roll-call, when she saw her master
and the strange gentleman coming toward her. She did
not, however, notice them. They were talking together
quite earnestly, and looking at her. Her master called
out, " Stop, Ratie ; come this way."

She obeyed the order with pleasing readiness.

" Ratie," said the master, " how do you like this gentleman ? "

The child smiled, but made no answer in words. The
master also smiled as he added : " He thinks that you
sing very prettily, and he has bought you. He will be
very kind and good to you ; and as soon as you have had
breakfast, you must get your things ready to go off with
him. Here is a present for you " ; and he tossed her a
bright, shining, silver coin.

The child seized the money, but did not seem to compre-
hend her master's words. To be sold to her implied some
sort of disgrace or hardship, which she did not think she

deserved; besides, she had always lived on the "old plantation." She knew no other home; she did not want to leave "the people" of the quarter; nor did she feel happy in going away from the "white folks," particularly the "young mistresses," who had always been so kind to her. She had also some vague yearning of heart to be close to her mammy's grave, rough as it was; and near also to Grandpap's cabin, where she roasted apples and potatoes on winter nights.

She looked around upon the familiar quarter, the well-known people, the row of cabins; and strained her gaze far away to the rolling fields in the distance, where the negroes, like a swarm of crows, were busy at their morning's work; and as she gazed, the whole landscape flushed with the bloom and beauty of the risen sun. Then the wild, pealing horn called the "sons of toil" from their morning hour's work to their frugal breakfast.

Ratie's little heart began to beat in its narrow limits as the word "sold" wrote itself there, and broke through her comprehension with all its horrors. She started quickly after her master, and, with the freedom of a petted slave, caught hold of the skirt of his coat. Colonel Williams turned suddenly round; and there, crouching on the earth at his feet, was the hunchback child. She held up the money which he had given her, and, in a sweet, tremulous voice, asked: "Massa, why has you sold me? I has not behaved bad, as de boys did dat you sold last year. I does n't steal nor tell lies. Is it bekase I 'se lazy? I do all de work dey gives me to do. I 'll do more. I 'll go into de fields. I 'll plant and pick de cotton. Please don't sell me. I does n't **want to** leave de ole place. Mammy is buried here; so I wants to be when I dies. I wants allers to live here."

The stranger and Colonel Williams were much moved. They did not venture to speak to the child, but tried to get away from the sound of her plaintive cries.

When the negroes drew around their morning meal, and learned that Ratie was sold, they were unhappy, and refused to eat anything. They looked sorrowfully at one another, and turned away from their untasted food. "Poor Ratie!" exclaimed the old negroes, as they shook their heads in mournful discontent, "we shall not hear any more her sweet songs in de evenin' time."

The young mistresses came to Ratie with kind gifts and kinder words. They told her, with tears in their eyes, how sorry they were to part with her, how good they knew she had been, and how much they wished their papa would allow her to stay. Words and acts like these softened the blow to the unfortunate child, and strengthened her for the coming trial. She looked up smilingly through her tears, as she said to her young mistresses: "Please not to cry for me. God is good, and de preacher says he is everywhar; so I shall not be fur from de ole plantation."

When she was starting away, each of the negroes brought her some little gift, such as cotton handkerchiefs, old ribbon-ends, bright-colored glass beads, or autumn berries, dried and strung on threads for neck ornaments. Each of these humble little tokens possessed an individual interest which touched some spring in Ratie's little heart. When the hour of separation came, she had nerved herself to the highest courage of which she was capable. She took leave of each of the slaves, all of them calling down the blessings of God upon her life. An old, lame negro man, whom the slaves addressed as Grandpap, hobbled from his cabin, on a broken crutch, to utter his farewell.

" Good by, Ratie," he began, and his voice choked with emotion; "good by, little Ratie, and may de good Lord be wid you. Him dat keres fur de poor, de lowly, and de despised, up yonder, way fur and high up dere, is a God dat loves all of his chillens alike. He does n't kere fur de color ob de skin or de quality ob de hair. In his sight, wool is jist as good as de fair, straight hair. He loves de heart, and looks straight and deep into dat, and keres fur nothin' else. Never you be afeard, Ratie, Him 'll take kere ob you, an' all sich as you, bekase He loves dem dat He smites and afflicts. Now, He did n't break your poor little back for nothin'. Him has Him's eye upon you. You is a lamb ob de fold, dat de great Shepherd will go fur and long to look arter. Him holds you in the holler ob Him's hand, an' He 'll keep you dar. Mind what I tell you. Good by, Ratie. God bless you. Allers trust Him. 'Member my last words; dat is, Allers trust Him. Look to Him, and He 'll never forget you."

As he uttered these words, in a slow, oracular manner, he brushed a tear from his eye with the back of his old, hard hand, and looking tenderly toward the child, his lips moved slowly, and the words seemed to melt unheard in the thin, morning air. He turned from her and hobbled off in the direction of his cabin.

The other slaves were more passionately demonstrative in their farewells; but little Ratie bore up with a beautiful and proud composure.

. . . . .

The new owner proved very kind to the gentle little creature; but her heart had received a blow from which it could not recover.

The master took her to New Orleans, intending to have her taught music, that she might make money for him;

6

but the poor child pined for "de ole plantation" and "de ole folks at home," — the kind people — "my people," as she fondly called them — with whom she had been brought up.

In the great city of New Orleans she was literally lost. She missed the free country air, the green trees, the sweet singing-birds, the fields blooming with early flowers, the meadows and the running brooks. It was easy to see that the little hunchback was not happy. She grew thinner and thinner, and her voice lost its flexible sweetness, its clear and liquid roundness of tone. At last she fell away to a mere skeleton; then sharp, burning fever set in, and little Ratie was taken down to her bed. Day and night, in the delirium of fever, she raved for "de ole plantation" and her own people.

The new master promised, when she got better, to take her back to her old home, — at least for a little while. But, alas! she never grew any better. She faded slowly away, until one evening, just at sundown, in the gay city of New Orleans, little Ratie breathed her last.

Just before she died, she lifted her head from the pillow, and, resting on her hand, she pointed eastward, saying: "Over dar is de ole plantation. Don't you see? How pretty and nice it looks! Dar is all de peoples at work. How busy dey is! But I'se not gwine dar. I does n't want to, any more. Dere up dar is God's plantation, and it is betterer far. Dere is no slaves dar, but all is free and happy, — loving friends; and it is dar dat I wants to go; and I hopes dat all de plantation folks will come to me."

And so little Ratie died.

From the New York Independent.

THE KINGDOM OF CHRIST.

BY JAMES MONTGOMERY.

HAIL to the Lord's anointed!
    Great David's greater Son!
Hail, in the time appointed,
    His reign on earth begun!
He comes to break oppression,
    To set the captive free,
To take away transgression,
    And rule in equity.

He comes, with succor speedy,
    To those who suffer wrong;
To help the poor and needy,
    And bid the weak be strong;
To give them songs for sighing,
    Their darkness turned to light,
Whose souls, condemned and dying,
    Were precious in his sight.

To him shall prayer unceasing,
    And daily vows ascend;
His kingdom still increasing, —
    A kingdom without end.
The tide of time shall never
    His covenant remove;
His name shall stand forever, —
    That name to us is Love.

THE BEGINNING AND PROGRESS OF EMANCI-
PATION IN THE BRITISH WEST INDIES.

NOTHING has ever been done in this world more wicked and cruel than the slave-trade on the coast of Africa. But the temptation to carry it on was very great; for hundreds of men and women could be bought for a cask of poor rum or a peck of cheap beads, and could be sold in the markets of America or the West Indies for thousands of dollars. A hundred years ago men were not at all ashamed of growing rich in this bad way. They were respected in society as much as other men. They were often members of churches and professed to be very pious. Perhaps they deceived themselves, as well as others, and really thought they were pious, because they observed all the ritual forms of religion. But, above all their prayers, God heard the groans and the cries of the poor tortured Africans. He put it into the heart of a young Englishman, named Thomas Clarkson, to inquire into the wicked business, that was going on under the sanction of the government, and unreproved by the Church. In the course of his investigations, this young man discovered that the most shocking cruelties were habitually practised. He found that poor creatures stolen from their homes were packed close, like bales of goods, in the dark holds of ships, where they were half choked by bad odors from accumulated filth, and where they could hardly breathe for want of air. The food allotted them was merely enough to keep them alive. Many died of grief and despair, and still more of burning fevers and other diseases.   Living and dead often remained huddled together for hours, and when the corpses were removed they were thrown out to the sharks.   But the sea-captains engaged in this horrid traffic were selfish as well as cruel.   They did not like to have their victims die, because every one they lost on the passage diminished the dollars they expected to get by selling them.   So at times they brought the poor half-dead wretches on deck and drove them round with a whip for exercise, and insulted their misery by compelling them to dance, and sing the songs they had sung in their native land.

Thomas Clarkson called public attention to the subject by publishing these things in a pamphlet.   More than thirty years before, the humane sect called Quakers had forbidden any of its members to be connected with the slave-trade.   But though the abominable traffic had been carried on more than two hundred and fifty years by various nations calling themselves Christian, there had been no attempt to excite general attention to the subject till Clarkson published his pamphlet in 1786, seventy-nine years ago.   He became so much interested in the question that he gave up all other pursuits in life, and wrote, and lectured, and talked about it incessantly. The assembled representatives of the people which we call a Congress, is called a Parliament in Great Britain.* He tried to bring the subject before that body, and succeeded in gaining the attention of some members, among whom the most conspicuous was the benevolent William Wilberforce.   He soon joined Mr. Clarkson in the formation of a Society for the Abolition of the Slave-trade.

* The northern part of Great Britain is called Scotland, the southern part England.   The entire people are called British.

This of course gave great offence to the sea-captains and merchants engaged in the profitable traffic. Clarkson met with all manner of insult and abuse, and his life was sometimes in danger. The British government did as governments are apt to do, — it sided with the rich and powerful as long as it was politic to do so. But, though many of the aristocracy were haughty and selfish, the generality of the common people were ready to sympathize with the poor and the oppressed. When they became aware of the outrages committed in the slave-trade, they determined that a stop should be put to it. They wrote, and talked, and petitioned Parliament, till the government was compelled to pay some attention to their demands. When the friends of the infernal traffic found that a resolution to abolish it was likely to be passed, they contrived to get the word "gradual" inserted into the resolution, and thus defeated the will of the people ; for the gradual abolition of crime is no abolition at all. It was as absurd as it would have been for them to say they would abolish murder gradually. But though the law was insufficient to accomplish the desired purpose, public opinion against the trade exerted an increasing influence. The friends of those who were engaged in it began to apologize for it as a necessary branch of trade, and pleaded that laborers could not be supplied in the hot climate of the West Indies in any other way. They were even shameless enough to defend it and praise it as a benevolent scheme to bring savages away from heathen Africa and make good Christians of them. Mr. Boswell, a well-known English writer of that period, went so far as to pronounce it "a trade which God had sanctioned"; and he declared that "to abolish it would be to shut the gates of mercy on mankind." Such pretences deceived some. But the English people have a great deal of good common sense; and it was not easy to convince them that stealing men, women, and children from their homes, torturing them on the ocean, and selling them in strange lands, to be whipped to incessant toil without wages, was a pious missionary enterprise.

Clarkson, Wilberforce, and others continued their unremitting labors to suppress the unrighteous traffic; the kindly sect of Quakers everywhere assisted them; and benevolent people in other sects became more and more convinced that it was their duty to do the same. All manner of obstacles were put in the way of the desired reformation; but at last, after twenty-two years of violent agitation, the slave-trade was entirely abolished by Great Britain, at the commencement of the year 1808. Sixteen years later, it was decreed by law that any British subject caught in the traffic should be punished as a pirate.

The king, George the Third, was opposed to the abolition, and so were all the royal family, except the Duke of Gloucester. The nobility and wealthy people, with a few honorable exceptions, took the same side. The measure was carried by the good sense and good feeling of the common people of Great Britain.

There were no slaves in Great Britain. It had been decided by law that any slave who landed in that country became free the moment he touched the shore. But many of the West India islands, lying between North and South America, were under the British government, and the laborers there were held in Slavery. The English people knew very little what was going on in those distant colonies. When West India planters visited their relatives and friends in Great Britain, they made out a very fair story for themselves. They said none but negroes could work in such a hot climate, that sugar must be made, and negroes would not work unless they were slaves. They represented themselves as very kind masters, and described their bondmen as a very contented and merry class of laborers. These planters were generally dashing men, who spent freely the money they did not earn ; and their fine manners and smooth talk gave the impression that they must be *gentle* men.

People were slow to believe the accounts of cruelties practised in the West Indies by these polished gentlemen. But more and more facts were brought to light to prove that there was little to choose between the slave-trade and the system of Slavery. When the honest masses of the British people became convinced that the slaves in the West Indies were entirely subject to the will of their masters, however licentious that will might be, and that they were kept in such brutal ignorance they could not read the Bible, they said at once that such a system ought to be abolished. They sent missionaries to the West Indies to teach the negroes. The planters considered this an impertinent interference with their affairs. They said if slaves were instructed they would rise in rebellion against their masters. The English people replied that it must be a very bad system which made it dangerous for human beings to read the Bible. The more closely they inquired into the subject, the more their indignation was roused. Brown faces and yellow faces among the slaves told a shameful story of licentious masters, while the chains and whips and other instruments of torture found on every plantation proved that severe treatment was universal. Again the honest masses of the English people rose up in their moral majesty and said that wrong should be righted. The government was unfavorable to the abolition of Slavery, and the aristocracy, with a few honorable exceptions, sympathized with the slaveholders. The West-Indian planters were boiling over with rage. They pulled down the chapels where the negroes met together to hear the words of Jesus; they mobbed the missionaries, they thrust them into dungeons, and two or three of them were killed. Some of the planters thought Slavery was a bad system, but they had to be very cautious in expressing such an opinion; for if they were even suspected of favoring abolition, their neighbors were sure to make them suffer for it in some way. Even women seemed to be filled with the spirit of Furies, whenever the subject of Slavery was mentioned. One of them said, if she could get hold of Mr. Wilberforce she would tear his heart out. Everywhere one heard mournful predictions of the ruin and desolation that would follow emancipation. They insisted that negroes would not work unless they were slaves, and of course no crops could be raised; and what was still more to be dreaded, they would murder all the whites and set fire to the towns. Sometimes they would present the subject from a benevolent point of view, and urge that it would be the greatest unkindness to the negroes to give them freedom; for when they had no kind masters to take care of them they would certainly starve.

The slaves of course found out that something in their favor was going on in England. They watched eagerly for the arrival of vessels; they took notice of everything that was said; if they could get hold of a scrap of newspaper they hid it away, and those who could read would read it privately to the others. If their masters were unusually cross, or swore more than common, they would

6 *   I

wink at each other and say, "There's good news for us from England."

The masters, on their part, watched the slaves closely. If they were more silent than common, or if they appeared to be in better spirits than common, they suspected them of plotting insurrections. But the negroes did more wisely than that. They believed that good people in England were working for them, and they tried to be patient till they were emancipated by law. There was but one exception to this. The planters in Jamaica were more bitter and furious than in the other islands. They formed societies to uphold Slavery, and made flaming speeches against the people and Parliament of Great Britain for "setting the slaves loose upon them," as they called it. They did not reflect that their colored servants, as they passed in and out, heard this violent language and had sense enough to draw conclusions from it. But they did draw from it a conclusion very dangerous to their masters. They had heard talk of emancipation for several years, and it seemed to them that the promised freedom was a long time coming. In 1832, the speeches of the planters were so furious against the doings in Parliament, that the slaves received the idea that the British government had already passed laws for their freedom, and that their masters were cheating them out of the legal rights that had been granted them. It was a sad mistake for the poor fellows, and brought a great deal of suffering upon themselves and others. They rose in insurrection, and it is said destroyed property to the amount of six millions of dollars. But instead of being protected by the British government, as they had expected, soldiers were sent over to put down the insurrection, and many of the negroes were shot and hung.

Meanwhile their friends in England were working for them zealously. They published pamphlets and papers and made speeches, and urgently petitioned Parliament to "let the people go." One petition alone was signed by eight hundred thousand women. One of the members, pointing to the enormous roll, said: "There is no use in trying longer to resist the will of the people. When all the women in Great Britain are knocking at the doors of Parliament, something must be done."

The government and the aristocracy were very reluctant to comply with the demand of the people. But at last, after eleven years of more violent struggle than it had taken to suppress the African slave-trade, Slavery itself was abolished in the British West Indies forever. The decree was to go into effect on the 1st day of August, 1834. Up to the very last day, the planters persisted in saying that the measure would ruin the islands. They said the emancipated slaves would do no work, but would go round in large gangs, robbing, stealing, murdering the whites, burning the houses, and destroying the fields of sugar-cane. If the negroes had been revengeful, they might have done a great deal of mischief; for there were five times as many colored people in the islands as there were whites. But they were so thankful to get their freedom at last, that there was no room in their hearts for bad feelings. The tears were in their eyes as they told each other the good news, and said, " Bress de Lord and de good English people."

But many of the masters really believed their own alarming prophesies. When they found that emancipation could not be prevented, numbers left the islands. Some of those who remained did not dare to undress and go to bed on the night of the 31st of July; and those who tried to sleep were generally restless and easily startled.

But while masters and mistresses were dreading to hear screams and alarms of fire, their emancipated slaves were flocking to the churches to offer up prayers and hymns of thanksgiving.

In the island of Antigua there were thirty thousand slaves when the midnight clock began to strive twelve, on the 31st of July, 1834; and when it had done striking they were all free men and free women. It was a glorious moment, never to be forgotten by them during the remainder of their lives. The Wesleyan Methodists kept watch-night in all their chapels. One of the missionaries who exhorted the emancipated people and prayed with them thus described the solemn scene : —

" The spacious house was filled with the candidates for liberty. All was animation and eagerness. A mighty chorus of voices swelled the song of expectation and joy; and as they united in prayer, the voice of the leader was drowned in the universal acclamations of thanksgiving and praise and blessing and honor and glory to God, who had come down for their deliverance. In such exercises the evening was spent, until the hour of twelve approached. The missionary then proposed that when the cathedral clock should begin to strike, the whole congregation should fall on their knees, and receive the boon of freedom in silence. Accordingly, as the loud bell tolled its first note, the crowded assembly prostrated themselves. All was silence, save the quivering, half-stifled breath of the struggling spirit. Slowly the tones of the clock fell upon the waiting multitude. Peal on peal, peal on peal, rolled over the prostrate throng, like angels' voices, thrilling their weary heartstrings.

Scarcely had the *last* tone sounded, when lightning
flashed vividly, and a loud peal of thunder rolled
through the sky. It was God's pillar of fire. His
trump of jubilee. It was followed by a moment of profound silence. Then came the outburst. They shouted
' Glory! Hallelujah!' They clapped their hands, they
leaped up, they fell down, they clasped each other in
their free arms, they cried, they laughed, they went to
and fro, throwing upward their unfettered hands. High
above all, a mighty sound ever and anon swelled up. It
was the utterance of gratitude to God.

" After this gush of excitement had spent itself, the
congregation became calm, and religious exercises were
resumed. The remainder of the night was spent in singing and prayer, in reading the Bible, and in addresses
from the missionaries, explaining the nature of the freedom
just received, and exhorting the people to be industrious,
steady, and obedient to the laws, and to show themselves
in all things worthy of the high boon God had conferred
upon them.

" The 1st of August came on Friday; and a release
from all work was proclaimed until the next Monday.
The great mass of the negroes spent the day chiefly in
the churches and chapels. The clergy and missionaries
throughout the island actively seized the opportunity to
enlighten the people on all the duties and responsibilities
of their new relation. The day was like a Sabbath. A
Sabbath, indeed, when 'the wicked ceased from troubling
and the weary were at rest.'

" The most kindly of the planters went to the chapels
where their own people were assembled, and shook hands
with them, and exchanged hearty good wishes.

" At Grace Hill, a Moravian missionary station, the

emancipated negroes begged to have a sunrise meeting on the 1st of August, as they had been accustomed to have at Easter; and as it was the Easter morning of their freedom, the request was granted. The people all dressed in white, and walked arm in arm to the chapel. There a hymn of thanksgiving was sung by the whole congregation kneeling. The singing was frequently interrupted by the tears and sobs of the melted people, until finally they were overwhelmed by a tumult of emotion.

"There was not a single dance by night or day; not even so much as a fiddle played. There were no drunken carousals, no riotous assemblies. The emancipated were as far from dissipation and debauchery as they were from violence and carnage. Gratitude was the absorbing emotion. From the hill-tops and the valleys the cry of a disenthralled people went upward, like the sound of many waters: ' Glory to God! Glory to God! ' "

Mr. Bleby, one of the Methodist missionaries in Jamaica, thus describes the same night in that island : —

"The church where the emancipated people assembled, at ten o'clock at night, was very large; but the aisles, the gallery stairs, the communion-place, the pulpit stairs, were all crowded ; and there were thousands of people round the building, at every open door and window, looking in. We thought it right and proper that our Christian people should receive their freedom as a boon from God, in the house of prayer; and we gathered them together in the church for a midnight service. Our mouths had been closed about Slavery up to that time. We could not quote a passage that had reference even to *spiritual* emancipation, without endangering our lives. The planters had a law of 'constructive treason,' that doomed any man to death who made use of language tending to excite a desire for liberty among the slaves; and they found treason in the Bible and sedition in the hymns of Watts and Wesley, and we had to be very careful how we used them. You may imagine with what feelings I saw myself emancipated from this thraldom, and free to proclaim 'liberty to the captive, and the opening of prison doors to them that were bound.' I took for my text, ' Proclaim liberty throughout all the land, unto all the inhabitants thereof. It shall be a jubilee unto you."

" A few minutes before midnight, I requested all the people to kneel down in silent prayer to God, as befitting the solemnity of the hour. I looked down upon them as they knelt. The silence was broken only by sobs of emotion, which it was impossible to repress. The clock began to strike. It was the knell of Slavery in all the British possessions! It proclaimed liberty to eight hundred thousand human beings! When I told them they might rise, what an outburst of joy there was among that mass of people! The clock had ceased to strike, and they were slaves no longer! Mothers were hugging their babes to their bosoms, old white-headed men embracing their children and husbands clasping their wives in their arms. By and by all was still again, and I gave out a hymn. You may imagine the feelings with which these people, just emerging into freedom, shouted

' Send the glad tidings o'er the sea!
His chains are broke, the slave is free! ' "

But though the dreaded 1st of August passed away so peacefully and pleasantly, the planters could not get rid of the idea that their laborers would not work after they were free. Mr. Daniell, who managed several estates in Antigua, talking of the subject, two years after-

ward, with an American gentleman from Kentucky, said:
"I expected some irregularities would follow such a pro-
digious change in the condition of the negroes. I supposed there would be some relaxation from labor during
the week that followed emancipation; but on Monday
morning, I found all my hands in the field, not one missing. The same day I received a message from another
estate, of which I was proprietor, that the negroes, to a
man, had refused to go into the field. I immediately
rode to the estate, and found the laborers, with hoes in
their hands, doing nothing. Accosting them in a friendly
manner, I inquired, 'What is the meaning of this? How
is it that you are not at work this morning?' They
immediately replied, 'It's not because we don't want to
work, massa; but we wanted to see you, first and fore-
most, to know what the *bargain* would be.' As soon as
that matter was settled, the whole body of negroes turned
out cheerfully." Another manager declared that the
largest gang he had ever seen in the field, on his property, turned out the week after emancipation. And
such in fact was the universal testimony of the managers
throughout Antigua.

In the days of Slavery, it had always been customary
to order out the militia during the Christmas holidays,
when the negroes were in the habit of congregating in
large numbers, to enjoy the festivities of the season. But
the December after emancipation, the Governor issued
a proclamation, that, "*in consequence of the abolition of
Slavery*," there was no further need of taking that pre-
caution. And it is a fact that there have been no soldiers out at Christmas from that day to this.

Unfortunately the British government had been so far
influenced by the representations of the planters, that the

plan of emancipation they adopted was a gradual one. All children under six years old were unconditionally free, the magistrates alone had power to punish, and no human being could be sold. But the slaves, under the new name of apprentices, were obliged to work for their masters six years longer without wages, except one day and a half in the week, which the law decreed should be their own. The number of hours they were to work each day was also stipulated by law. This was certainly a great improvement in their condition; but it was not all they had expected. They were peaceable, and worked more cheerfully than they had done while they were slaves; for now a definite date was fixed when they should own all their time, and they knew that every week brought them nearer to it. Still they felt that entire justice had not been done to them. Sometimes white men asked them if they would work when they were entirely free. They answered, "In Slavery time we work; now we work better; den how you tink we work when we *free*, when we get *paid* for work!" Sometimes people said to them, "I suppose you expect to do just as you please when you are your own masters?" They replied: "We 'spect to 'bey de law. In oder countries where dey is all free dey hab de law. We could n't get along widout de law. In Slavery time, massa would sometimes slash we when we do as well as we could; but de law don't do harm to anybody dat behaves himself. 'Prenticeship is bad enough; but we know de law make it so, and for peace' sake we will be satisfy. But we murmur in we minds."

In the island of Antigua, planters rejected the plan of apprenticeship. They said, "If the negroes *must* be free, let them be free at once, without any more fuss and trouble." The result proved that they judged wisely for their own interest, as well as for the comfort and encouragement of their laborers. When the negroes found that they were paid for every day's work, they put their whole hearts into it. So zealous were they to earn wages, that they sometimes worked by moonlight, or by the light of fires kindled among the dry cane-stalks. In all respects, the change from the old order of things to the new went on more smoothly in Antigua than it did anywhere else.

In the islands where apprenticeship was tried, the irritability of the masters made it work worse than it would otherwise have done. All that most of them seemed to care for was to get as much work out of their servants as they could, during the six years that they were to work without wages, and it vexed them that they could not use the lash whenever they pleased. They took away various little privileges which they had been accustomed to grant; while during four days and a half of the week the apprentices received no wages to compensate them for the loss of those privileges. Being deprived of the power to sell the children, they refused to supply them with any food. In fact, they contrived every way to make the colored people think they had better have remained slaves. But if they called out, "Work faster, you black rascal, or I'll flog you!" the apprentices would sometimes lose patience, and answer, "You can't flog we now." That would make the master very angry, and he would send the apprentice to a magistrate to be punished for impudence. The magistrates were the associates of the planters; they ate their good dinners, and rode about in their carriages. Consequently, they were more inclined to believe them than they were to believe their servants. The laborers became so well aware of this, that they were accustomed to say to each other, " It's of no use for us to apply to the magistrates. They are so poisoned by massa's turtle-soup." It has been computed by missionaries that, in the course of two years, sixty thousand apprentices received, among them all, two hundred and fifty thousand lashes, besides fifty thousand other legalized punishments, such as the tread-mill and the chain-gang.

The planters were full of complaints to travellers who visited the West Indies. If they were asked, " Why don't you emancipate your laborers entirely, and give them wages, as they do in Antigua, — they have no such troubles there?" the prejudiced men would shake their heads and answer: " Negroes will not work without being flogged. We must get what we can out of them before 1840; for when they are their own masters they will rob, murder, or starve, rather than labor."

Planters who manifested a more kind and considerate disposition had pleasanter relations with their servants, and they never found any difficulty in procuring as much labor as they wanted. Some made it easy for their apprentices to buy the remainder of their time; and it was soon observed that those who owned all their time worked faster and better than those who were without that stimulus. The idea gained ground that unconditional emancipation would be better both for masters and servants. The Marquis of Sligo, the humane Governor of Jamaica, set a good example by emancipating all his apprentices. People in England began to petition Parliament to abolish the apprenticeship, on the ground that it proved unsatisfactory and troublesome to all parties. The result was that all the apprentices in the British

West Indies were made entirely free on the 1st of August, 1838. Mr. Phillippo, a Baptist missionary in Jamaica, thus describes the observance of the day in that island : "On the preceding evening, the missionary stations throughout the island were crowded with people, filling all the places of worship. They remained at their devotions till the day of liberty dawned, when they saluted it with joyous acclamations. Then they dispersed through the towns and villages, singing ' God save the queen,' and rending the air with their shouts, — ' Freedom 's come !' ' We 're free ! we 're free !' ' Our wives and children are free !' During the day, the places of worship were crowded to suffocation. The scenes presented exceeded all description. Joyous excitement pervaded the whole island. At Spanish Town, the Governor, Sir Lionel Smith, addressed the emancipated people, who formed a procession of seven thousand, and escorted the children of the schools, about two thousand in number, to the Government House. They bore banners and flags with various inscriptions, of which the following are samples : ' Education, Religion, and Social Order'; 'August First, 1838, — the Day of our Freedom'; ' Truth and Justice have at last prevailed.' The children sang before the Government House, and his Excellency made a speech characterized by simplicity and kindness, which was received with enthusiastic cheers. The procession then escorted their pastor to his house. In front of the Baptist Chapel were three triumphal arches, decorated with leaves and flowers, and surmounted by flags bearing the inscriptions, ' Freedom has come !' ' Slavery is no more !' ' The chains are broken, Africa is free !' There were many flags bearing the names of their English benefactors, — Clarkson, Wilberforce, Sligo,

Thompson, etc. When these were unfurled, the enthusiasm of the multitude rose to the highest pitch. For nearly an hour the air rang with exulting shouts, in which the shrill voices of two thousand children joined, singing, 'We're free! we're free!' Several of the kindly disposed planters gave rural *fêtes* to the laborers. Long tables were spread in the lawns, arches of evergreens were festooned with flowers, and on the trees floated banners bearing the names of those who had been most conspicuous in bringing about this blessed result. Songs were sung, speeches made, prayers offered, and a plentiful repast eaten. Mr. Phillippo says: "The conduct of the newly emancipated peasantry would have done credit to Christians of the most civilized country in the world. They were clean in their persons, and neat in their attire. Their behavior was modest, unassuming, and decorous in a high degree. There was no crowding, no vulgar familiarity, but all were courteous and obliging to each other, as members of one harmonious family. There was no dancing, gambling, or carousing. All seemed to have a sense of the obligations they owed to their masters, to each other, and to the civil authorities. The masters who were present at these *fêtes* congratulated their former dependents on the boon they had received, and hopes were mutually expressed that all past differences and wrongs might be forgiven."

On some of the estates where these festivals were held the laborers, with few individual exceptions, went to work as usual on the following day. *Many of them gave their first week of free labor as an offering of good-will to their masters.* Thus the period from which many of the planters had apprehended the worst consequences passed away in peace and harmony.

It is now twenty-seven years since the laborers in the British West Indies have been made entirely free; and the missionaries, the magistrates, and even the masters agree that the laborers are much more faithful and industrious under the new system than they were under the iron rule of Slavery. It is true, some of the old planters growled as long as they lived. They had always predicted that freedom would bring ruin on all classes, and it vexed them to see the negroes behaving so well. They, however, made the most of the fact that there was less sugar made than in former years. It was their own fault. The emancipated slaves wanted to stay and work on the plantations where they had always lived. But the masters could not give up their old habits of meanness and tyranny. Their laborers could scarcely support life with the very small wages they received; and yet they took from them the little patches of provision-ground which they had formerly had, and charged them enormously high rent for their miserable little huts. It seemed as if they wanted to drive them to robbery, that they might say, "We told you it would be so, if you set them free."

But the freedmen disappointed them. Under all discouragements, they persisted in behaving well. When they found that they could not get a living on the old plantations where they wanted to stay, they went to work on railroads, and wherever they could find employment. They laid up as much as they could of their wages, and bought bits of land, on which they built comfortable cabins for themselves, and laid out little gardens. Their wives and children raised poultry and tended a cow, and carried vegetables and butter and eggs to market, in baskets poised on their heads. With the money thus earned they bought more land and added to their little stock of furniture. Though the men received only from eighteen to twenty-four cents a day, out of which they boarded themselves, they were so industrious and saving that in four years the freedmen in Jamaica alone had bought and paid for one hundred thousand acres of land, and put up dwellings thereon. Mr. Phillippo states, that during that time as many as two hundred new villages of freedmen were formed. These villages generally received the names of benefactors, such as Clarkson, Wilberforce, Thompson, &c. To their own little homes they also gave names indicative of their gratitude and contentment. They called them "Save Rent," "A Little of My Own," "Heart's Love," "Liberty and Content," "Happy Retreat," "Jane's Delight," "Thank God to see It," &c.

Mr. Phillippo says : —

"These free villages are regularly laid out. The houses are small, many of them built of stone or wood, with shingled roofs, green blinds, and verandahs, to shield them from the sun. Most of them are neatly thatched, and generally plastered and whitewashed both outside and in. They now have looking-glasses, chairs, and sideboards decorated with pretty articles of glass and crockery. Each dwelling has its little plot of vegetables, generally neatly kept; and many of them have flowergardens in front, glowing with all the bright hues of the tropics. The groups often presented are worthy of the painter's pencil or the poet's song. Amid the stillness of a Sabbath evening, many families, after their return from the house of God, may be seen gathered together in the shadow of the trees, which overhang their cottages, singing hymns, or listening to the reading of the Scriptures, with none to molest or make them afraid."

Mr. Charles Tappan of Boston, who visited Jamaica several years after emancipation, writes : —

"On landing at Kingston, I must confess I was half inclined to believe the story so industriously circulated, that the emancipated slave is more idle and vicious than any other of God's intelligent creatures ; but when I rode through the valleys and over the mountains, and found everywhere an industrious, sober people, I concluded all the vagabonds of the island had moved to the sea-shore, to pick up a precarious living by carrying baggage, begging, &c. ; and such, upon inquiry, I found to be the fact. Wherever I went in the rural districts, I found contented men and women, cultivating sugar-cane, and numerous vegetables and fruits, on their own account. Their neat, well-furnished cottages compared well with the dwellings of pioneers in our own country. I found in them mahogany furniture, crockery and glass ware, and shelves of useful books. I saw Africans, of unmixed blood, grinding their own sugar-cane in their own mills, and making their own sugar.

"I attended a large meeting called to decide the question about inviting a schoolmaster to settle among them. There was only one man who doubted the expediency of taking the children from work and sending them to school. One said, 'My little learning enabled me to see that a note, given to me in payment for a horse was not written according to contract.' Another said, 'I should have been wronged out of forty pounds of coffee I sold in Kingston the other day, if I had n't known how to cipher.' Another said, 'I shall not have much property to leave my children ; but if they have learning they can get property.' Another said, 'Those that can read will be more likely to get religion.' All these people had been slaves, or were the children of slaves. I saw no intoxicated person in Jamaica; and when it is considered that every man there can make rum, it strikes me as very remarkable."

One of the most striking characteristics of this colored peasantry is their desire to obtain education for themselves and their children. After a hard day's work, women would often walk miles, with babies in their arms, to learn the alphabet. With the first money they can spare they build school-houses and chapels and hire teachers. They also form charitable societies and contribute money to help the aged and sick among them. In the days of Slavery they herded together like animals; but now it is considered disreputable and wrong to live together without being married. In the days of Slavery they wore ragged and filthy garments, but freedom has made them desirous of making a neat appearance. Their working-clothes are generally well mended and clean, and they keep a pretty suit to attend meeting and other festival occasions. They are very careful of their best clothes. When they go to dances, or social gatherings, they carry them in a basket, nicely folded and covered up, and put them on when they arrive; and when they are about to return home they again pack them up carefully. When they have far to walk to meeting, over rough and dusty roads, they carry their shoes and stockings till they come in sight of the church.

This is not at all like what the old planters prophesied, when they said that if the negroes were freed they would skulk in the woods and steal yams to keep them from starving. But all that silly talk has passed away. Everybody in the British West Indies acknowledges that emancipation has proved a blessing both to the white and the black population. There is not a planter to be found there who would restore Slavery again, if his own wish could do it.

THE LAST NIGHT OF SLAVERY.

BY JAMES MONTGOMERY.

LET the floods clap their hands!
    Let the mountains rejoice!
Let all the glad lands
    Breathe a jubilant voice!
The sun, that now sets on the waves of the sea,
Shall gild with his rising the land of the free!

Let the islands be glad!
    For their King in his might,
Who his glory hath clad
    With a garment of light,
In the waters the beams of his chambers hath laid,
And in the green waters his pathway hath made.

Dispel the blue haze,
    Golden Fountain of Morn!
With meridian blaze
    The wide ocean adorn!
The sunlight has touched the glad waves of the sea,
And day now illumines the land of the FREE!

MADISON WASHINGTON.

BY L. MARIA CHILD.

THIS man was a slave, born in Virginia. His lot was more tolerable than that of many who are doomed to bondage; but from his early youth he always longed to be free. Nature had in fact made him too intelligent and energetic to be contented in Slavery. Perhaps he would have attempted to escape sooner than he did, had he not become in love with a beautiful octoroon slave named Susan. She was the daughter of her master, and the blood of the white race predominated in several of her ancestors. Her eyes were blue, and her glossy dark hair fell in soft, silky ringlets. Her lover was an unmixed black, and he also was handsome. His features were well formed, and his large dark eyes were very bright and expressive. He had a manly air, his motions were easy and dignified, and altogether he looked like a being that would never consent to wear a chain.

If he had hated Slavery before, he naturally hated it worse after he had married Susan; for a handsome woman, who is a slave, is constantly liable to insult and wrong, from which an enslaved husband has no power to protect her. They laid plans to escape; but unfortunately their intention was discovered before they could carry it into effect. To avoid being sold to the far South, where he could have no hopes of ever rejoining his beloved Susan, he ran to the woods, where he re-

mained concealed several months, suffering much from
privation and anxiety. His wife knew where he was,
and succeeded in conveying some messages to him, without being detected. She persuaded him not to wait for a
chance to take her with him, but to go to Canada and
earn money enough to buy her freedom, and then she
would go to him.

He travelled only in the night, and by careful management, after a good deal of hardship, he reached the
Northern States, and passed into Canada. There he
let himself out to work on the farm of a man named
Dickson. He was so strong, industrious, intelligent, and
well behaved, that the farmer hoped to keep him a long
time in his employ. He never mentioned that he was
born a slave; for the idea was always hateful to him,
and he thought also that circumstances might arise
which would render it prudent to keep his own secret.
He showed little inclination for conversation, and occupied every leisure moment in learning to read and
write. He remained there half a year, without any
tidings from his wife; for there are many difficulties in
the way of slaves communicating with each other at a
distance. He became sad and restless. His employer
noticed it, and tried to cheer him up. One day he said
to him: "Madison, you seem to be discontented. What
have you to complain of? Do you think you are not
treated well here? Or are you dissatisfied with the
wages I give you?"

"I have no complaint to make of my treatment, sir,"
replied Madison. "You have been just and kind to me;
and since you manifest so much interest in me, I will tell
you what it is that makes me so gloomy."

He then related his story, and told how his heart was

homesick for his dear Susan. He said she was so handsome that they would ask a high price for her, and he
had been calculating that it would take him years to
earn enough to buy her; meanwhile, he knew not what
might happen to her. There was no law to protect a
slave, and he feared all sorts of things; especially, he
was afraid they might sell her to the far South, where
he could never trace her. So he said he had made
up his mind to go back to Virginia and try to bring
her away. Mr. Dickson urged him not to attempt it.
He reminded him of the dangers he would incur: that he
would run a great risk of getting back into Slavery,
and that perhaps he himself would be sold to the far
South, where he never would be able to communicate
with his wife. But Madison replied, " I am well aware
of that, sir; but freedom does me no good unless Susan
can share it with me."

He accordingly left his safe place of refuge, and started
for Virginia. He had free-papers made out, which he
thought would protect him till he arrived in the neighborhood where he was known. He also purchased several small files and saws, which he concealed in the lining of his clothes. With these tools he thought he could
effect his escape from prison, if he should be taken up on
the suspicion of being a runaway slave. Passing through
the State of Ohio, he met several who had previously
seen him on his way to Canada. They all tried to per-
suade him not to go back to Virginia; telling him there
were nine chances out of ten that he would get caught
and carried back into Slavery again. But his answer
always was, " Freedom does me no good while my wife
is a slave."

When he came to the region where he was known, he

hid in woods and swamps during the day, and travelled only in the night. At last he came in sight of his master's farm, and hid himself in the woods near by. There he remained several days, in a dreadful state of suspense and anxiety. He could not contrive any means to obtain information concerning his wife. He was afraid they might have sold her, for fear she would follow him. He prowled about in the night, in hopes of seeing some old acquaintance, who would tell him whether she was still at the old place; but he saw no one whom he could venture to trust. At last fortune favored him. One evening he heard many voices singing, and he knew by their songs that they were slaves. As they passed up the road, he came out from the woods and joined them. There were so many of them that the addition of one more was not noticed. He found that they were slaves from several plantations, who had permits from their masters to go to a corn-shucking. They were merry, for they were expecting to have a lively time and a comfortable supper. Being a moonless evening, they could not see Madison's face, and he was careful not to let them discover who he was. He went with them to the corn-shucking; and, keeping himself in the shadow all the time, he contrived, in the course of conversation, to find out all he wanted to know. Susan was not sold, and she was living in the same house where he had left her. He was hungry, for he had been several days without food, except such as he could pick up in the woods; but he did not dare to show his face at the supper, where dozens would be sure to recognize him. So he skulked away into the woods again, happy in the consciousness that his Susan was not far off.

He resolved to attempt to see her the next night. He

was afraid to tap at her window after all the people in
the Great House were abed and asleep; for, as she supposed he was in Canada, he thought she might be frightened and call somebody.　He therefore ventured to
approach her room in the evening.　Unfortunately, the
overseer saw him, and called a number of whites, who
rushed into the room just as he entered it.　He fought
hard, and knocked down three of them in his efforts to
escape.　But they struck at him with their bowie-knives
till he was so faint with loss of blood that he could resist
no longer.　They chained him and carried him to Richmond, where he was placed in the jail.　His prospects
were now dreary enough.　His long-cherished hope of
being reunited to his dear wife vanished away in the
darkness of despair.

There was a slave-trader in Richmond buying a gang
of slaves for the market of New Orleans.　Madison
Washington was sold to him, and carried on board the
brig Creole, owned by Johnson and Eperson, of Richmond, and commanded by Captain Enson.　The brig was
lying at the dock waiting for her cargo, which consisted
of tobacco, hemp, flax, and slaves.　There were two
separate cabins for the slaves : one for the men and the
other for the women.　Some of the poor creatures belonged to Johnson and Eperson, some to Thomas Mc-
Cargo, and some to Henry Hewell.　Each had a little
private history of separation and sorrow.　There was
many a bleeding heart there, beside the noble heart that
was throbbing in the bosom of Madison Washington.
His purchasers saw that he was intelligent, and they
knew that he was sold for having escaped to Canada.
He was therefore chained to the floor of the cabin and
closely watched.　He seemed quiet and even cheerful,

and they concluded that he was reconciled to his fate. On the contrary, he was never further from such a state of mind. He closely observed the slaves who were in the cabin with him. His discriminating eye soon selected those whom he could trust. To them he whispered that there were more than a hundred slaves on board, and few whites. He had his saws and files still hidden in the lining of his clothes. These were busily used to open their chains, while the captain and crew were asleep. They still continued to wear their chains, and no one suspected that they could slip their hands and feet out at their pleasure.

When the Creole had been nine days out they encountered rough weather. Most of the slaves were sea-sick, and therefore were not watched so closely as usual. On the night of November 7, 1841, the wind was blowing hard. The captain and mate were on deck, and nearly all the crew. Mr. Henry Hewell, one of the owners of the cargo of slaves, who had formerly been a slave-driver on a plantation, was seated on the companion, smoking a cigar. The first watch had just been summoned, when Madison Washington sprang on deck, followed by eighteen other slaves. They seized whatever they could find to use as weapons. Hewell drew a pistol from under his coat, fired at one of the slaves and killed him. Madison Washington struck at him with a capstan-bar, and he fell dead at his feet. The first and second mates both attacked Madison at once. His strong arms threw them upon the deck wounded, but not killed. He fought for freedom, not for revenge; and as soon as they had disarmed the whites and secured them safely, he called out to his accomplices not to shed blood. With his own hands he dressed the wounds of the crew, and told them they had nothing to fear if they would obey his orders. The man who had been a chained slave half an hour before was now master of the vessel, and his grateful companions called him Captain Washington. Being ignorant of navigation, he told Merritt, the first mate, that he should have the freedom of the deck, if he would take an oath to carry the brig faithfully into the nearest port of the British West Indies; and he was afraid to do otherwise.

The next morning Captain Washington ordered the cook to prepare the best breakfast the store-room could furnish, for it was his intention to give all the freed slaves a good meal. The women, who had been greatly frightened by the tumult the night before, were glad enough to come out of their close cabin into the fresh air. And who do you think was among them? Susan, the beautiful young wife of Madison, was there! She had been accused of communicating with her husband in Canada, and being therefore considered a dangerous person, she had been sold to the slave-trader to be carried to the market of New Orleans. Neither of them knew that the other was on board. With a cry of surprise and joy they rushed into each other's arms. The freed slaves threw up their caps and hurrahed again and again, till the sea-gulls wondered at the noise. O, it was a joyful, joyful time! Captain Washington was repaid for all he had suffered. He had gained his own liberty, after having struggled for it in vain for years; he had freed a hundred and thirty-four of his oppressed brethren and sisters; and he had his beloved Susan in his arms, carrying her to a land where the laws would protect their domestic happiness. He felt richer at that moment than any king with a golden crown upon his head.

7 *

There had been but two lives lost. One white man was killed in the affray, and he was the slave-driver who shot down one of the slaves. Captain Enson and others who were wounded were kindly cared for by Captain Washington. They proved ungrateful, and tried to regain possession of the vessel and the slaves. The blacks were so exasperated by this attempt, that they wanted to kill all the whites on board. But Captain Washington called out to them: "We have got our liberty, and that is all we have been fighting for. Let no more blood be shed! I have promised to protect these men. They have shown that they are not worthy of it; but let us be magnanimous."

Next morning the Creole arrived at Nassau, in the island of New Providence. Captain Washington and his companions sprang out upon free soil. There he and his beloved Susan are living under the protection of laws which make no distinctions on account of complexion.

EXTRACT FROM THE VIRGINIA BILL OF RIGHTS.

"THE election of members to serve as representatives of the people in Assembly ought to be free; and all men having sufficient evidence of permanent common interest with, and attachment to, the community have the right of suffrage; and they cannot be taxed, or deprived of their property for public uses, without their own consent, or that of their representatives so elected; nor can they be bound by any law to which they have not assented, in like manner, for the public good."

The Virginia Bill of Rights was unanimously adopted by the people, in June, 1776; and when they met, in January, 1830, to amend the constitution of the State, they voted that the Bill of Rights needed no amendment.

PRAISE OF CREATION.

BY GEORGE HORTON.

CREATION fires my tongue!
Nature, thy anthems raise,
And spread the universal song
Of thy Creator's praise.

When each revolving wheel
Assumed its sphere sublime,
Submissive Earth then heard the peal,
And struck the march of time.

The march in heaven begun,
And splendor filled the skies,
When Wisdom bade the morning sun
With joy from chaos rise.

The angels heard the tune
Throughout creation ring;
They seized their golden harps as soon,
And touched on every string.

When time and space were young,
And music rolled along,
The morning stars together sung,
And heaven was drowned in song.

FREDERICK DOUGLASS.

BY L. MARIA CHILD.

CAPTAIN ANTHONY owned two or three farms on the eastern shore of Maryland, and held about thirty slaves. One of them, a black woman named Betsy, married a free black man named Isaac Baily; and they had a numerous family of children, all of whom were, of course, slaves to Captain Anthony. When she became an old widow she lived in a hut separate from the other slaves, and was principally employed in nursing troops of babies, which her children brought into the world for the benefit of their master. Somewhere about the year 1817, Harriet, the youngest of her five daughters, gave birth to a boy, on whom she bestowed the high-sounding name of Frederick Augustus Washington Baily. As she could not be spared from field-work, baby Frederick joined the band of little slaves that were under his grandmother's care. Her hut was made of logs, with no windows, a clay floor, and a mud chimney. But the children were as well satisfied with it as if it had been a palace. They were too young to know that they were slaves, and they were as happy as little wild animals. They imitated the noises made by cats, dogs, pigs, and barn-yard fowls, and rolled over and over on the ground, laughing at their own fun. If the mud or dust made them uncomfortable, they walked into the river without undressing; for the short tow shirt, which was their only garment, was washed by swimming, and soon dried in the sunshine. There was a wood close by, and it was one of their greatest pleasures to watch the squirrels as they frisked about, or sat on the stumps eating nuts. Near the hut was a well, with its beam placed between the boughs of an old tree, and so well balanced that the children could easily help themselves to water. Down in a valley, not far off, was a water-mill, where people went to get their corn ground. It was capital sport to play at fishing in the mill-pond, with thread lines, and hooks made of bent pins; and they were never tired of seeing the big wheel turn round, throwing off great drops of water that sparkled in the sunshine. They lived mostly on corn mush, which they ate from a big wooden tray, with oyster-shells for spoons. But they were as healthy as little pigs, and enjoyed their coarse food as well.

The greatest of their blessings was their good grand-mother, who nursed them kindly and did all she could to make them happy. They loved her dearly; and when she was obliged to leave them for a short time, they greeted her return with merry shouts. She was advanced in years, and the hair that peeped from under the folds of her turban was very gray. But she was remarkably strong for her age, straight in her figure, and quick in her motions. She was very expert at catching fish, and sometimes spent half the day in the water She also made excellent nets to catch shad and herring; and, as these nets sold extremely well, Captain Anthony still found the old slave profitable. She had the name of being born to good luck, because whatever business she undertook prospered in her hands. She raised such excellent sweet potatoes that people often sent for her to plant for them, saying, " If Gran'ma Betty touches them they 'll be sure to flourish." But the secret of her good luck was her intelligence and carefulness. When she dug potatoes she took pains not to cut or bruise them; and in winter she protected them from frost in a hole under her hearth.

Freddy's poor mother was not allowed the comfort of being with her child. She was let out to work in the fields, twelve miles off. Whenever she went to see her little boy she had to walk over all those miles twice in the night-time, after a hard day's work; for if she was not back in the field by sunrise she was severely whipped. Freddy saw her but four or five times, and never by daylight. Sometimes she would lie down beside him and talk to him till he fell asleep, but when he woke she was always gone. He always remembered that she once took him on her knee and gave him a cake in the shape of a heart. Her rare visits made such an impression on him that he never forgot her personal appearance. She was tall and finely proportioned, with regular features and a deep black glossy complexion. Her manners were very sedate, her countenance downcast, and her eyes very sad. When he was nearly seven years old she died; but he knew nothing about it till long afterward. In later years he heard that she could read, and that she was the only one of all the slaves in the neighborhood who possessed that advantage. He never discovered how she had learned. When she died he was too young to have heard anything from her lips concerning his father. He was always told that he was the son of a white man, and some whispered the name of his master. But he never knew who was his father, and could only conjecture why the eyes of his poor mother had such a sad expression.

Captain Anthony did not carry on any of his own farms. He employed overseers for that purpose; and

however cruelly the slaves might be treated by the overseers, they never could obtain any protection by applying
to the "old master," as they called him. All the interest
he took in them was to have as much work as possible
forced out of them, and to sell one every year to add to
his income. He himself managed the affairs of Colonel
Lloyd, a wealthy gentleman with numerous plantations
and a thousand slaves. His home-plantation, on the river
Miles, where he resided with his family, was about twelve
miles from the hut where Frederick had been nursed.
His manager, Captain Anthony, lived in a house on the
same plantation, and was personally a stranger to his own
little slaves. But the children had seen and heard of
things which made the name of the "old master" a terror
to them. Frederick's first great trouble was when he
discovered that he was a slave, and that, as soon as he
was big enough to work, he would have to go to "old
master." Nothing could exceed his dread of leaving the
dear old home, and being separated from the kind friend
of his childhood. When he was about eight years old,
Captain Anthony sent for him; but his grandmother kept
it a secret, knowing how it would frighten him. One
bright summer morning she told him she was going to
Colonel Lloyd's plantation, and invited him to go with
her. He had a curiosity to see the grand place of which
he had heard so much; so she took him by the hand and
led him away from the happy home of his childhood, to
which he never returned. She carefully concealed from
him how her heart was swelling, and her tender ways did
not lead him to suspect it. When the unconscious little
boy began to be overcome with fatigue she "toted" him
on her strong shoulders. She scarcely seemed to feel the
burden, and insisted upon carrying him a long way; but he

felt too much of a man to permit it. He was, however, a little afraid as they walked through the thick, dark woods; for sometimes the old knotted and gnarled stumps, when seen from a distance, looked like creatures with eyes and legs; and he kept a tight hold of her gown till the monstrous things were safely passed.

It was afternoon before they reached the famous Home Plantation of Colonel Lloyd. There he found everything very different from the solitude and poverty to which he had been accustomed. The plantation seemed like a village, there were so many large houses, and stables, and out-buildings, and mechanics' shops, and such a long row of huts for the "slaves' quarters." Children were shouting and singing, and a great many men and women were hoeing in the fields. The children came crowding round Frederick, and asked him to go and play with them. He looked in his grandmother's face, and seeing that she seemed very sad, he begun to suspect that he was going to live with the "old master." He was unwilling to lose sight of her for a moment; but she patted him on the head, and said, "Be a good boy, and go and play with the children. That one is your brother Perry, that is your sister Sarah, and that is your sister Eliza." He had heard of these brothers and sisters before, but he had never seen them, and they seemed like strangers. He kept close to his grandmother; but at last she persuaded him to follow the children to the back part of the house. He felt so shy that he stood leaning against the wall, looking on, while the others played. After a while, a little boy, who had been left in the kitchen, ran up to him, exclaiming, "Fed! Fed! Grandmammy's gone!" He rushed after her, and when he found that she was gone far out of sight, he threw himself on the ground and sobbed. His brother and sisters brought him peaches and pears, but he flung them away, and continued sobbing, till, overcome with sorrow and fatigue, he fell into a deep sleep.

As Colonel Lloyd's plantation was not near any town, the barrels, wheels, shoes, and cloth that were needed by the numerous slaves were manufactured by themselves. Large crops of grain and tobacco were raised and shipped for Baltimore. All the business of twenty or thirty other farms was transacted at this plantation, which was distinguished by the name of "The Great House Farm"; and as Captain Anthony was overseer of all the overseers, he was kept very busy all the time. He took no notice of Freddy at first, but when told who the newcomer was, he patted him on the head and said, "You are my little Indian boy." Occasionally when he met him he would speak affectionately to him; but he was a violent-tempered man, and Freddy soon learned to watch him closely when he saw him coming. If he was shaking his head or muttering to himself, he hastened to get out of his way, lest he should catch a blow without knowing what it was for. The slave children had no one to care for them but cross Katy, the cook, who cuffed them about, and kept all, except her own children, in such a half-starved condition, that Freddy often had a tussle with the dogs and cats for the bones that were thrown to them. Summer and winter, they had no clothing but a coarse tow shirt that reached to the knees. They were provided with two a year; and if they wore out before allowance-day came round, they went naked. They slept anywhere on the floor without covering. Freddy suffered much from cold. His naked feet were cracked open in great gashes in the winter. When he could get a chance, he would creep into the meal-bag at night. So much for the care taken of their bodies; and it fared no better with their souls. All the instruction they received was from Uncle Isaac, a crippled slave, who, being unable to work, taught the children to say the Lord's Prayer after him by rote, and switched them whenever they made a mistake.

But Freddy was at an age to bear privations and troubles lightly, and to enjoy thoughtlessly whatever pleasant things came in his way. He had never seen anything so grand as The Great House, in which Colonel Lloyd resided. It was a large white building, with piazza and columns in front, surrounded by arbors, and grain-houses, and turkey-houses, and pigeon-houses, interspersed with grand old trees. There was an extensive lawn, kept as smooth as velvet, and ornamented with flowering shrubs. The carriage-road to and from the house made a circle round the lawn, and was paved with white pebbles from the beach. Outside of this enclosed space were extensive parks, where rabbits, deer, and other wild animals frisked about. Flocks of red-winged blackbirds made the trees look gay, and filled the air with melody. Vessels on their way to Baltimore were continually in sight, and a sloop belonging to Colonel Lloyd lay in the river, with its pretty little boat bobbing about in the sparkling water. There was a windmill not far off, and the little slaves were never tired of watching the great wings go whirling round. There was a creek to swim in, and crabs and clams and oysters to be got by wading and digging and raking for them. Freddy was glad enough to catch them when he had a chance, for he never had half enough to eat. He had one friend at The Great House. Daniel Lloyd, the Colonel's youngest son, liked to have him assist in his sports. He protected him when bigger boys wanted to make war upon him, and sometimes he gave him a cake. Captain Anthony's family consisted of a son, Andrew, and a daughter, Lucretia, who had married Captain Thomas Auld. Mrs. Lucretia took a fancy to bright little Freddy. She liked to hear him sing, and often spoke a kind word to him. This emboldened him so much, that when he was very hungry he would go and sing under the window where she sat at work, and she would generally give him a piece of bread, sometimes with butter on it. That was a great treat for a boy who was fed all the time on corn mush, and could not get half enough of that. His business was to clean the front yard, to keep fowls out of the garden, to drive the cows home from pasture, and to run of errands. He had a good deal of time to play with his little relatives, and with the young slaves at Colonel Lloyd's, who called him " Captain Anthony Fed." He was such a mere boy, that it is no wonder so many new people and things soon cured him of homesickness for his grandmother, who could very seldom get time to trudge twelve miles to see him.

But though his slave-life was not without gleams of enjoyment, he saw and heard much that was painful. At one time he would see Colonel Lloyd compel a faithful old slave get down upon his knees to be flogged for not keeping the hair of his horses sufficiently smooth. At another time, the overseer would shoot a slave dead for refusing to come up to be whipped. Ever and anon some of them were sold to Georgia slave-traders, and there was weeping and wailing in the families they left behind. On the premises of his own master, he was not unfrequently wakened in the night by the screams and groans of slaves who were being lashed.   One of Captain Anthony's slaves, named Esther, was the sister of Freddy's mother.   She had a pretty face and a graceful shape.   She and a handsome young slave of Colonel Lloyd's were much attached, and wished to marry.   But her old master, for reasons of his own, forbade her to see her lover, and if he suspected them of meeting he would abuse the poor girl in a most shocking manner. Freddy was too young at the time to understand the full significance of this cruel treatment; but when he thought of it in after years, it explained to him why his poor mother had always looked so downcast and sad.   As for himself, he managed to escape very severe punishment, though Captain Anthony not unfrequently whipped him for some carelessness or mischief.   But when he saw the plantation-laborers, even of so rich a man as Colonel Lloyd, driven out to toil from early morning to dusk, shivering in the cold winds, or dripping with rain, with no covering but a few coarse tow rags, he could not help thinking that such was likely to be his fate when he was older.   Young as he was, he had a great dread of being a field-hand.   Therefore he was rejoiced when Mrs. Lucretia told him he was to be sent to Baltimore, to live with her husband's brother, Mr. Hugh Auld.   She told him if he would make himself very clean, she would give him a pair of new trousers.   The prospect of exchanging his little tow shirt for new trousers delighted him so much that he was ready to scrub his skin off to obtain them.   He was, moreover, very eager to see Baltimore; for slaves who had been there told fine stories about the grand houses and the multitude of ships.   He had been only two years at Captain Anthony's, and he had formed no attachment so strong as that he had felt for his old grandmother. It was with a joyful heart that he went forth to view the wonders of thê city. When he arrived in Baltimore, his new mistress met him at the door with a pleasant smile. She said to her son, " There's little Freddy, who has come to take care of you"; and to him she said, " You must be kind to little Tommy." Mrs. Sophia Auld had earned her own living before her marriage, and she had not yet acquired the ways of slaveholders toward servants. While her own little Tommy was on her knee, Freddy was often seated by her side, and sometimes her soft hand would rest upon his head in a kind, motherly way. He had never been treated so since he left his good old grandmother. In a very short time he loved her with all his heart, and was eager to do anything to please her. It was his business to go of errands and take care of Tommy. The boys became as much attached to each other as if they were brothers. There was nothing to remind Freddy of being a slave. He had plenty of wholesome food to eat, clean clothes to wear, and a good straw bed with warm covering. Mrs. Auld was much in the habit of singing hymns and reading the Bible aloud; and Freddy, who was not at all afraid of " Miss Sophy," as he called her, said to her one day that he wished she would teach him to read. She consented; and he was so quick at learning that he was soon able to spell small words. His kind mistress was so much pleased with his progress, that she told her husband about it, and remarked, with much satisfaction, that Freddy would soon be able to read the Bible. Mr. Auld was displeased, and forbade her giving any more lessons. " It is contrary to law to teach a nigger to read," said he. "It is unsafe, and can only lead to mischief. If you teach him to read the Bible, it will make him discontented, and there will be no keeping him. Next thing, he will be wanting to learn to write; and then he 'll be running away with himself." This was said in the presence of Freddy, and it set his active mind to thinking. He had often before wondered why black children were born to be slaves; and now he heard his master say that if he learned to read it would spoil him for a slave. He resolved that he *would* learn to read. He carried a spelling-book in his pocket when he went of errands, and persuaded some of the white boys who played with him to give him a lesson now and then. He was soon able to read. With some money that he earned for himself, he bought a book called "The Columbian Orator." It contained many speeches about liberty. The reading of them made him discontented. He was no longer light-hearted and full of fun. He became thoughtful and serious. When he played with white boys, he would ask, "Why have n't I as good a right to be free, and go where I please, as you have?" And sometimes a generous-hearted boy would answer, "I believe, Fred, you *have* just as good a right to be free as I have."

He knew that his present situation was uncommonly favorable; but the idea of being a slave for life became more and more hateful to him. He had not been in Baltimore quite four years when an event occurred which proved to him the extreme uncertainty of a slave's condition, even when circumstances seemed the most favorable. His old master, Captain Anthony, died; and his slaves were to be divided between his son Andrew and his daughter Mrs. Lucretia Auld. Frederick was in terror lest it should be decided that he belonged to Andrew, who was a confirmed drunkard, and excessively cruel to the slaves. It was a month before the division of the estate was decided by law; and the anxiety of his mind was so great that it seemed to him half a year. He felt as if saved from sentence of death, when he was informed that he belonged to Mrs. Lucretia, who had been kind to him in his hungry boyhood. As she had no occasion for his services, it was agreed that he should remain in Mr. Hugh Auld's family; a circumstance which pleased Master Tom and his mother about as much as it did Freddy.

But in a short time he was again painfully reminded of the uncertainty of his condition. Mrs. Lucretia and her brother Andrew both died, each of them leaving one child. Neither Captain Anthony nor his children left any of the slaves free. Even Frederick's old grandmother, who had nursed her master when he was a baby, waited upon him through his boyhood, worked faithfully for him during all her life, and reared up a multitude of children and grandchildren to toil for him, — even she was left in Slavery, with no provision made for her. The children she had tended so lovingly were sold, or let out in distant places; all were unable to write to inform her where they had gone; all were unable to help her, because they were not allowed to have their own earnings. When her old master and his children were dead, the owners of the property thought Gran'ma Betty was too old to be of any further use; so they put up a hut with a mud chimney in the woods, and left her there to find food for herself as she could, with no mortal to render her any service in her dying hour. This brutal proceeding increased the bitterness of Frederick's feeling against Slavery.

By the blessing of God the consolations of religion came to him, and enabled him to look beyond this trou-

bled and transitory world. A pious colored man, called
Uncle Lawson, became interested in him. They attended prayer-meetings together, and Frederick often
went to his house on Sundays. They had refreshing
times together, reading the Bible, praying, and singing
hymns. Uncle Lawson saw that his young friend had
uncommon intelligence, and he often said to him, " The
Lord has a great work for you to do, and you must prepare yourself for it." Frederick replied that he did not
see how a slave could prepare himself for any great
work; but the pious old man always answered, " Trust
in the Lord. He will bring it about in his own good
time. You must go on reading and studying Scripture."
This prophecy inspired him with hope, and he seized
every opportunity to improve himself. But he had many
obstacles to contend with. His master, Mr. Hugh Auld,
was made irritable by an increasing love for brandy.
When he found out that Frederick read and spoke at
religious meetings, he threatened to flog him if he continued to do it. His kind mistress, who used to pat him
on the head and call him " Little Freddy," was changed
by the habit of having slaves and talking with slaveholders. The pleasant, motherly expression of her face
had become severe. She watched Frederick very closely,
and if she caught him with a book or newspaper in his
hand, she would rush at him in a great rage and snatch
it away. Master Tommy had grown to be a tall lad, and
began to feel that he was born to be a master and Fred
to be a slave. Frederick would probably have tried to
run away, had it not been for the friendships he had
formed for Uncle Lawson and the religious young men
he met at the meetings. Notwithstanding his master's
threat, he contrived to find opportunities to read and

pray with good Uncle Lawson; and it had a blessed influence on his spirit, making him feel at peace with all men. Now that he had a taste of knowledge, it was impossible to prevent his getting more. His master sent him of errands to the shipyard almost daily. He noticed that the carpenters marked their boards with letters. He asked the name of the letters, and copied them with a bit of chalk. When the family went from home, he diligently copied from the writing-books Master Tommy had brought from school; and his zeal was so great that in a short time he could write as well as his master. He picked up bits of newspapers wherever he could find them, and he listened attentively when he heard slave-holders talking about the Northern States and cursing the Abolitionists. He did not at first know what was the meaning of "abolitionists"; but when he read in a newspaper that petitions were sent into Congress for the abolition of Slavery, light dawned upon him. He told trustworthy colored friends about it, and they were comforted by the thought that there were people at the North trying to help them out of bondage.

But a new blow fell upon him. Captain Thomas Auld married again, after the death of his wife Mrs. Lucretia, and removed to St. Michael's, — an old village, the principal business of which was oyster fishing. He got into a quarrel with his brother, Mr. Hugh Auld of Baltimore, and demanded that Frederick should be sent back to him. So he was put on board a ship for St. Michael's. When swift steamboats on their way to Philadelphia passed the sloop that carried him, he bitterly regretted that he had not escaped to the Free States from Baltimore, where he could have had so many more opportunities for doing it than he could at the old fishing-village.

8

Captain Thomas Auld and his new wife were both great
professors of religion. He was an exhorter and class-
leader in the Methodist Church. But their religion was
not of a kind that taught them humanity to their fellow-
creatures. They worked their slaves very hard, and
kept them half fed and half clothed. Scolding and flogging were going on incessantly. Frederick soon discovered that they were violently opposed to colored people's
knowing how to read; but when a pious young man in
the neighborhood asked him to assist in a Sunday school
for colored children, he resolved to seize the opportunity
of being useful. When his master found out what he
was doing, he was very angry; and the next Sunday he
and two other Methodist class-leaders went to the school,
armed with clubs and whips, and drove off both teachers
and scholars. It was agreed that Frederick had been
spoiled by living in Baltimore, and that it was necessary
to cure him of his dangerous thirst for knowledge. For
that purpose he was sent to a famous "negro-breaker" in
the neighborhood named Covey. He was a great profes-
sor of religion, but a monster of cruelty. Frederick was
almost killed by hard labor, and not a week passed without his being cruelly cut up with the whip. Escape was
impossible, for Covey was on the watch at all times of
day and night. Six months of such treatment wellnigh
crushed all manhood out of him. But cruelty was carried so far that at last he became desperate, and when
his master attempted to beat him, he struggled with him
and threw him down. He expected to be hung for it,
according to the laws of Maryland; but Covey prided
himself on his reputation as a "negro-breaker," and he
was ashamed to have it known that he had been con-
quered by a lad of seventeen. Frederick's time was not

out for six month's longer, but Covey never attempted to whip him again.

The next two years Frederick was let out to do field-work for Mr. Freeland, who fed his slaves well, and never worked them beyond their strength. Some of his slaves were intelligent, and desirous to learn to read. On Sundays they had meetings in the woods, and twenty or thirty young men were taught by Frederick. After a while they formed a plan of escaping in a canoe. But some unknown men excited suspicion against them, and they were seized and thrust into prison. They kept their secrets so well, however, that no proof could be obtained against them, and they were released without even a whipping. But some of the neighboring slave-holders said Frederick was a dangerous fellow; that he knew too much, — they would not have him tampering with their slaves; and if he was not sent out of the neighborhood they would shoot him. Captain Thomas Auld talked of selling him to Alabama; but he finally concluded to let him out again to his brother Hugh, with a promise that if he behaved well he should be free at twenty-five years old.

When he returned to Baltimore he was let out to work at calking vessels; and he soon became so expert at the business that he earned from seven to nine dollars a week. He was trusted to make his own contracts, but was required to pay Mr. Hugh Auld his earnings every Saturday night. On such occasions a sixpence or a shilling was sometimes given him, for which he was expected to be grateful; but it naturally occurred to him that the whole of the money rightfully belonged to him who earned it. He was attached to a worthy girl named Anna, but he was reluctant to form family ties while he was subject to the vicissitudes of Slavery. He often thought of escaping to the Free States, but the regulations were so strict that it seemed a hopeless undertaking, unless he had money. When Captain Thomas Auld visited Baltimore, he tried to make a bargain with him to buy his time for a specified sum each week, being free to earn as much more as he could. The reply was, " You are planning to run away. But, wherever you go, I shall catch you." The master then tried to coax him with promises of freedom in the future ; but Frederick thought it very uncertain when they would be willing to give up a man who brought them in nine dollars a week. He concluded to go to the Free States. How he accomplished it he never told, for he was afraid of bringing trouble upon those who helped him.

When he arrived in New York, he says he felt as he should suppose a man would feel who had escaped from a den of hungry lions. But the joyful feeling was soon checked. He met an acquaintance who had recently escaped from Slavery. He told him the city was full of Southerners, who had agents out in every direction to catch runaway slaves ; and then he hurried away, as if afraid of being betrayed. This made Frederick feel very desolate. He was afraid to seek employment as a calker, lest spies from his master should be on the watch for him. He bought a loaf of bread, and hid away for the night among some barrels on a wharf. In the morning, he met a sailor, who looked so good-natured and honest that he ventured to tell him he was a fugitive slave, and to ask him for advice. He was not deceived in the expression of the man's face. He invited him to his house, and went in search of Mr. David Ruggles, a worthy colored man, well known as a zealous friend of his oppressed race.

The fugitive was kept hidden for a few days, during which time Anna was sent for, and they were married. By help of Mr. Ruggles, employment at calking was obtained in New Bedford, a large town in Massachusetts, where a great many ships are constantly employed. There he found many intelligent colored people, not a few of whom had been slaves. They lived in convenient houses, took newspapers, bought books, and sent their children to good schools. They had various societies for improvement; and when he attended their meetings, he was surprised to hear their spirited discussions on various subjects. His bright mind was roused into full activity by the influences around him. He changed his name to Frederick Douglass. He was called Mr. Douglass now, and felt like it. He worked hard, but that was a pleasure, now that he could enjoy his own earnings. He felt safe; for there were so many Abolitionists and so many intelligent colored people in New Bedford, that slaveholders did not venture to go there to hunt for fugitives. The cruel treatment he had received from hypocritical professors of religion had not destroyed his faith in the excellence of real religion. He joined a church of colored people, called Zion Methodists, and became a class-leader and preacher among them. He took a newspaper called "The Liberator," edited by William Lloyd Garrison, wherein he found the rights of the colored people vindicated with great zeal and ability. His wife proved a neat and industrious helpmate, and a little family of children began to gather round him. Thus furnished with healthy employment for his mind, his heart, and his hands, he lived over three years in New Bedford.

At the end of that period, in the year 1841, a great

Anti-Slavery meeting was held in the vicinity, and Mr. Douglass went to hear Mr. Garrison and others speak. He did not suppose that any one in the meeting knew him; but a gentleman was present who had heard him preach in Zion Church, and he went to him and urged him to address the Anti-Slavery meeting. He was bashful about speaking before such a large and intelligent audience; and when he was persuaded to mount the platform he trembled in every limb. But what he said flowed right out from the depths of his heart; and when people of any intelligence speak in that way, they are always eloquent. The audience were greatly moved by what he told them of his experiences. It was the beginning of a great change in his life. The Anti-Slavery Society employed him to travel in the Free States to lecture against Slavery; and that you may be sure he could do with a will. Crowds went to hear him, and his ministration was greatly blessed. The prophecy of good Uncle Lawson was fulfilled. The Lord *had* a great work for him to do; and in His own good time he had brought it about.

People who were in favor of Slavery said he was an impostor; that he did not look like a slave, or speak like a slave; and that they did not believe he had ever been in the Southern States. To prove that he was not an impostor he wrote and published an account of his life, with the names of his masters and the places where they resided. The book was ably written, and produced almost as great an effect as his lectures. Slaveholders were very angry that one of their escaped chattels should produce such an excitement. There was great danger that some of their agents would kidnap him as he went about the country lecturing. It was therefore concluded that

he had better go to England. In 1845 he took passage
for Liverpool in the English steamship Cambria. He
was invited to deliver a lecture on deck. Some slaveholders from New Orleans and Georgia, who were a little under the influence of brandy, swore they would throw
him overboard if he did; but the captain of the vessel
threatened to put them in irons if they behaved in a dis-
orderly manner. When they arrived in England they
tried to injure Mr. Douglass by publishing that he was
an insolent, lying negro; but their efforts only served to
make him famous. He delivered a great number of lectures, and attracted crowds everywhere. In the Free
States of his own country he had been excluded from
many places of improvement, and often insulted on account of his color; but he had no such prejudice to en-
counter in England. He behaved like a gentleman, and
was treated like a gentleman. Many distinguished and
wealthy people invited him to their houses, as a mark
of respect for his natural abilities and the efforts he had
made to improve himself. But he felt that his labors
were needed in America, in behalf of his oppressed brethren, and he wanted to return. His friends in England
entered into negotiations with Captain Thomas Auld for
the purchase of his freedom, which they succeeded in obtaining for little more than seven hundred dollars.

After an absence of two years he returned to the United
States a freeman. He established himself with his family
in Rochester, New York. There he edited a weekly
newspaper, called "The North Star," and from time to
time travelled about the country to deliver lectures, which
were always fully attended. After he was free he wrote
a spirited letter to his old master, Captain Thomas Auld,
in which he asks : " What has become of my dear old

grandmother, whom you turned out, like an old horse, to die in the woods? If she is still alive, she must be near eighty years old, — too old to be of any service to you. O, she was father and mother to me, so far as hard toil for my comfort could make her so. Send her to me at Rochester, and it shall be the crowning happiness of my life to take care of her in her old age." I never heard that any answer was received to this letter.

During the Rebellion Mr. Douglass labored zealously to raise colored regiments, and one of his sons enlisted in the service of the United States. After the Proclamation of Emancipation he was invited to Baltimore, where he delivered an address before a large audience of respectable citizens. How different was free Maryland from the Slavery-ridden State which he had left, secretly and in terror, nearly thirty years before!

HOW THE GOOD WORK GOES ON.

IN the spring of 1865 an association of colored men was formed in Baltimore for moral and intellectual improvement. They bought a building formerly used by the Newton University, for which they paid sixteen thousand dollars. In honor of their able pioneer, Frederick Douglass, they named it "The Douglass Institute." On the day of its dedication he delivered an address before the association in Baltimore, in the course of which he said: "The mission of this institution is to develop manhood; to build up manly character among the colored people of this city and State. It is to teach them the true idea of manly independence and self-respect. It is to be a dispenser of knowledge, a radiator of light. In a word, we dedicate this institution to virtue, temperance, knowledge, truth, liberty, and justice."

DEDICATION HYMN.

BY J. M. WHITEFIELD.

Written for the Vine Street Methodist Episcopal Church of colored
people, in Buffalo, N. Y.

GOD of our sires! before thy throne
  Our humble offering now we bring;
Deign to accept it as thine own,
  And dwell therein, Almighty King!
Around thy glorious throne above
  Angels and flaming seraphs sing;
Archangels own thy boundless love,
  And cherubim their tribute bring.

And every swiftly rolling sphere,
  That wends its way through boundless space,
Hymns forth, in chorus loud and clear,
  Its mighty Maker's power and grace.
It is not ours to bear the parts
  In that celestial song of praise;
But here, O Lord! with grateful hearts,
  This earthly fane to Thee we raise.

O let thy presence fill this house,
  And from its portals ne'er depart!
Accept, O Lord! the humble vows
  Poured forth by every contrite heart!
No sacrifice of beast or bird,
  No clouds of incense here shall rise,

8 *   L

But, in accordance with thy word,
  We 'll bring a holier sacrifice.

Here shall the hoary-headed sire
  Invoke thy grace, on bended knee ;
While youth shall catch the sacred fire,
  And pour its song of praise to Thee.
Let childhood, too, with stammering tongue,
  Here lisp thy name with reverent awe ;
And high and low, and old and young,
  Learn to obey thy holy law.

And when our spirits shall return
  Back to the God who gave them birth,
And these frail bodies shall be borne
  To mingle with their kindred earth, —
Then, in that house not made with hands,
  New anthems to thy praise we 'll sing,
To Thee, who burst our slavish bands,
  Our Saviour, Prophet, Priest, and King.

A PRAYER.

GRANT, O Father, that the time
  Of earth's deliverance may be near,
When every land and tongue and clime
  The message of Thy love shall hear ;
When, smitten as with fire from heaven,
  The captive's chain shall sink in dust,
And to his fettered soul be given
  The glorious freedom of the just.

JOHN G. WHITTIER.

WILLIAM AND ELLEN CRAFTS.

BY L. MARIA CHILD.

WILLIAM CRAFTS is a black man, born in Georgia. His master had the reputation of being a humane man and a pious Christian. Yet, when some of his slaves were getting old, he had no scruples about selling them away from their families, and buying a young lot. Among those sold were the father and mother of William. They were sold to different purchasers from different places, and never saw each other again. They were much attached to each other, and it was a consolation to their son to think how happy would be their reunion in another world; for he says he never knew people who more humbly placed their trust in God than his parents did. William was apprenticed to a cabinet-maker, and his brother to a blacksmith; because slaves who worked well at a trade could be let out with more profit to their masters, and would also bring a higher price if sold. Before their time was out, their master became hard pressed for money. Accordingly, he sold the young blacksmith, and mortgaged William and his sister, a girl of fourteen. When the time of the mortgage was up, their master had no money to redeem them, and they were placed on the auction-block, to be sold to the highest bidder. The girl was sold first, and bought by a planter who lived some distance in the country. William was strongly attached to his sister; and when he saw her put into a cart, to be carried away from

him forever, it seemed as if his heart would burst. He
knelt down and begged and entreated to be allowed to go
and speak to her before she was taken away; but they
handled him roughly, and ordered him to stay on the
auction-block. As he stood there awaiting his own fate,
he saw the cart moving slowly away. The tears were
rolling down his sister's cheeks, and she stretched her
hands toward him with a movement of despair. The
thought that he could do nothing for her, and that they
might never meet more, almost killed him. His eyes
were blinded with tears; and when he could see again,
the cart was gone.

He was bought by the man to whom he had been
mortgaged, and ordered to return to the cabinet-maker's
shop to work. After a while his new master took him
to Macon, where he was let out to work at his trade.
There he became acquainted with a quadroon girl named
Ellen, whom he afterward married.

Ellen was the daughter of her master, but her mother
was a slave. Her handsome dark eyes were apt to attract attention; her hair was straight, and her skin was so
nearly white that strangers often mistook her for one of
her master's own white family. This was very vexatious
to her mistress, who treated her so harshly that the poor
child had no comfort of her life. When she was eleven
years old she was given to a daughter of her mistress,
who was about to be married to a gentleman living in
Macon. It was painful to part from her poor mother,
but she was glad to get away from the incessant cruelty
of her old mistress. Her new mistress proved more
humane. In her service Ellen grew up without being
exposed to some of the most degrading influences of
Slavery.

She and the intelligent young cabinet-maker formed an attachment for each other soon after they were acquainted. But Ellen had seen so much of the separation of families in Slavery, that she was very reluctant to marry. Whenever William said anything about it, she reminded him that they were both slaves; and that if they were married either of their masters could separate them whenever they chose. William remembered, with bitterness of heart, how his father and mother and brother had been sold, and how his sister had been torn from him without his being allowed to bid her good by. He had not been tortured in his own person, but he had seen other slaves cruelly whipped and branded with hot iron, hunted and torn by bloodhounds, and even burned alive, merely for trying to get their freedom. In view of these things, he had a great horror of bringing children into the world to be slaves. He and Ellen often talked together about escaping to the North and being married there. But they reflected that they would have to travel a thousand miles before they could reach any Free State. They knew that bloodhounds and slave-hunters would be put upon their track; that if they were taken, they would be subjected to terrible tortures; and that, even if they succeeded in reaching the Free States, they would still be in danger of being delivered up to their masters. They talked over a variety of plans; but the prospect of escape seemed so discouraging, that at last they concluded to ask their owner's consent to their marriage; and they resolved to be as contented as they could in the situation to which they were born. But they were too intelligent not to know that a great wrong was done to them by keeping them in slavery. William shuddered to think into what cruel and licentious hands his dear wife might

fall if she should be sold by her present owners; and
Ellen was filled with great anguish whenever she thought
what might happen to her children, if she should be a
mother. They were always thinking and talking about
freedom, and they often prayed earnestly to God that
some way of escape might be opened for them.

In December, 1848, a bold plan came into William's
mind. He thought that if his wife were dressed in men's
clothes she could easily pass for a white gentleman, and
that he could accompany her on her travels as her negro
slave. Ellen, who was very modest and timid, at first
shrank from the idea. But, after reflecting more upon
their hopeless situation, she said: " It seems too difficult
for us to undertake; but I feel that God is on our side,
and with His help we may carry it through. We will
try."

It was contrary to law for white men in the Southern
States to sell anything secretly to slaves; but there were
always enough ready to do it for the sake of getting
money, — especially as they knew that no colored man
was allowed to testify against a white man. William
was skilful and diligent at his trade; and though his
wages all went to his master, he had contrived to lay up
money by doing jobs for others in extra hours. He
therefore found little difficulty in buying the various articles of a gentleman's dress, at different times and in different parts of the town. He had previously made Ellen
a chest of drawers, with locks and key; and as she was
a favorite and trusted slave, she was allowed to keep it
for her own use in the little room where she slept. As
fast as the articles were bought they were secretly conveyed to her, and she locked them up. The next important thing was to obtain leave of absence for a few days.

It was near Christmas-time, when kind slaveholders sometimes permit favorite slaves to be absent on a visit to
friends or relatives.   But Ellen's services were very
necessary to her mistress, and she had to ask many times
before she could obtain a written permission to be gone
for a few days.   The cabinet-maker for whom William
worked was persuaded to give him a similar paper, but
he charged him to be sure and return as soon as the time
was up, because he should need him very much.   There
was still another difficulty in the way.   Travellers were
required to register their names at the custom-houses
and hotels, and to sign a certificate for the slaves who
accompanied them.   When Ellen remembered this, it
made her weep bitterly to think that she could not write.
But in a few moments she wiped her eyes and said, with
a smile, "I will poultice my right hand and put it in a
sling, and then there will be a good excuse for asking
the officers to write my name for me."   When she was
dressed in her disguise, William thought she could easily
pass for a white gentleman, only she looked young enough
for a mere boy; he therefore bought a pair of green
spectacles to make her look older.   She, on her part,
was afraid that the smoothness of her chin might betray
her; she therefore resolved to tie a bandage round her
face, as if she were troubled with toothache.

In four days after they first thought of the plan, all
was in readiness.   They sat up all night, whispering over
to each other the parts they were to act in case of various supposable difficulties.   William cut off Ellen's glossy
black hair, according to the fashion of gentlemen.   When
all was carefully arranged, they knelt together and
prayed that God would protect them through their peril-
ous undertaking.   They raised the latch of the door very

softly, and looked out and listened.   Nobody was stirring abroad, and all was still.   But Ellen trembled and threw herself on her husband's breast.   There she wept for a few moments, while he tried to comfort her with whispered words of encouragement, though he also felt that they were going forth into the midst of terrible dangers. She soon recovered her calmness, and said, " Let us go." They stepped out on tiptoe, shook hands in silence, and parted to go to the railway station by different routes. William deemed it prudent to take a short cut across the fields, to avoid being recognized ; but his wife, who was now to pass for his young master, went by the public road.   Under the name of Mr. William Johnson, she purchased tickets for herself and slave for Savannah, which was about two hundred miles off.   The porter who took charge of the luggage at the station had formerly wished to marry Ellen ; but her disguise was so complete that he called her " Young massa," and respectfully obeyed her orders concerning the baggage.   She gave him a bit of money for his trouble, and he made his best bow.

The moment William arrived at the station, he hid himself in the " negro car " assigned to servants.   It was lucky that he did so ; for, just before the train started, he saw upon the platform the cabinet-maker, who had given him a pass for quite a different purpose than an excursion to Savannah.   He was looking round, as if searching for some one ; and William afterward heard that he suspected him of attempting to escape.   Luckily, the train started before he had time to examine the " negro car."

Ellen had a narrow escape on her part ; for a gentleman who took the seat beside her proved to be Mr. Cray, who frequently visited at her master's house, and who had known her ever since she was a child. Her first thought was that he had come to seize her and carry her back; but it soon became evident that he did not recognize her in a gentleman's dress, with green spectacles, bandaged face, and her arm in a sling. After the cars started, he remarked, "It is a very fine morning, sir." Ellen, being afraid that her voice would betray her, continued to look out of the window, and made no reply. After a little while, he repeated the remark in a louder tone. The passengers who heard him began to smile, and Mr. Cray turned away, saying, "I shall not trouble that deaf fellow any more." To her great relief, he left the cars at the next station.

They arrived at Savannah early in the evening, and William having brought his master something to eat, they went on board a steamer bound for Charleston, South Carolina. Mr. Johnson, as Ellen was now called, deemed it most prudent to retire to his berth immediately. William, fearing this might seem strange to the other passengers, made a great fuss warming flannels and opodeldoc at the stove, informing them that his young master was an invalid travelling to Philadelphia in hopes of getting cured. He did not tell them the disease was Slavery; he called it inflammatory rheumatism. The next morning, at breakfast, Mr. Johnson was seated by the captain of the boat, and, as his right hand was tied in a sling, his servant, William, cut up his food for him. The captain remarked, "You have a very attentive boy, sir; but I advise you to watch him like a hawk when you get North. Several gentlemen have lately lost valuable niggers among them cut-throat Abolitionists."

A hard-looking slave-trader, with red eyes, and bristly

beard, was sitting opposite. He laid down a piece of
chicken he was eating, and with his thumbs stuck in the
arm-holes of his waistcoat, said : " I would n't take a nigger North under no consideration. Now, if you 'd like
to sell that 'ere boy, I 'll pay you for him in silver dollars, on this 'ere board. What do you say, stranger ? "
Mr. Johnson replied, " I do not wish to sell him, sir ;
I could not get on well without him." " You 'll *have* to
get on without him, if you take him to the North," continued the slave-trader. " I am an older cove than you
are, and I reckon I have had more dealings with niggers.
I tell you, stranger, that boy will never do you any good
if you take him across Mason and Dixon's line. I can
see by the cut of his eye that he is bound to run away as
soon as he can get a chance." Mr. Johnson replied, " I
think not, sir. I have great confidence in his fidelity."
Whereupon the slave-trader began to swear about niggers in general. A military officer, who was also travelling with a servant, said to Mr. Johnson : " Excuse me,
sir, for saying I think you are likely to spoil that boy of
yours by saying ' thank you' to him. The only way to
make a nigger toe the mark, and to keep him in his
place, is to storm at him like thunder. Don't you see
that when I speak to my Ned, he darts like lightning ?
If he did n't, I 'd skin him."

When the steamboat arrived at Charleston, the hearts
of the fugitives beat almost loud enough to be heard ;
they were so afraid their flight had been discovered, and
a telegraph sent from Savannah to have them arrested.
But they passed unnoticed among the crowd. They took
a carriage and drove to a fashionable hotel, where the
invalid gentleman received every attention befitting his
supposed rank. He was seated at a luxurious table in a

brilliant dining-room, while William received some fragments of food on a broken plate, and was told to go into the kitchen. Mr. Johnson gave some pieces of money to the servants who waited upon him; and they said to William, " Your massa is a big-bug. He is de greatest gentleman dat has been dis way dis six months."

Notwithstanding the favorable impression he had made, Mr. Johnson found some difficulty in obtaining tickets to Philadelphia for himself and his slave. The master of the ticket-office refused to write the invalid gentleman's name for him. But the military officer who had breakfasted with him stepped up and said he knew the gentleman, and all was right. The captain of the North Carolina steamer hearing this, and not wishing to lose a passenger, said, " I will register the gentleman's name, and take the responsibility upon myself." Mr. Johnson thanked him politely, and the captain remarked : " No disrespect was intended to you, sir; but they are obliged to be very strict in Charleston. Some Abolitionist might take a valuable nigger along with him, and try to pass him off as his slave."

They arrived safely at Wilmington, North Carolina, and took the cars to Richmond, Virginia. On the way, an elderly lady in the cars, seeing William on the platform, cried out, in great excitement, " There goes my nigger Ned!" Mr. Johnson said, very politely, " No, madam, that is my boy." But the lady, without paying any attention to what he said, called out, " Ned, you runaway rascal, come to me, sir." On nearer inspection she perceived that she was mistaken, and said to Mr. Johnson : " I beg your pardon, sir. I was sure it was my Ned. I never saw two black pigs look more alike."

From Petersburg, a Virginia gentleman with two handsome daughters were in the same car with Mr. Johnson. Supposing him to be a rich, fashionable young Southerner, they were very attentive and sympathizing. The old gentleman told him he knew how to pity him, for he had had inflammatory rheumatism himself. He advised him to lie down to rest; which he was very willing to do, as a good means of avoiding conversation. The ladies took their extra shawls and made a comfortable pillow for his head, and their father gave him a piece of paper which he said contained directions for curing the rheumatism. The invalid thanked him politely; but not knowing how to read, and fearing he might hold the paper upside down, prudently put it in his pocket. When they supposed him to be asleep, one of the ladies said, " Papa, he seems to be a very nice young gentleman"; and the other responded, "I never felt so much for any gentleman in my life."

At parting the Virginian gave him his card and said: "I hope you will call upon me when you return. I should be much pleased to see you, and so would my daughters." He gave ten cents to William, and charged him to be attentive to his master. This he promised to do, and he very faithfully kept his word.

They arrived at Baltimore with the joyful feeling that they were close upon the borders of a Free State. William saw that his master was comfortably placed in one of the best cars, and was getting into the servants' car when a man tapped him on the shoulder and asked where he was going. William replied humbly, "I am going to Philadelphia, sir, with my master, who is in the next car." "Then you had better get him out, and be mighty quick about it," said the man; "for the train is going to start, and no man is allowed to take a slave past here till he has satisfied the folks in the office that he has a right to take him along."

William felt as if he should drop down on the spot; but he controlled himself, and went and asked his master to go back to the office. It was a terrible fright. As Mr. Johnson stepped out he whispered, in great agitation, "O William, is it possible we shall have to go back to Slavery, after all we have gone through?" It was very hard to satisfy the station-master. He said if a man carried off a slave that did not belong to him, and the rightful owner could prove that he escaped on that road, they would be obliged to pay for the slave. Mr. Johnson kept up a calm appearance, though his heart was in his throat. "I bought tickets at Charleston to pass us through to Philadelphia," said he; "therefore you have no right to detain us here." "Right or no right, we shall not let you go," replied the man. Some of the spectators sympathized with the rich young Southerner, and said it was a pity to detain him when he was so unwell. While the man hesitated, the bell rang for the cars to start, and the fugitives were in an agony. "I don't know what to do," said the man. "It all seems to be right; and as the gentleman is so unwell, it is a hard case for him to be stopped on the way. Clerk, run and tell the conductor to let this gentleman and his slave pass."

They had scarcely time to scramble into the cars, before the train started. It was eight o'clock in the evening, and they expected to arrive in Philadelphia early the next morning. They did not know that on the way the passengers would have to leave the cars and cross the river Susquehanna in a ferry-boat. They had slept very little for several nights before they left Georgia, and they had been travelling day and night for four days.

William, overcome with fatigue, and feeling that their greatest dangers were now over, fell sound asleep on a heap of baggage. When they arrived at the ferry, it was cold, dark, and rainy; and for the first time during their hazardous journey the invalid found no faithful servant at hand when the cars stopped. He was in great distress, fearing that William had been arrested or kidnapped. He anxiously inquired of the passengers whether they had seen his boy. There were a good many Northerners on board, and, supposing his slave had run away, they rather enjoyed his perplexity. One gruffly replied, "I am no slave-hunter." Another smiled as he said, "I guess he is in Philadelphia before now."

When they had crossed the ferry one of the guard found William still sound asleep on the baggage, which had been rolled into the boat. He shook him and bawled out: "Wake up, you boy! Your master has been half scared to death. He thought you had run away." As soon as William was enough awake to understand what had happened, he said, "I am sure my good master does not think that of me." He hastened to explain to Mr. Johnson how he happened to be out of the way. He was received with a great leap of the heart; but the passengers only thought that the master was very glad to recover his lost property. Some of them took a convenient opportunity to advise William to run away when they reached Philadelphia. He replied, "I shall never run away from such a good master as I have." They laughed, and said, "You will think differently when you get into a Free State." They told him how to proceed in case he wanted to be free, and he thanked them. A colored man also entered into conversation with him, and told him of a certain boarding-house in Philadelphia, the keeper of which was very friendly to slaves who wanted their freedom.

On Christmas-day, just as morning was about to dawn, they came in sight of the flickering lights of Philadelphia. William procured a cab as quick as possible, hurried their baggage into it, and told the driver to take them to the boarding-house which had been recommended to them. While Ellen had been obliged to act the part of Mr. Johnson, she had kept her mind wonderfully calm and collected. But now that she was on free soil she broke down with the excess of her emotions. "Thank God, William, we are safe, we are safe!" she exclaimed; and sinking upon her husband's breast, she burst into a passion of tears. When they arrived at the boarding-house, she was so faint she had no further occasion to act being an invalid. As soon as a room was provided, they entered and fastened the door. Then kneeling down side by side, folded in each other's arms, with tears flowing freely, they thanked God for having brought them safely through their dangerous journey, and having permitted them to live to see this happy Sabbath day, which was Christmas-day also.

When they had rested and refreshed themselves with a wash, Ellen put on her womanly garments and went to the sitting-room. When the landlord came at their summons, he was very much surprised and perplexed. "Where is your master?" inquired he; and when William pointed to his wife, he thought it was a joke; for he could not believe she was the same person who came into the house in the dress of a gentleman. He listened to their singular story with great interest and sympathy. He told them he was afraid it would not be safe for them to remain in Philadelphia, but he would send for some

Abolitionists who knew the laws better than he did. Friends soon came, and gave them a hearty welcome; but they all agreed that it would not be safe for them to remain long in Philadelphia, and advised them to go to Boston. Barclay Ivens, a kind-hearted Quaker farmer, who lived some distance in the country, invited them to rest a few weeks at his house. They went accordingly. But Ellen, who had not been accustomed to receive such attentions from white people, was a little flurried when they arrived. She had received the impression that they were going to stay with colored people; and when she saw a white lady and three daughters come out to the wagon to meet her, she was much disturbed, and said to William, "I thought they were colored people." "It is all the same as if they were," replied he. "They are our good friends." "It is *not* all the same," said Ellen, decidedly. "I have no faith in white people. They will be sending us back into Slavery. I am going right off." She had not then become acquainted with the Abolitionists. She had heard her master and other Southerners talk about them as very bad men, who would make slaves believe they were their friends, and then sell them into distant countries. The Quaker lady saw that she was afraid, and she went up to her and took her very kindly by the hand, saying: "How art thou, my dear? We are very glad to see thee and thy husband. We have heard about thy marvellous escape from Slavery. Come in and warm thyself. I dare say thou art cold and hungry after thy journey." Ellen thanked her, and allowed herself to be led into the house. Still she did not feel quite safe in that strange place, away from all her people. When Mrs. Ivens attempted to remove her bonnet, she said, "No, I thank you. I am not going to stop long." "Poor child!" said the good Quaker mother, "I don't wonder thou art timid. But don't be afraid. Thou art among friends who would as soon sell their own daughters into Slavery as betray thee. We would not harm a hair of thy head for the world." The kindly face and the motherly tones melted the heart of the poor frightened fugitive, and the tears began to flow. They stayed several weeks in that hospitable house, and the son and daughters took so much pains to teach them to read and write, that before they left they could spell a little, and write their names quite legibly. They were strongly urged to stay longer, and would have done so had they not been very desirous to be earning their own living. When they left this excellent family it seemed like parting with near and dear relatives.

In Boston they were introduced to William Lloyd Garrison, Wendell Phillips, Francis Jackson, Rev. Theodore Parker, and other good men, who had for years been laboring for the emancipation of the slaves. The fugitives made a favorable impression on strangers at first sight. They both looked intelligent and honest. William had a very manly air, and Ellen was modest and ladylike in her manners.

Their marriage in Georgia had been, like other slave marriages, without a certificate; therefore they were desirous to have the ceremony performed again, with all the forms of law, now that they were in a free land. They were accordingly married by the Rev. Mr. Parker, at the house of a respectable colored citizen of Boston, named Lewis Hayden. Mr. Crafts was employed at his trade, and his wife obtained work as a seamstress. They lived in Boston two years, during which time they established an excellent character by their honest industry and

correct deportment. They earned a comfortable living,
and might have laid by some money if circumstances
had permitted them to remain in Massachusetts.

But in 1850 the Congress of the United States, under
the influence of slaveholders, passed a very wicked act
called the Fugitive Slave Bill. There was in Boston at
that time a celebrated lawyer named Daniel Webster.
He wanted to be President of the United States, and for
many years no man had been able to get elected to that
office unless he pleased the slaveholders.   He accordingly used his great influence to help the passage of the
bill, and advised the people of Massachusetts to get over
their scruples about hunting slaves. He died without being
President ; and I hope God forgave the great sin into
which his ambition led him. By that cruel act of Congress, everybody, all over the country, was required to
send back fugitive slaves to their masters. Whoever
concealed them or helped them in any way became
liable to a year's imprisonment and a fine of a thousand
dollars, besides paying the price of the slave. In all the
Northern cities there were many honest, industrious colored people who had escaped from Slavery years before,
and were now getting a comfortable living. Many of
them had married at the North and reared families.
But when slaveholders gained this victory over the conscience of the North, they were compelled to leave their
business and their homes, and hide themselves whereso-
ever they could. Mr. and Mrs. Crafts had many zealous
friends in Boston, but the friends of the slaveholders
were more numerous. For some time past, Southerners
had been rather reluctant to hunt slaves in Massachusetts, because the public opinion of the people was
so much opposed to Slavery, that they found it a difficult

and disagreeable job. But after the passage of that un-righteous bill, they and their pro-slavery accomplices at the North became more bold.

One day, while Mr. Crafts was busy in his shop, he received a visit from a man by the name of Knight, who used to work in the same shop with him in Georgia. He professed to be much pleased to see William again, and invited him to walk round the streets and show him the curiosities of Boston. Mr. Crafts told him he had work to do, and was very busy. The next day he tried again; but finding Mr. Crafts still too busy to walk with him, he said: "I wish you would come to see me at the United States Hotel, and bring your wife with you. She would like to hear from her mother. If you want to send letters to Georgia, I will take them for you." This was followed by a badly spelled note to Mr. Crafts, informing him that he was going to leave Boston early the next morning, and if he wanted to send a letter to Georgia he must bring it to him at the hotel after tea. Mr. Crafts smiled that he should think him silly enough to walk into such an open trap. Mr. Knight had told him that he came to Boston alone; but when he questioned the hotel-servant who brought the note, he was told that a Mr. Hughes from Georgia accompanied him. Mr. Hughes was a notorious slave-catcher, and the jailer of Macon. Mr. Crafts continued to work at his shop; but he kept the door locked, and a loaded pistol beside him.

Finding that his intended victim was too much on his guard to be caught by trickery, Mr. Hughes applied to the United States Court in Boston and obtained a war-rant to arrest William and Ellen Crafts as fugitive slaves. This produced tremendous excitement. The

Abolitionists were determined that they should not be carried back into Slavery. They had people everywhere on the watch, and employed lawyers to throw all manner of difficulties in the way of the slave-hunters, whose persons and manners were described in the newspapers in a way by no means agreeable to them. The colored people held large meetings, and passed various spirited resolutions, among which was the following: " *Resolved*, Man wills us slaves, but God wills us free. We will as God wills. God's will be done." Two hundred of them armed themselves and vowed that they would defend William and Ellen Crafts to the death. Mr. Crafts said very calmly, but very resolutely, that they should never take him alive. Hughes the slave-catcher swore: "I'll have 'em if I stay in Boston to all eternity. If there a'n't men enough in Massachusetts to take 'em, I'll bring men from Georgia." Merchants in Boston, thinking only of their trade with the South, sympathized with those men engaged in such a base calling; and the United States officials did all they could to help them. But though they received countenance and aid from many influential men in Boston, those hirelings of Slavery could not help feeling ashamed of their business. They complained that the boys in the streets hooted after them, and that wherever they made their appearance, people called out, "There go the slave-hunters!" They heard that the Abolitionists were preparing to arrest them and try them as kidnappers; and the number of colored people who watched their movements with angry looks made them wish themselves back in Georgia. During all this commotion, the conduct of Mr. Crafts excited universal admiration. He was resolute, but very calm. If there had been any law to protect him, he would have appealed to the law, rather than have harmed a hair of any man's head; but left defenceless as he was among a pack of wolves hunting him and his innocent wife, he was determined to defend his freedom at any cost.

Ellen was secretly conveyed out of the city. Mr. and Mrs. Ellis Gray Loring of Boston were excellent people, always kind to the poor and true friends to the oppressed slaves. They spent their summers in the neighboring town of Brookline. A Boston physician, who was an Abolitionist, carried Ellen to their house in the evening. Mr. and Mrs. Loring were both absent from home for a few days, but a lady who was staying in the house received her with great kindness. She stayed there two days, assisting the lady very industriously and skilfully with her needle. Her mind was full of anxiety about her husband, whom she had left in the city exposed to the most fearful danger. She was very wakeful through the night, listening to every noise. As soon as she became drowsy, she would wake with a sudden start from some bad dream. She dreamed that she and William were running from the Georgia slave-catcher, and that Daniel Webster was close behind them, pointing a pistol at them. It was a sad thing that a man of such intellectual ability as Mr. Webster, and with so much influence in society, should make such bad use of his great power that he haunted the dreams of the poor and the oppressed. Ellen rose in the morning with a feeling of weariness and a great load upon her heart. But she kept back the tears that were ready to flow, and was so quiet and sweet-tempered that she completely gained the hearts of her protectors. Early the next evening, the same friend who carried Ellen from the city brought her husband to her. He also had been sleepless, and was worn down with fatigue and anxiety. They were advised to retire to rest immediately, to remain in their room with the door locked, and be careful not to show themselves at the window. They followed these directions, and the lady was hoping they would both have peaceful and refreshing slumber, when Ellen came to say that her husband wanted to speak with her. She found him standing by the fireplace looking very sad, but with a dignified calmness that seemed to her truly noble in the midst of such dreadful danger. As she entered he said, "Ellen has just told me that Mr. and Mrs. Loring are absent from home. If we should be found in his house, he would be liable to imprisonment and a heavy fine. It is wrong for us to expose him to this danger without his knowledge and consent. We must seek shelter elsewhere." The lady replied: "Mr. Loring would feel troubled to have you leave his house under such circumstances. He is the best and kindest of men, and a great friend of the colored people." "That makes it all the more wrong for us to bring him into trouble on our account, without his knowledge," replied Mr. Crafts. Ellen had kept up bravely all day, but now her courage began to fail. She looked up with tears swimming in her handsome eyes and said: "O William, it is so dark and rainy to-night, and it seems so safe here! We may be seen and followed, if we go out. You said you did n't sleep last night. I started up from a little nap, dreaming that Daniel Webster was chasing us with a loaded pistol. I thought of all manner of horrid things that might be happening to you, and I could n't sleep any more. Don't you think we might stay here just this one night?" He looked at her with pity in his eyes, but said, very firmly, "Ellen, it would n't be right." Without another word she prepared to go, though the tears were falling fast. The lady, finding his mind too fixed to be changed by her persuasions, sent a guide with them to the house of Mr. Philbrick, a worthy, kind-hearted gentleman, who lived about half a mile off. She herself told me the story; and she said she never felt so much respect and admiration for any human beings as she did for those two hunted slaves when she saw them walk out into the darkness and rain because they thought it wrong to endanger, without his consent, a friend of their persecuted people. She felt anxious lest the slave-catcher or his agents might seize them on the road, and it was a great relief to her mind when the guide returned and said Mr. Philbrick received them gladly.

After a few more days of peril they were secretly put on board a vessel, which conveyed them to England. They carried letters which introduced them to good people, who contributed money to put them to school for a while. Their intelligence, industry, and good conduct confirmed the favorable impression made by their first appearance. In 1860, Mr. Crafts published a little book giving an account of their " Running a Thousand Miles for Freedom." They have now been living in England fifteen years. By their united industry and good management they earned a comfortable living, and laid by a little, year after year, until they had enough to buy a small house in the village of Hammersmith, not far from the great city of London. There they keep their children at the best of schools, and pay taxes which help to support the poor in the country which protected them in their time of danger and distress.

The honesty, energy, and good sense of Mr. Crafts inspired so much respect and confidence in England, that the Quakers and other benevolent people, who wish to do good to Africa, also merchants, who want to open trade with that region, sent him out there with a valuable cargo of goods, in November, 1862. The mission he is performing is very important to the well-being of the world, as you will see by the following explanation.

Africa is four thousand miles across the Atlantic Ocean from the United States. It is inhabited by numerous tribes of black people, each tribe with a separate government. These tribes vary in degrees of intelligence and civilization; but they are generally of a peaceable and kindly disposition, unless greatly provoked by wrongs from others. Where they are safe from attack they live in little villages of huts, and raise yams, rice, and other grain for food. They weave coarse cloth from cotton, merely by means of sticks stuck in the ground, and in some places they color it with gay patterns. They make very pretty baskets and mats from grasses, and some of the tribes manufacture rude tools of iron and ornaments of gold. But a constant state of warfare has hindered the improvement of the Africans; for men have very little encouragement to build good houses, and make convenient furniture, and plant grain, if enemies are likely to come any night and burn and trample it all to the ground. These continual wars have been largely caused by the slave-trade. Formerly the African chiefs sold men into Slavery only in punishment for some crime they had committed, or to work out a debt they had failed to pay, or because they were prisoners taken in war. These customs were barbarous enough, but they were not so bad as what they were afterward taught to do by nations calling themselves Christians. In various countries of Europe and America there were white people too proud and lazy to work, but desirous to dress in the best and live on the fat of the land. They sent ships out to Africa to bring them negroes, whom they compelled to work without wages, with coarse, scanty food, and scarcely any clothing. They grew rich on the labor of these poor creatures, and spent their own time in drinking, gambling, and horse-racing. Slave-traders, in order to supply them with as many negroes as they wanted, would steal all the men, women, and children they could catch on the coast of Africa; and would buy others from the chiefs, paying them mostly in rum and gunpowder. This made the different tribes very desirous to go to war with each other, in order to take prisoners to sell to the slave-traders; and the more rum they drank, the more full of fight they were. This mean and cruel business has been carried on by white men four hundred years; and all that while African villages have been burned in the night, and harvests trampled, and men, women, and children carried off to hopeless Slavery in distant lands. This continual violence, and intercourse with such bad white men as the slave-traders, kept the Africans barbarous; and made them much more barbarous than they would otherwise have been. Such a state of things made it impossible for them to improve, as they would have done if the nations called Christians had sent them spelling-books and Bibles instead of rum, teachers instead of slave-traders, and tools and machinery instead of gun-powder.

Of all the African chiefs the King of Dahomey is the most powerful. He sends armed men all about the country to carry off people and sell them to Europeans and Americans. In that bad way he has grown richer than other chiefs, and more hard-hearted. Benevolent people

9 *

in England have long desired to stop the ravages of the slave-trade and to teach the Africans better things. The dearth of cotton in the United States, occasioned by the Rebellion of the planters, turned the attention of English merchants in the same direction. It was accordingly agreed to send Mr. Crafts to Dahomey to open a trade, and try to convince the king that it would be more profitable to him to employ men in raising cotton than to sell them for slaves. He was well received by the King of Dahomey, who shows a disposition to be influenced by his judicious counsels. This is a great satisfaction to Mr. Crafts, desirous as he is of elevating people of his own color. Numbers who were destined to be sold into foreign Slavery are already employed in raising cotton in their native land. Wars will become less frequent; and the African tribes will gradually learn that the arts of peace are more profitable, as well as more pleasant. This will bring them into communication with a better class of white men ; and I hope that, before another hundred years have passed away, there will be Christian churches all over Africa, and school-houses for the children.

Mr. Crafts sold all the goods he carried out in the first vessel, and managed the business so well that he was sent out with another cargo. He is now one of the most enterprising and respected merchants in that part of the world; and his labors produce better results than mere money, for they are the means of making men wiser and better. How much would have been lost to himself and the world if he had remained a slave in Georgia, not allowed to profit by his own industry, and forbidden to improve his mind by learning to read !

Mr. M. D. Conway, the son of a slaveholder in Virginia, but a very able and zealous friend of the colored people, recently visited England, and sent the following letter to Boston, where it was read with great interest by the numerous friends of William and Ellen Crafts : —

"LONDON, October 29th, 1864.

"A walk one pleasant morning across a green common, then through a quiet street of the village called Hammersmith, brought me to the house of an American whom I respect as much as any now in Europe ; namely, William Crafts, once a slave in Georgia, then a hunted fugitive in Massachusetts, but now a respected citizen of England, and the man who is doing more to redeem Africa from her cruel superstitions than all other forces put together.   He lately came home from Dahomey, the ship-load of goods that he had taken out to Africa from Liverpool having been entirely sold.   The merchants who sent him are preparing another cargo for him, and he will probably leave the country this week.   His theory is, that commerce is to destroy the abominations in the realm of Dahomey.   He is very black, but he finds the color which was so much against him in America a leading advantage to him in Africa.   Ellen, his wife, told us that she was too white to go with him. He was absent on business in Liverpool, and thus, to my regret, I missed the opportunity of seeing him.   There was a pretty little girl, and three unusually handsome boys.   They all inherit the light complexion and beauty of their mother.   We found Mrs. Crafts busy packing her husband's trunk for his next voyage.   She showed us a number of interesting things which he had brought from Africa.   Among them were birds of bright plumage, a belt worn by the Amazons in war, a sword made by the Africans, breastpins, and other excellent specimens of work in metals. I remembered that years ago the sight of similar things inspired Clarkson with his strong faith in the improvability of the African race.

"William and Ellen Crafts own the house in which they live. After that brave flight of a thousand miles for freedom, after the dangers which surrounded them in Massachusetts, it did my heart good to see them enjoying their own simple but charming home, to see them thus living under their own vine and fig-tree, none daring to molest or make them afraid.

"M. D. Conway."

Mrs. Crafts has used her needle diligently to make garments for the colored people of the United States emancipated by President Lincoln's Proclamation. She has had the pleasure of hearing that her mother is among them, healthy, and still young looking for her years. As soon as arrangements can be made she will go to England to rejoin her daughter, whom she has not seen since her hazardous flight from Georgia.

I think all who read this romantic but true story will agree with me in thinking that few white people have shown as much intelligence, moral worth, and refinement of feeling as the fugitive slaves William and Ellen Crafts.

In February, 1861, the Emperor of Russia proclaimed freedom to twenty-three millions of serfs. Finding their freedom was not secure in the hands of their former masters, he afterward completed the good work by investing the freedmen with civil and political rights; including the right to testify in court, the right to vote, and the right to hold office.

SPRING.

BY GEORGE HORTON.

HAIL, thou auspicious vernal dawn!
　　Ye birds, proclaim that winter's gone!
　　Ye warbling minstrels, sing!
Pour forth your tribute as ye rise,
And thus salute the fragrant skies,
　　The pleasing smiles of spring!

Coo sweetly, O thou harmless dove,
And bid thy mate no longer rove
　　In cold hybernal vales!
Let music rise from every tongue,
Whilst winter flies before the song
　　Which floats on gentle gales.

Ye frozen streams, dissolve and flow
Along the valley sweet and slow!
　　Divested fields, be gay!
Ye drooping forests, bloom on high,
And raise your branches to the sky;
　　And thus your charms display!

Thou world of heat! thou vital source!
The torpid insects feel thy force,
　　Which all with life supplies.
Gardens and orchards richly bloom,
And send a gale of sweet perfume,
　　To invite them as they rise.

Near where the crystal waters glide
The male of birds escorts his bride,
    And twitters on the spray ;
He mounts upon his active wing,
To hail the bounty of the spring,
    The lavish pomp of May.

THE GOOD GRANDMOTHER.

BY HARRIET JACOBS.

I HAD a great treasure in my maternal grandmother,
who was a remarkable woman in many respects.
She was the daughter of a planter in South Carolina,
who, at his death, left her and her mother free, with
money to go to St. Augustine, where they had relatives.
It was during the Revolutionary War, and they were
captured on their passage, carried back, and sold to different purchasers.   Such was the story my grandmother
used to tell me.   She was sold to the keeper of a large
hotel, and I have often heard her tell how hard she fared
during childhood.   But as she grew older she evinced
so much intelligence, and was so faithful, that her master
and mistress could not help seeing it was for their interest to take care of such a valuable piece of property.
She became an indispensable person in the household,
officiating in all capacities, from cook and wet-nurse to
seamstress.   She was much praised for her cooking ; and
her nice crackers became so famous in the neighborhood
that many people were desirous of obtaining them.   In

consequence of numerous requests of this kind, she asked permission of her mistress to bake crackers at night, after all the household work was done; and she obtained leave to do it, provided she would clothe herself and the children from the profits. Upon these terms, after working hard all day for her mistress, she began her midnight bakings, assisted by her two oldest children. The business proved profitable; and each year she laid by a little, to create a fund for the purchase of her children. Her master died, and his property was divided among the heirs. My grandmother remained in the service of his widow, as a slave. Her children were divided among her master's children; but as she had five, Benjamin, the youngest, was sold, in order that the heirs might have an equal portion of dollars and cents. There was so little difference in our ages, that he always seemed to me more like a brother than an uncle. He was a bright, handsome lad, nearly white; for he inherited the complexion my grandmother had derived from Anglo-Saxon ancestors. His sale was a terrible blow to his mother; but she was naturally hopeful, and she went to work with redoubled energy, trusting in time to be able to purchase her children. One day, her mistress begged the loan of three hundred dollars from the little fund she had laid up from the proceeds of her baking. She promised to pay her soon; but as no promise or writing given to a slave is legally binding, she was obliged to trust solely to her honor.

In my master's house very little attention was paid to the slaves' meals. If they could catch a bit of food while it was going, well and good. But I gave myself no trouble on that score; for on my various errands I passed my grandmother's house, and she always had something to spare for me. I was frequently threatened with punishment if I stopped there ; and my grandmother, to avoid detaining me, often stood at the gate with something for my breakfast or dinner. I was indebted to her for all my comforts, spiritual or temporal. It was *her* labor that supplied my scanty wardrobe. I have a vivid recollection of the linsey-woolsey dress given me every winter by Mrs. Flint. How I hated it ! It was one of the badges of Slavery. While my grandmother was thus helping to support me from her hard earnings, the three hundred dollars she lent her mistress was never repaid. When her mistress died, my master, who was her son-in-law, was appointed executor. When grandmother applied to him for payment, he said the estate was insolvent, and the law prohibited payment. It did not, however, prohibit him from retaining the silver candelabra which had been purchased with that money. I presume they will be handed down in the family from generation to generation.

My grandmother's mistress had always promised that at her death she should be free ; and it was said that in her will she made good the promise. But when the estate was settled, Dr. Flint told the faithful old servant that, under existing circumstances, it was necessary she should be sold.

On the appointed day the customary advertisement was posted up, proclaiming that there would be " a public sale of negroes, horses, &c." Dr. Flint called to tell my grandmother that he was unwilling to wound her feelings by putting her up at auction, and that he would prefer to dispose of her at private sale. She saw through his hypocrisy, and understood very well that he was ashamed of the job. She was a very spirited woman ; and if he was base enough to sell her, after her mistress had made her free by her will, she was determined the public should know it. She had, for a long time, supplied many families with crackers and preserves; consequently "Aunt Marthy," as she was called, was generally known; and all who knew her respected her intelligence and good character. It was also well known that her mistress had intended to leave her free, as a reward for her long and faithful services. When the day of sale came, she took her place among the chattels, and at the first call she sprang upon the auction-block. She was then fifty years old. Many voices called out: "Shame! shame! Who's going to sell *you*, Aunt Marthy? Don't stand there. That's no place for *you*." She made no answer, but quietly awaited her fate. No one bid for her. At last a feeble voice said, "Fifty dollars." It came from a maiden lady, seventy years old, the sister of my grandmother's deceased mistress. She had lived forty years under the same roof with my grandmother; she knew how faithfully she had served her owners, and how cruelly she had been defrauded of her rights, and she resolved to protect her. The auctioneer waited for a higher bid; but her wishes were respected; no one bid above her. The old lady could neither read nor write; and when the bill of sale was made out, she signed it with a cross. But of what consequence was that, when she had a big heart overflowing with human kindness? She gave the faithful old servant her freedom.

My grandmother had always been a mother to her orphan grandchildren, as far as that was possible in a condition of Slavery. Her perseverance and unwearied industry continued unabated after her time was her own, and she soon became mistress of a snug little home, and surrounded herself with the necessaries of life. She would have been happy, if her family could have shared them with her. There remained to her but three children and two grandchildren; and they were all slaves. Most earnestly did she strive to make us feel that it was the will of God; that He had seen fit to place us under such circumstances, and though it seemed hard, we ought to pray for contentment. It was a beautiful faith, coming from a mother who could not call her children her own. But I and Benjamin, her youngest boy, condemned it. It appeared to us that it was much more according to the will of God that we should be free, and able to make a home for ourselves, as she had done. There we always found balsam for our troubles. She was so loving, so sympathizing! She always met us with a smile, and listened with patience to all our sorrows. She spoke so hopefully, that unconsciously the clouds gave place to sunshine. There was a grand big oven there, too, that baked bread and nice things for the town; and we knew there was always a choice bit in store for us. But even the charms of that old oven failed to reconcile us to our hard lot. Benjamin was now a tall, handsome lad, strongly and gracefully made, and with a spirit too bold and daring for a slave.

One day his master attempted to flog him for not obeying his summons quickly enough. Benjamin resisted, and in the struggle threw his master down. To raise his hand against a white man was a great crime, according to the laws of the State; and to avoid a cruel, public whipping, Benjamin hid himself and made his escape. My grandmother was absent, visiting an old friend in the country, when this happened. When she returned, and found her youngest child had fled, great was her sorrow.

But, with characteristic piety, she said, "God's will be done." Every morning she inquired whether any news had been heard from her boy. Alas! news did come, — sad news. The master received a letter, and was rejoicing over the capture of his human chattel.

That day seems to me but as yesterday, so well do I remember it. I saw him led through the streets in chains to jail. His face was ghastly pale, but full of determination. He had sent some one to his mother's house to ask her not to come to meet him. He said the sight of her distress would take from him all self-control. Her heart yearned to see him, and she went; but she screened herself in the crowd, that it might be as her child had said.

We were not allowed to visit him. But we had known the jailer for years, and he was a kind-hearted man. At midnight he opened the door for my grandmother and myself to enter, in disguise. When we entered the cell, not a sound broke the stillness. "Benjamin," whispered my grandmother. No answer. "Benjamin!" said she, again, in a faltering tone. There was a jingling of chains. The moon had just risen, and cast an uncertain light through the bars. We knelt down and took Benjamin's cold hands in ours. Sobs alone were heard, while she wept upon his neck. At last Benjamin's lips were unsealed. Mother and son talked together. He asked her pardon for the suffering he had caused her. She told him she had nothing to forgive; that she could not blame him for wanting to be free. He told her that he broke away from his captors, and was about to throw himself into the river, but thoughts of her came over him and arrested the movement. She asked him if he did not also think of God. He replied: "No, mother, I did not. When a man is hunted like a wild beast, he forgets that there *is* a God."

The pious mother shuddered, as she said : " Don't talk so, Benjamin. Try to be humble, and put your trust in God."

" I wish I had some of your goodness," he replied. " You bear everything patiently, just as though you thought it was all right. I wish I could."

She told him it had not always been so with her; that once she was like him; but when sore troubles came upon her, and she had no arm to lean upon, she learned to call on God, and he lightened her burdens. She besought him to do so likewise.

The jailer came to tell us we had overstayed our time, and we were obliged to hurry away. Grandmother went to the master and tried to intercede for her son. But he was inexorable. He said Benjamin should be made an example of. That he should be kept in jail till he was sold. For three months he remained within the walls of the prison, during which time grandmother secretly conveyed him changes of clothes, and as often as possible carried him something warm for supper, accompanied with some little luxury for her friend the jailer. He was finally sold to a slave-trader from New Orleans. When they fastened irons upon his wrists to drive him off with the coffle, it was heart-rending to hear the groans of that poor mother, as she clung to the Benjamin of her family, — her youngest, her pet. He was pale and thin now, from hardships and long confinement; but still his good looks were so observable that the slave-trader remarked he would give any price for the handsome lad, if he were a girl. We, who knew so well what Slavery was, were thankful that he was not.

Grandmother stifled her grief, and with strong arms and unwavering faith set to work to purchase freedom

for Benjamin. She knew the slave-trader would charge
three times as much as he gave for him; but she was not
discouraged. She employed a lawyer to write to New
Orleans, and try to negotiate the business for her. But
word came that Benjamin was missing; he had run away
again.

Philip, my grandmother's only remaining son, inherited
his mother's intelligence. His mistress sometimes trusted
him to go with a cargo to New York. One of these occasions occurred not long after Benjamin's second escape.
Through God's good providence the brothers met in the
streets of New York. It was a happy meeting, though
Benjamin was very pale and thin; for on his way from
bondage he had been taken violently ill, and brought nigh
unto death. Eagerly he embraced his brother, exclaiming: "O Phil! here I am at last. I came nigh dying
when I was almost in sight of freedom; and O how I
prayed that I might live just to get one breath of free
air! And here I am. In the old jail, I used to wish I
was dead. But life is worth something now, and it would
be hard to die." He begged his brother not to go back
to the South, but to stay and work with him till they
earned enough to buy their relatives.

Philip replied: "It would kill mother if I deserted her
She has pledged her house, and is working harder than
ever to buy you. Will you be bought?"

"Never!" replied Benjamin, in his resolute tone.
"When I have got so far out of their clutches, do you
suppose, Phil, that I would ever let them be paid one
red cent? Do you think I would consent to have mother
turned out of her hard-earned home in her old age? And
she never to see me after she had bought me? For you
know, Phil, she would never leave the South while any

of her children or grandchildren remained in Slavery.
What a good mother! Tell her to buy *you*, Phil. You
have always been a comfort to her; and I have always
been making her trouble."

Philip furnished his brother with some clothes, and
gave him what money he had. Benjamin pressed his
hand, and said, with moistened eyes, "I part from all my
kindred." And so it proved. We never heard from him
afterwards.

When Uncle Philip came home, the first words he said,
on entering the house, were: "O mother, Ben is free!
I have seen him in New York." For a moment she
seemed bewildered. He laid his hand gently on her
shoulder and repeated what he had said. She raised
her hands devoutly, and exclaimed, "God be praised!
Let us thank Him." She dropped on her knees and
poured forth her heart in prayer. When she grew calmer,
she begged Philip to sit down and repeat every word her
son had said. He told her all, except that Benjamin had
nearly died on the way and was looking very pale and
thin.

Still the brave old woman toiled on to accomplish the
rescue of her remaining children. After a while she
succeeded in buying Philip, for whom she paid eight
hundred dollars, and came home with the precious document that secured his freedom. The happy mother and
son sat by her hearthstone that night, telling how proud
they were of each other, and how they would prove to
the world that they could take care of themselves, as they
had long taken care of others. We all concluded by saying, "He that is *willing* to be a slave, let him be a slave."

My grandmother had still one daughter remaining in
Slavery. She belonged to the same master that I did;

and a hard time she had of it. She was a good soul, this old Aunt Nancy. She did all she could to supply the place of my lost mother to us orphans. She was the *factotum* in our master's household. She was house-keeper, waiting-maid, and everything else : nothing went on well without her, by day or by night. She wore her-self out in their service. Grandmother toiled on, hoping to purchase release for her. But one evening word was brought that she had been suddenly attacked with paraly-sis, and grandmother hastened to her bedside. Mother and daughter had always been devotedly attached to each other; and now they looked lovingly and earnestly into each other's eyes, longing to speak of secrets that weighed on the hearts of both. She lived but two days, and on the last day she was speechless. It was sad to witness the grief of her bereaved mother. She had always been strong to bear, and religious faith still sup-ported her; but her dark life had become still darker, and age and trouble were leaving deep traces on her withered face. The poor old back was fitted to its bur-den. It bent under it, but did not break.

Uncle Philip asked permission to bury his sister at his own expense; and slaveholders are always ready to grant *such* favors to slaves and their relatives. The arrangements were very plain, but perfectly respectable. It was talked of by the slaves as a mighty grand funeral. If Northern travellers had been passing through the place, perhaps they would have described it as a beauti-ful tribute to the humble dead, a touching proof of the attachment between slaveholders and their slaves; and very likely the mistress would have confirmed this im-pression, with her handkerchief at her eyes. *We* could have told them how the poor old mother had toiled, year

after year, to buy her son Philip's right to his own earnings; and how that same Philip had paid the expenses
of the funeral which they regarded as doing so much
credit to the master.

There were some redeeming features in our hard destiny. Very pleasant are my recollections of the good
old lady who paid fifty dollars for the purpose of making
my grandmother free, when she stood on the auction-
block. She loved this old lady, whom we all called
Miss Fanny. She often took tea at grandmother's
house. On such occasions, the table was spread with a
snow-white cloth, and the china cups and silver spoons
were taken from the old-fashioned buffet. There were
hot muffins, tea-rusks, and delicious sweetmeats. My
grandmother always had a supply of such articles, because she furnished the ladies of the town with such
things for their parties. She kept two cows for that
purpose, and the fresh cream was Miss Fanny's delight.
She invariably repeated that it was the very best in
town. The old ladies had cosey times together. They
would work and chat, and sometimes, while talking over
old times, their spectacles would get dim with tears, and
would have to be taken off and wiped. When Miss
Fanny bade us " Good by," her bag was always filled
with grandmother's best cakes, and she was urged to
come again soon.

[Here follows a long account of persecutions endured
by the granddaughter, who tells this story. She finally
made her escape, after encountering great dangers and
hardships. The faithful old grandmother concealed her
for a long time at great risk to them both, during which
time she tried in vain to buy free papers for her. At
last there came a chance to escape in a vessel Northward
bound. She goes on to say:—]

" All arrangements were made for me to go on board at
dusk. Grandmother came to me with a small bag of
money, which she wanted me to take. I begged her to
keep at least part of it ; but she insisted, while her tears
fell fast, that I should take the whole. 'You may be
sick among strangers,' said she ; 'and they would send
you to the poor-house to die.' Ah, that good grandmother ! Though I had the blessed prospect of freedom
before me, I felt dreadfully sad at leaving forever that
old homestead, that had received and sheltered me in so
many sorrows. Grandmother took me by the hand and
said, 'My child, let us pray.' We knelt down together,
with my arm clasped round the faithful, loving old
friend I was about to leave forever. On no other occasion has it been my lot to listen to so fervent a suppli-
cation for mercy and protection. It thrilled through my
heart and inspired me with trust in God. I staggered
into the street, faint in body, though strong of purpose.
I did not look back upon the dear old place, though I
felt that I should never see it again."

[The granddaughter found friends at the North, and,
being uncommonly quick in her perceptions, she soon did
much to supply the deficiencies of early education.
While leading a worthy, industrious life in New York,
she twice very narrowly escaped becoming a victim to
the infamous Fugitive Slave Law. A noble-hearted
lady purchased her freedom, and thereby rescued her
from further danger. She thus closes the story of her
venerable ancestor : —]

" My grandmother lived to rejoice in the knowledge of
my freedom ; but not long afterward a letter came to me
with a black seal. It was from a friend at the South,
who informed me that she had gone 'where the wicked

10

cease from troubling, and where the weary are at rest.'
Among the gloomy recollections of my life in bondage
come tender memories of that good grandmother, like a
few fleecy clouds floating over a dark and troubled sea."

H. J.

NOTE. — The above account is no fiction. The author,
who was thirty years in Slavery, wrote it in an interesting book entitled " Linda." She is an esteemed friend
of mine; and I introduce this portion of her story here
to illustrate the power of character over circumstances.
She has intense sympathy for those who are still suffering in the bondage from which she escaped. She has
devoted all her energies to the poor refugees in our
camps, comforting the afflicted, nursing the sick, and
teaching the children. On the 1st of January, 1863,
she wrote me a letter, which began as follows: " I have
lived to hear the Proclamation of Freedom for my suffering people. All my wrongs are forgiven. I am more
than repaid for all I have endured. Glory to God in
the highest!"

L. M. CHILD.

"THEY CANNOT TAKE CARE OF THEMSELVES."

OUR tobacco they plant, and our cotton they pick,
    And our rice they can harvest and thrash;
They feed us in health, and they nurse us when sick,
    And they earn — while we pocket — our cash.
They lead us when young, and they help us when old,
    And their toil loads our tables and shelves;
But they're " niggers "; and *therefore* (the truth must be told)
    They cannot take care of *themselves*.

REV. JOHN PIERPONT.

THE COLORED MOTHER'S PRAYER.

GREAT Father! who created all,
   The colored and the fair,
O listen to a mother's call;
   Hear Thou the negro's prayer!

Yet once again thy people teach,
   With lessons from above,
That they may *practise* what they *preach*,
   And *all* their neighbors love.

Again the Gospel precepts give;
   Teach them this rule to know, —
Such treatment as ye should *receive*,
   Be willing to *bestow*.

Then my poor child, my darling one,
   Will never feel the smart
Of their unjust and cruel scorn,
   That withers all the heart.

Great Father! who created all,
   The colored and the fair,
O listen to a mother's call;
   Hear Thou the negro's prayer!

WILLIAM COSTIN.

MR. WILLIAM COSTIN was for twenty-four years porter of a bank in Washington, D. C. Many millions of dollars passed through his hands, but not a cent was ever missing, through fraud or carelessness. In his daily life he set an example of purity and benevolence. He adopted four orphan children into his family, and treated them with the kindness of a father. His character inspired general respect; and when he died, in 1842, the newspapers of the city made honorable mention of him. The directors of the bank passed a resolution expressive of their high appreciation of his services, and his coffin was followed to the grave by a very large procession of citizens of all classes and complexions. Not long after, when the Honorable John Quincy Adams was speaking in Congress on the subject of voting, he said : " The late William Costin, though he was not white, was as much respected as any man in the District; and the large concourse of citizens that attended his remains to the grave — as well white as black — was an evidence of the manner in which he was estimated by the citizens of Washington. Now, why should such a man as that be excluded from the elective franchise, when you admit the vilest individuals of the white race to exercise it ? "

STRAIN every nerve, wrestle with every power God and nature have put into your hands, for your place among the races of this Western world. — WENDELL PHILLIPS.

EDUCATION OF CHILDREN.

BY L. MARIA CHILD.

PEOPLE of all colors and conditions love their off-
spring; but very few consider sufficiently how
much the future character and happiness of their children depend on their own daily language and habits.   It
does very little good to teach children to be honest if the
person who teaches them is not scrupulous about taking
other people's property or using it without leave.   It
does very little good to tell them they ought to be
modest, if they are accustomed to hear their elders use
unclean words or tell indecent stories.   Primers and
catechisms may teach them to reverence God, but the
lesson will lose half its effect if they habitually hear their
parents curse and swear.   Some two hundred years ago
a very learned astronomer named Sir Isaac Newton
lived in England.   He was so devout that he always
took off his hat when the name of God was mentioned.
By that act of reverence he taught a religious lesson to
every child who witnessed it.   Young souls are fed by
what they see and hear, just as their bodies are fed with
daily food.   No parents who knew what they were doing
would give their little ones poisonous food, that would
produce fevers, ulcers, and death.   It is of far more
consequence not to poison their souls; for the body
passes away, but the soul is immortal.

When a traveller pointed to a stunted and crooked
tree and asked what made it grow so, a child replied,

"I suppose somebody trod on it when it was little." It is hard for children born in Slavery to grow up spiritually straight and healthy, because they are trodden on when they are little. Being constantly treated unjustly, they cannot learn to be just. Their parents have no power to protect them from evil influences. They cannot prevent their continually seeing cruel and indecent actions, and hearing profane and dirty words. Heretofore, you could not educate your children, either morally or intellectually. But now that you are freemen, responsibility rests upon you. You will be answerable before God for the influence you exert over the young souls intrusted to your care. You may be too ignorant to teach them much of book-learning, and you may be too poor to spend much money for their education, but you can set them a pure and good example by your conduct and conversation. This you should try your utmost to do, and should pray to the Heavenly Father to help you; for it is a very solemn duty, this rearing of young souls for eternity. That you yourselves have had a stunted growth, from being trodden upon when you were little, will doubtless make you more careful not to tread upon them.

It is necessary that children should be made obedient to their elders, because they are not old enough to know what is good for themselves; but obedience should always be obtained by the gentlest means possible. Violence excites anger and hatred, without doing any good to counterbalance the evil. When it is necessary to punish a child, it should be done in such a calm and reasonable manner as to convince him that you do it for his good, and not because you are in a rage.

Slaves, all the world over, are generally much addicted

to lying. The reason is, that if they have done any mischief by carelessness or accident, they dare not tell the truth about it for fear of a cruel flogging. Violent and tyrannical treatment always produces that effect. Wherever children are abused, whether they are white or black, they become very cunning and deceitful; for when the weak are tortured by the strong, they have no other way to save themselves from suffering. Such treatment does not cure faults; it only makes people lie to conceal their faults. If a child does anything wrong, and confesses it frankly, his punishment ought to be slight, in order to encourage him in habits of truthfulness, which is one of the noblest attributes of manhood. If he commits the same fault a second time, even if he confesses it, he ought not to be let off so easily, because it is necessary to teach him that confession, though a very good thing, will not supply the place of repentance. When children are naughty, it is better to deprive them of some pleasant thing that they want to eat or drink or do, than it is to kick and cuff them. It is better to attract them toward what is right than to drive them from what is wrong. Thus if a boy is lazy, it is wiser to promise him reward in proportion to his industry, than it is to cuff and scold him, which will only make him shirk work as soon as you are out of sight. Whereas, if you tell him, "You shall have six cents if you dig one bushel of potatoes, and six cents more if you dig two," he will have a motive that will stimulate him when you are not looking after him. If he is too lazy to be stimulated by such offers, he must be told that he who digs no potatoes must have none to eat.

The moral education which you are all the time giving your children, by what they hear you say and see you do, is of more consequence to them than reading and writing and ciphering. But the education they get at school is also very important; and it will be wise and kind in you to buy such books as they need, and encourage them in every way to become good scholars, as well as good men. By so doing you will not only benefit them, but you will help all your race. Every colored man or woman who is virtuous and intelligent takes away something of prejudice against colored men and women in general; and it likewise encourages all their brethren and sisters, by showing what colored people are capable of doing.

The system of Slavery was all penalty and no attraction; in other words, it punished men if they did *not* do, but it did not reward them for *doing*. In the management of your children you should do exactly the opposite of this. You should appeal to their manhood, not to their fears. After emancipation in the West Indies, planters who had been violent slaveholders, if they saw a freedman leaning on his hoe, would say, "Work, you black rascal, or I'll flog you"; and the freedman would lean all the longer on his hoe. Planters of a more wise and moderate character, if they saw the emancipated laborers idling away their time, would say, "We expect better things of free men"; and that appeal to their manhood made the hoes fly fast.

Old men and women have been treated with neglect and contempt in Slavery, because they were no longer able to work for the profit of their masters. But respect and tenderness are peculiarly due to the aged. They have done much and suffered much. They are no longer able to help themselves; and we should help them, as they helped us in the feebleness of our infancy, and as we may again need to be helped in the feebleness of age.

Any want of kindness or civility toward the old ought to be very seriously rebuked in children; and affectionate attentions should be spoken of as praiseworthy.

Slavery in every way fosters violence. Slave-children, being in the habit of seeing a great deal of beating, early form the habit of kicking and banging each other when they are angry, and of abusing poor helpless animals intrusted to their care. On all such occasions parents should say to them: " Those are the ways of Slavery. We expect better things of free children."

AN HONORABLE RECORD.

In 1837 the colored population in Philadelphia numbered eighteen thousand seven hundred and sixty-eight. Many of them were poor and ignorant, and some of them were vicious; as would be the case with any people under such discouraging influences. But, notwithstanding they were excluded by prejudice from all the most profitable branches of industry, they had acquired property valued at one million three hundred and fifty thousand dollars; five hundred and fifty thousand was in real estate, and eight hundred thousand was personal property. They had built sixteen churches, valued at one hundred and fourteen thousand dollars, for the support of which they annually paid over six thousand dollars. The pauper tax they paid was more than enough to support all the colored paupers in the city. They had eighty benevolent societies, and during that year they had expended fourteen thousand one hundred and seventy-two dollars for the relief of the sick and the helpless. A number of them who had been slaves had paid, in the course of that year, seventy thousand seven hundred and thirty-three dollars to purchase their own freedom, or that of their relatives.

10 *   o

THANK GOD FOR LITTLE CHILDREN.

BY FRANCES E. W. HARPER.

THANK God for little children!
 Bright flowers by earth's wayside, —
The dancing, joyous life-boats
 Upon life's stormy tide.

Thank God for little children!
 When our skies are cold and gray,
They come as sunshine to our hearts,
 And charm our cares away.

I almost think the angels,
 Who tend life's garden fair,
Drop down the sweet wild blossoms
 That bloom around us here.

It seems a breath of heaven
 "Round many a cradle lies,"
And every little baby
 Brings a message from the skies.

The humblest home, with children,
 Is rich in precious gems;
Better than wealth of monarchs,
 Or golden diadems.

Dear mothers, guard these jewels
 As sacred offerings meet, —
A wealth of household treasures,
 To lay at Jesus' feet.

SAM AND ANDY.

BY HARRIET BEECHER STOWE.

A BEAUTIFUL slave in Kentucky, named Eliza, had a very handsome little boy. One day she overheard her master making a bargain with a slave-trader by the name of Haley to sell them both. She made her escape that night, taking her child with her. Her mistress, who was much attached to her, and did not want to have her sold, was glad when she heard that Eliza was gone; but her master, who was afraid the trader would think he had helped her off after he had taken the money for her, ordered the horses Bill and Jerry to be brought, and two of his slaves, called Sam and Andy, to go with the slave-trader in pursuit of the fugitive. The way they contrived how *not* to overtake Eliza is thus told in " Uncle Tom's Cabin " : —

" ' Sam ! Halloo, Sam !' said Andy. ' Mas'r wants you to cotch Bill and Jerry.'

" ' High ! what 's afoot now ? ' said Sam.

" ' Why I s'pose you don't know that Lizy 's cut stick, and clared out, with her young un ? '

" ' You teach your granny !' replied Sam, with infinite contempt; 'knowed it a heap sooner than *you* did. This nigger a'n't so green, now.'

" ' Wal, anyhow, Mas'r wants Bill and Jerry geared right up; and you and I 's to go with Mas'r Haley, to look arter her,' said Andy.

" Sam, who had just been contriving how he could make

himself of importance on the plantation, exclaimed: 'Good, now! dat's de time o' day! It's Sam dat's called for in dese yere times. *He*'s de nigger. Mas'r 'll see what Sam can do!'

"'Ah, you'd better think twice,' said Andy; 'for Missis don't want her cotched, and she'll be in yer wool.'

"'High! how you know dat?' said Sam, opening his eyes.

"'Heard her say so, my own self, dis blessed mornin', when I bring in Mas'r's shaving-water. She sent me to see why Lizy did n't come to dress her; and when I telled her she was off, she jes ris up, and ses she, "The Lord be praised!" Mas'r he seemed rael mad; and ses he, "Wife, you talk like a fool." But, Lor! she'll bring him to. I knows well enough how that'll be. It's allers best to stand Missis's side the fence, now I tell yer,' said Andy.

"Sam scratched his woolly pate, and gave a hitch to his pantaloons, as he had a habit of doing when his mind was perplexed. 'Der a'n't never no sayin' 'bout no kind o' thing in dis yere world,' said he at last. 'Now I'd a said sartin that Missis would a scoured the varsal world after Lizy.'

"'So she would,' said Andy; 'but can't ye see through a ladder, ye black nigger? Missis don't want dis yer Mas'r Haley to get Lizy's boy; dat's de go. And I 'specs you'd better be making tracks for dem hosses, — mighty sudden too, — for I hearn Missis 'quirin' arter yer; so you've stood foolin' long enough.'

"Sam, upon this, began to bestir himself in earnest, and after a while appeared, bearing down gloriously towards the house, with Bill and Jerry in a full canter. Adroitly throwing himself off before they had any idea of stopping, he brought them up alongside the horse-post like a tornado. Haley's horse, which was a skittish young colt, winced and bounced, and pulled hard at his halter.

"'Ho! ho!' said Sam, 'skeery, ar ye?' and his black face lighted up with a curious, mischievous gleam. 'I'll fix ye now,' said he.

"There was a large beech-tree overshadowing the place, and the small, sharp, triangular beech-nuts lay scattered thickly on the ground. Sam stroked and patted the colt, and while pretending to adjust the saddle, he slipped under it a sharp little nut, in such a manner that the least weight brought upon the saddle would annoy the nervous animal, without leaving any perceptible wound.

"'Dar, me fix 'em,' said he, rolling his eyes with an approving grin.

"At this moment Mrs. Shelby appeared on the balcony and beckoned to him. 'Why have you been loitering so, Sam?' said she. 'I sent Andy to tell you to hurry.'

"'Bress you, Missis, hosses won't be cotched all in a minit. They done clared out down to the south pasture, and everywhar,' said Sam.

"'Well, Sam,' replied his mistress, 'you are to go with Mr. Haley to show him the road, and help him. Be careful of the horses, Sam. You know Jerry was a little lame last week. *Don't ride them too fast.*' She spoke the last words in a low voice, and with strong emphasis.

"'Let dis chile alone for dat,' said Sam, rolling up his eyes with a look full of meaning. 'Yes, Missis, I'll look out for de hosses.'

"Sam returned to his stand under the beech-tree, and said to Andy, 'Now, Andy, I would n't be 't all surprised if dat ar gen'lman's crittur should gib a fling, by and by, when he comes to be a gettin' up. You know, Andy, critturs *will* do such things'; and Sam poked Andy in the side, in a highly suggestive manner.

"'High!' exclaimed Andy, with an air that showed he understood instantly.

"'Yes, you see, Andy, Missis wants to make time,' said Sam; 'dat ar 's cl'ar to der most or'nary 'bserver. I jis make a little for her. Now, you see, get all dese yere hosses loose, caperin' permiscus round dis yere lot, and down to de wood dar, and I 'spec Mas'r won't be off in a hurry.

"Andy grinned.

"'You see, Andy,' said Sam, 'if any such thing should happen as that Mas'r Haley's hoss *should* begin to act contrary, and cut up, you and I jist lets go of *our'n* to help him! O yes, we 'll *help* him!' And Sam and Andy laid their heads back on their shoulders, and broke into a low, immoderate laugh, snapping their fingers, and flourishing their heels with exquisite delight.

"While they were enjoying themselves in this style, Haley appeared on the verandah. Some cups of very good coffee had somewhat mollified him, and he came out smiling and talking in tolerably restored humor. Sam and Andy clawed for their torn hats, and flew to the horse-posts to be ready to 'help Mas'r.' The brim of Sam's hat was all unbraided, and the slivers of the palm-leaf started apart in every direction, giving it a blazing air of freedom and defiance. The brim had gone entirely from Andy's hat; but he thumped the crown on his head, and looked about well pleased, as if to ask, 'Who says I have n't got a hat?'

"'Well, boys,' said Haley, 'be alive now. We must lose no time.'

"'Not a bit of him, Mas'r,' said Sam, putting Haley's

rein into his hand and holding his stirrup, while Andy was untying the other two horses.

"The instant Haley touched the saddle the mettlesome creature bounded from the earth with a sudden spring, that threw his master sprawling some feet off, on the dry, soft turf With frantic ejaculations Sam made a dive at the reins, but only succeeded in brushing the torn slivers of his hat into the horse's eyes, which by no means tended to allay the confusion of his nerves. With two or three contemptuous snorts he upset Sam, flourished his heels vigorously in the air, and pranced away toward the lower end of the lawn. He was followed by Bill and Jerry, whom Andy had not failed to let loose, according to contract, speeding them off with various direful cries. And now there was a scene of great confusion. Sam and Andy ran and shouted ; dogs ran barking here and there ; Mike, Mose, Mandy, Fanny, and all the smaller specimens on the place, raced, whooped, shouted, and clapped their hands with outrageous zeal. Haley's fleet horse entered into the spirit of the scene with great gusto. He raced round the lawn, which was half a mile in extent, and seemed to take a mischievous delight in letting his pursuers come within a hand's breadth of him, and then whisking off again with a start and a snort.

"Sam's torn hat was seen everywhere. If there seemed to be the least chance that a horse could be caught, down he bore upon him full tilt, shouting, ' Now for it ! Cotch him ! cotch him !' in a way that set them all to racing again.

" Haley ran up and down, stamped, cursed, and swore. The master in vain tried to give some directions from the balcony, and the mistress looked from her chamber window and laughed. She had some suspicion that Sam was the cause of all this confusion.

"At last, about twelve o'clock, Sam appeared, mounted on Jerry, leading Haley's horse, reeking with sweat, but with flashing eyes and dilated nostrils, showing that the spirit of freedom had not yet entirely subsided.

"'He's cotched!' exclaimed Sam, triumphantly. 'If it hadn't been for me they might a bust themselves, all on 'em; but I cotched him.'

"'*You!*' growled Haley. 'If it hadn't been for *you,* this never would have happened.'

"'Bress us, Mas'r!' exclaimed Sam; 'when it's me that's been a racin' and chasin' till the swet jist pours off me.'

"'Well, well!' said Haley, 'you've lost me near three hours with your cursed nonsense. Now let's be off, and have no more fooling.'

"'Why, Mas'r,' said Sam, in a deprecating tone, 'I do believe you mean to kill us all clar, — hosses and all. Here we are all jist ready to drop down, and the critturs all in a reek o' sweat. Sure Mas'r won't think of startin' now till arter dinner. Mas'r's hoss wants rubben down. See how he's splashed hisself! — and Jerry limps, too. Don't think Missis would be willing to have us start dis yere way, no how. Bress you, Mas'r, we can ketch up, if we stop. Lizy nebber was no great of a walker.'

"The mistress, who, greatly to her amusement, overheard this conversation from the verandah, now came forward and courteously urged Mr. Haley to stay to dinner, saying that the cook should bring it on the table immediately. All things considered, the slave-trader concluded it was best to do so. As he moved toward the parlor, Sam rolled his eyes after him with unutterable meaning, and gravely led the horses to the stable.

"When he had fairly got beyond the shelter of the

barn, and fastened the horse to a post, he exclaimed, 'Did you see him, Andy? *Did* yer see him? O Lor', if it war n't as good as a meetin', now, to see him a dancin' and a kickin', and swarin' at us! Did n't I hear him? Swar away, ole fellow! says I to myself. Will you have yer hoss now, or wait till you cotch him? says I.' And Sam and Andy leaned up against the barn, and laughed to their hearts' content.

"'Yer oughter seen how mad he looked when I brought the hoss up. Lor', he 'd a killed me if he durs' to; and there I was a standin' as innercent and humble.'

"'Lor', I seed you,' said Andy. 'A'n't you an old hoss, Sam?'

"'Rather 'specs I am,' said Sam. 'Did you see Missus up stars at the winder? I seed her laughin'.'

"'I 'm sure I was racin' so I did n't see nothin',' said Andy.

"'Wal, yer see, I 'se 'quired a habit o' bobservation,' said Sam. 'It 's a very 'portant habit, Andy; and I 'commend yer to be cultivatin' it, now yer young. Bobservation makes all de difference in niggers. Did n't I see what Missis wanted, though she never let on? Dat ar 's bobservation, Andy. I 'specs it 's what yer may call a faculty. Faculties is different in different peoples; but cultivation of 'em goes a great way.'

"'I guess if I had n't helped your bobservation dis mornin', yer would n't have seen yer way so smart,' said Andy.

"'You 's a promisin' chile, Andy, der a'n't no manner o' doubt,' said Sam. 'I think lots of yer, Andy; and I don't feel no ways ashamed to take idees from yer. Let 's go up to the house now, Andy. I 'll be boun' Missis 'll give us an uncommon good bite dis yere time.'"

"The mistress had promised that dinner should be brought on the table in a hurry, and she had given the orders in Haley's hearing. But the servants all seemed to have an impression that Missis would not be disobliged by delay. Aunt Chloe, the cook, went on with her operations in a very leisurely manner. Then it was wonderful what a number of accidents happened. One upset the butter; another tumbled down with the water, and had to go to the spring for more; another spilled the gravy; then Aunt Chloe set about making new gravy, watching it and stirring it with the greatest precision. If reminded that the orders were to hurry, she answered shortly that she 'war n't a going to have raw gravy on the table, to help nobody's catchin's.'

"From time to time there was giggling in the kitchen, when news was brought that 'Mas'r Haley was mighty oneasy, and that he could n't set in his cheer no ways, but was a walkin' and stalkin' to the winders and through the porch.'

"'Sarves him right!' said Aunt Chloe. 'He 'll git wus nor oneasy, one of these days, if he don't mend his ways.'

"At last the dinner was sent in, and the mistress smiled and chatted, and did all she could to make the time pass imperceptibly.

"At two o'clock, Sam and Andy brought the horses up to the posts, apparently greatly refreshed and invigorated by the scamper of the morning. As Haley prepared to mount, he said, 'Your master don't keep no dogs, I s'pose?'

"'Heaps on 'em,' said Sam, triumphantly. 'Thar's Bruno, — he 's a roarer; and besides that, 'bout every nigger of us keeps a pup o' some natur' or uther.'

" ' But does your master keep any dogs for tracking out niggers?' said Haley.

" Sam knew very well what he meant, but he kept on a look of desperate simplicity. 'Wal,' said he, 'our dogs all smells round considerable sharp. I 'spect they 's the *kind*, though they ha'n't never had no *practice*. They 's far dogs at most anything though, if you 'd get 'em started.' He whistled to Bruno, a great lumbering Newfoundland dog, who came pitching tumultuously toward them.

" ' You go hang!' exclaimed Haley, mounting his horse. 'Come, tumble up, now.'

Sam tumbled up accordingly, contriving to tickle Andy as he did so. This made Andy split out into a laugh, greatly to Haley's indignation, who made a cut at him with his riding-whip. 'I 'se 'stonished at yer, Andy,' said Sam, with awful gravity. 'This yere 's a seris bisness, Andy. Yer must n't be a makin' game. This yere a'n't no way to help Mas'r.'

" When they came to the boundaries of the estate, Haley said : ' I shall take the road to the river. I know the way of all of 'em. They always makes tracks for the underground.'

" ' Sartin, dat 's de idee,' said Sam. 'Mas'r Haley hits de thing right in de middle. Now, der 's two roads to de river, — de dirt road and der pike. Which Mas'r mean to take?'

" Andy looked up innocently at Sam, surprised at hearing this new geographical fact; but he instantly confirmed what Sam said.

" ' I 'd rather be 'clined to 'magine that Lizy 'd take der dirt road, bein' it 's the least travelled,' said Sam. Though Haley was an old bird, and inclined to be sus-

picious of chaff, he was rather brought up by this view
of the case. He pondered a moment, and said, 'If yer
was n't both on yer such cussed liars, now !'

"The pensive tone in which this was spoken amused
Andy prodigiously. He fell a little behind, and shook so
with laughter as to run a great risk of falling from his
horse. But Sam's face was immovably composed into
the most doleful gravity.

"'Course, Mas'r can do as he'd ruther,' said Sam.
'It's all one to us. When I study 'pon it, I think de
straight road is de best.'

"'She would naturally go a lonesome way,' said
Haley.

"'I should 'magine so,' said Sam ; 'but gals is pecular.
Dey nebber does nothin' ye thinks they will ; mose
gen'lly de contrar ; so if yer thinks they 've gone one
road, it 's sartin you 'd better go t'other, and then you 'll
be sure to find 'em. So I think we 'd better take de
straight road.'

"Haley announced decidedly that he should go the
other, and asked when they should come to it.

"'A little piece ahed,' said Sam, giving a wink to
Andy. He added gravely, 'I 've studded on de matter,
and I 'm quite clar we ought not to go dat ar way. I
nebber been over it no way. It 's despit lonesome, and
we might lose our way. And now I think on 't, I hearn
'em tell dat ar road was all fenced up down by der creek.
A'n't it, Andy ?'

"Andy was n't certain ; he 'd only 'hearn tell' about
that road, but had never been over it.

"Haley thought the first mention of the road was in-
voluntary on Sam's part, and that, upon second thoughts,
he had lied desperately to dissuade him from taking that

direction because he was unwilling to implicate Eliza. Therefore he struck briskly into the road, and was followed by Sam and Andy.

"The road in fact had formerly been an old thoroughfare to the river, but after the laying of the new pike it had been abandoned. It was open for about an hour's ride, and after that it was cut across by various farms and fences. Sam knew this perfectly well; indeed, the road had been so long closed that Andy had never heard of it. He therefore rode along with an air of dutiful submission, only groaning occasionally, and saying it was 'desp't rough, and bad for Jerry's foot.'

"'Now, I jest give yer warning, I know yer,' said Haley. 'Yer won't get me to turn off this yere road, with all yer fussin'; so you shet up.'"

"'Mas'r will go his own way,' said Sam, with rueful submission, at the same time winking portentously to Andy, whose delight now was very near the explosive point. Sam was in wonderful spirits. He professed to keep a very brisk lookout. At one time he exclaimed that he saw 'a gal's bunnet' on the top of some distant eminence; at another time, he called out to Andy to ask if 'that thar was n't Lizy down in the holler.' He was always sure to make these exclamations in some rough or craggy part of the road, where the sudden quickening of speed was a special inconvenience to all parties concerned, thus keeping Haley in a state of constant commotion.

"After riding about an hour in this way, the whole party made a precipitate and tumultuous descent into a barn-yard belonging to a large farming establishment. Not a soul was in sight, all the hands being employed in the fields; but as the barn stood square across the road, it was evident that their journey in that direction had reached its end.

"'You rascal!' said Haley; 'you knew all about this.'

"'Did n't I *tell* yer I knowed, and yer would n't believe me?' replied Sam. 'I telled Mas'r 't was all shet up, and fenced up, and I did n't 'spect we could git through. Andy heard me.'

"This was too true to be disputed, and the unlucky man had to pocket his wrath as well as he could. All three faced to the right about, and took up their line of march for the highway."

[The consequence of all these delays was, that they reached the Ohio River only in season to see Eliza and her child get safely on the other side, by jumping from one mass of floating ice to the other.]

"'The gal's got seven devils in her I believe,' said Haley. 'How like a wild-cat she jumped!'

"'Wal, now,' said Sam, scratching his head, 'I hope Mas'r 'scuse us tryin' dat ar road. Don't think I feel spry enough for dat ar, no way'; and Sam gave a hoarse chuckle.

"'*You* laugh!' exclaimed the slave-trader, with a growl.

"'I could n't help it now, Mas'r,' said Sam, giving way to the long pent-up delight of his soul. 'She looked so curis, a leapin' and springin'; ice a crackin' — and only to hear her! plump! ker chunk! ker splash!' and Sam and Andy laughed till the tears rolled down their cheeks.

"'I'll make yer laugh t' other side yer mouths!' exclaimed the trader, laying about their heads with his riding-whip. Both ducked, and ran shouting up the bank. They were on their horses before he could come up with them.

"With much gravity Sam called out: 'Good evening, Mas'r Haley. Won't want us no longer. I 'spect Missis be anxious 'bout Jerry. Missis would n't hear of our ridin' the critturs over Lizy's bridge to-night.' With a poke into Andy's ribs, they started off at full speed, their shouts of laughter coming faintly on the wind.

"Sam was in the highest possible feather. He expressed his exultation by all sorts of howls and ejaculations, and by divers odd motions and contortions of his whole system. Sometimes he would sit backward with his face to the horse's tail; then, with a whoop and a somerset, he would come right side up in his place again; and, drawing on a grave face, he would begin to lecture Andy for laughing and playing the fool. Anon, slapping his sides with his arms, he would burst forth in peals of laughter, that made the old woods ring as they passed. With all these evolutions, he contrived to keep the horses up to the top of their speed, until, between ten and eleven, their heels resounded on the gravel at the end of the balcony.

"His mistress flew to the railings, and called out, 'Is that you, Sam? Where are they?'

"'Mas'r Haley 's a restin' at the tavern,' said Sam. 'He 's drefful fatigued, Missis.'

"'And Eliza, where is she, Sam?'

"'Wal, Missis, de Lord he persarves his own. Lizy 's done gone over the river into 'Hio; as 'markably as if de Lord took her over in a chariot of fire and two hosses.'

"His master, who had followed his wife to the verandah, said, 'Come up here, and tell your mistress what she wants to know.'

"Sam soon appeared at the parlor-door, hat in hand. In answer to their questions, he told his story in lively style. 'Dis yere's a providence, and no mistake,' said Sam, piously rolling up his eyes. 'As Missis has allers been instructin' on us, thar's allers instruments ris up to do de Lord's will. Now if it had n't been for me to-day, Lizy 'd been took a dozen times. War n't it I started off de hosses, dis yere mornin', and kept 'em chasin' till dinner time? And did n't I car Mas'r Haley five miles out of de road dis evening? else he 'd a come up with Lizy, as easy as a dog arter a coon. Dese yere's all providences!'

"With as much sternness as he could command under the circumstances, his master said, 'They are a kind of providences that you'll have to be pretty sparing of, Sam. I allow no such practices with gentlemen on my place.'

"Sam stood with the corners of his mouth lowered, in most penitential style. 'Mas'r's quite right,' said he. 'It was ugly on me; thar's no disputin' that ar; and of course Mas'r and Missis would n't encourage no such works. I'm sensible ob dat ar. But a poor nigger like me 's 'mazin' tempted to act ugly sometimes, when fellers will cut up such shines as dat ar Mas'r Haley. He a'n't no gen'l'man no way. Anybody 's been raised as I 've been can't help a seein' dat ar.'

"'Well, Sam,' said his mistress, 'as you seem to have a proper sense of your errors, you may go now and tell Aunt Chloe she may get you some of that cold ham that was left of dinner to-day. You and Andy must be hungry.'

"'Missis is a heap too good for us,' said Sam, making his bow with alacrity and departing.

"Having done up his piety and humility, to the satisfaction of the parlor, as he trusted, he clapped his palm-leaf on his head with a sort of free-and-easy air, and proceeded to the dominions of Aunt Chloe, with the intention of flourishing largely in the kitchen."

JOHN BROWN AND THE COLORED CHILD.

BY L. MARIA CHILD.

[When John Brown went from the jail to the gallows, in Charlestown, Virginia, December 2, 1859, he stooped to kiss a little colored child.]

A WINTER sunshine, still and bright,
   The Blue Hills bathed with golden light,
And earth was smiling to the sky,
When calmly he went forth to die.

Infernal passions festered there,
Where peaceful Nature looked so fair;
And fiercely, in the morning sun,
Flashed glitt'ring bayonet and gun.

The old man met no friendly eye,
When last he looked on earth and sky;
But one small child, with timid air,
Was gazing on his hoary hair.

As that dark brow to his upturned,
The tender heart within him yearned;
And, fondly stooping o'er her face,
He kissed her for her injured race.

11   P

The little one she knew not why
That kind old man went forth to die;
Nor why, 'mid all that pomp and stir,
He stooped to give a kiss to *her*.

But Jesus smiled that sight to see,
And said, " He did it unto *me*."
The golden harps then sweetly rung,
And this the song the angels sung:

"Who loves the poor doth love the Lord;
Earth cannot dim thy bright reward:
We hover o'er yon gallows high,
And wait to bear thee to the sky."

JOHN BROWN, on his way to the scaffold, stooped to take
up a slave-child. That closing example was the legacy of the
dying man to his country. That benediction we must continue and fulfil. In this new order, equality, long postponed,
shall become the master-principle of our system, and the very
frontispiece of our Constitution. — HON. CHARLES SUMNER.

CHRIST told me to remember those in bonds as bound
with them; to do toward them as I should wish them to do
toward me in similar circumstances. My conscience bade me
to do that. Therefore I have no regret for the transaction for
which I am condemned. I think I feel as happy as Paul did
when he lay in prison. He knew if they killed him it would
greatly advance the cause of Christ. That was the reason he
rejoiced. On that same ground " I do rejoice, yea, and will
rejoice." — JOHN BROWN.

THE AIR OF FREEDOM.

BY FRANCES E. W. HARPER.

[Written at Niagara Falls in 1856.]

I HAVE just returned from Canada. I have gazed for the first time upon free land. Would you believe it? the tears sprang to my eyes, and I wept. It was a glorious sight to gaze, for the first time, on the land where a poor slave, flying from our land of boasted liberty, would in a moment find his fetters broken and his shackles loosed. Whatever he was in the land of Washington, in the shadow of Bunker Hill Monument, or even upon Plymouth Rock, *here* he becomes "a man and a brother."

I had gazed on Harper's Ferry, or rather the Rock at the Ferry, towering up in simple grandeur, with the gentle Potomac gliding peacefully at its feet; and I felt that it was God's masonry. My soul expanded while gazing on its sublimity. I had heard the ocean singing its wild chorus of sounding waves, and the living chords of my heart thrilled with ecstasy. I have since seen the rainbow-crowned Niagara, girdled with grandeur and robed with glory, chanting the choral hymn of omnipotence; but none of these sights have melted me, as did the first sight of free land.

Towering mountains, lifting their hoary summits to catch the first faint flush of day, when the sunbeams kiss the shadows from morning's drowsy face, may expand and exalt your soul; the first view of the ocean may

fill you with strange delight; the great, the glorious
Niagara may hush your spirit with its ceaseless thunder,
— it may charm you with its robe of crested spray, and
with its rainbow crown: but the land of freedom has
a lesson of deeper significance than foaming waves and
towering mountains. It carries the heart back to that
heroic struggle in Great Britain for the emancipation of
the slaves, in which the great heart of the people throb-
bed for liberty, and the mighty pulse of the nation beat
for freedom, till eight hundred thousand men, women,
and children in the West Indies arose redeemed from
bondage and freed from chains.

EMANCIPATION IN THE DISTRICT OF COLUMBIA, APRIL 16, 1862.

BY JAMES MADISON BELL.

UNFURL your banners to the breeze!
   Let Freedom's tocsin sound amain,
Until the islands of the seas
   Re-echo with the glad refrain!
Columbia's free! Columbia's free!
   Her teeming streets, her vine-clad groves,
Are sacred now to Liberty,
   And God, who every right approves.

Thank God, the Capital is free!
   The slaver's pen, the auction-block,
The gory lash of cruelty,
   No more this nation's pride shall mock;

No more, within those ten miles square,
    Shall men be bought and women sold;
Nor infants, sable-hued and fair,
    Exchanged again for paltry gold.

To-day the Capital is free!
    And free those halls where Adams stood
To plead for man's humanity,
    And for a common brotherhood;
Where Sumner stood, with massive frame,
    Whose eloquent philosophy
Has clustered round his deathless name
    Bright laurels for eternity;

Where Wilson, Lovejoy, Wade, and Hale,
    And other lights of equal power,
Have stood, like warriors clad in mail,
    Before the giant of the hour, —
Co-workers in a common cause,
    Laboring for their country's weal,
By just enactments, righteous laws,
    And burning, eloquent appeal.

To them we owe and gladly bring
    The grateful tributes of our hearts;
And while we live to muse and sing,
    These in our songs shall claim their parts.
To-day Columbia's air doth seem
    Much purer than in days agone;
And now her mighty heart, I deem,
    Hath lighter grown by marching on.

THE LAWS OF HEALTH.

BY L. MARIA CHILD.

THERE are three things peculiarly essential to health, — plenty of fresh water, plenty of pure air, and enough of nourishing food.

If possible, the human body should be washed all over every day; but if circumstances render that difficult, the operation should be performed at least two or three times a week. People in general are not aware how important frequent bathing is. The cuticle, or skin, with which the human body is covered, is like fine net-work, or lace. By help of a magnifying-glass, called a microscope, it can be seen that there are a thousand holes in every inch of our skin. In the skin of a middle-sized man there are two millions three hundred and four thousand of these holes, called pores. Those pores are the mouths of exceedingly small vessels made to carry off fluids, which are continually formed in the human body, and need to be continually carried off. This process is going on all the time, whether we are sleeping or waking, hot or cold. When we are cool and at rest, that which passes off is invisible; and because we see no signs of it, and are not sensible of it, it is called insensible perspiration. But in very hot weather, or when we exercise violently, a saltish fluid passes through our pores in great drops, which we call sweat; and because we can see and feel it, it is called sensible perspiration. If the pores of the body are filled up with dust, or any kind of dirt, the fluids cannot pass off through them, as Nature intended; and, being shut up, they become corrupt and produce fevers and bad humors. This is the reason why physicians always advise people to be careful and keep their pores open. In order to do this, dust and dirt should be frequently washed away. Many a fever and many a troublesome sore might be prevented by frequent bathing. Moreover, the skin looks smoother and handsomer when it is washed often. If a pond or river is near by, it is well to swim a few minutes every day or two; if not, the body should be washed with a pail of water and a rag. But it is not safe to go into cold water, or to apply it to the skin, when you are very much heated; nor is it safe to drink much cold water until you get somewhat cool. The best way is to plunge into water when you first get up in the morning, and then rub yourself with a cloth till you feel all of a glow. It takes but a few minutes, and you will feel more vigorous for it all day. Cool water is more healthy to wash in than warm water. It makes a person feel stronger, and it is not attended with any danger of catching cold afterward. But water directly from the well is too chilly; it is better to use it when it has been standing in the house some hours. Garments worn next to the skin, and the sheets in which you sleep, imbibe something of the fluids all the time passing from the body; therefore they should be washed every week. I am aware that, as slaves, you had no beds or sheets; but as free men I hope you will gradually be able to provide yourselves with such comforts. Meanwhile, sleep in the cleanest way that you can; for that is one way to avoid sickness. When the skin is hot and feverish, it does a great deal of good to wipe the face, arms, and legs with a cloth moistened with

cool water, changed occasionally. Headache is often
cured by placing the feet in cool water a minute or two,
and then rubbing them smartly with a dry cloth. Sitting in cool water fifteen or twenty minutes is also a
remedy for headache or dizziness. A cut or bruise
heals much quicker if it is soaked ten or fifteen minutes
in cool water, then wrapped in six or eight folds of wet
rag, and covered with a piece of dry cloth. The rag
should be moistened again when it gets dry. This simple process subdues the heat and fever of a wound.
When the throat is sore, it is an excellent thing to wash
the outside freely with cold water the first thing in the
morning, and then wipe it very dry. A wet bandage at
night, covered with a dry cloth, to keep it from the air,
often proves very comforting when the throat is inflamed.
Indeed, it is scarcely possible to say too mnch in favor of
using cool water freely, at suitable times.

Fresh air is as important as good water. The lungs
of the human body are all the time drawing in air and
breathing out air. What we breathe out carries away
with it something from our bodies. Therefore it is un-
healthy to be in a room with many people, without doors
or windows open ; for the people draw in all the fresh air,
and what they breathe out is more or less corrupted by
having passed through their bodies. It is very important to health to have plenty of pure fresh air to breathe.
No dirty things, or decaying substances, such as cab-
bage-leaves or mouldy vegetables, or pools of stagnant
water, should be allowed to remain anywhere near a
dwelling. The pools should be filled up, and the decaying things should be carried away from the house, heaped
up and covered with earth to make manure for the garden. If there is not room enough to do that, they should

be buried in the ground. Whole families often have fevers from breathing the bad odors that rise from such things. It is morally wrong to indulge in any habits that injure the health or well-being of others. The bed, and the coverings of the bed, should have fresh air let in upon them every day; otherwise, they retain the fluids which are passing from the body all the time. In England, children that worked in large manufactories became pale and sickly and died off fast. When doctors inquired into it, they found that the poor little creatures crept into the same bedclothes week after week, and month after month, without having them washed or aired.

Occasional change in articles of food is healthy, as well as agreeable; but it is injurious to eat a great variety of things at the same meal. There are two good rules, so very simple that everybody, rich or poor, can observe them: First, never indulge yourself in eating what you have found by experience does not agree with you; secondly, when you have eaten enough, do not continue to eat merely because the food tastes good. It is foolish to derange the stomach for a long time to please the palate for a short time.

-If you have oppressed feelings in the head, or sour and bitter tastes in the mouth, or a tendency to sickishness, take nothing but bread and water for two or three days, and you will be very likely to save yourself from a fever.

People might spare themselves many a toothache if they would rinse their mouths after every meal, and every night, before going to bed, remove every particle of food from between the teeth, and rinse them thoroughly with water. New toothpicks should be made often, for the sake of cleanliness.

Dirt was a necessity of Slavery; and that is one

reason, among many others, why freemen should hate it, and try to put it away from their minds, their persons, and their habitations.

PRESIDENT LINCOLN'S PROCLAMATION OF EMANCIPATION, JANUARY 1, 1863.

BY FRANCES E. W. HARPER.

IT shall flash through coming ages,
　It shall light the distant years;
And eyes now dim with sorrow
　Shall be brighter through their tears.

It shall flush the mountain ranges,
　And the valleys shall grow bright;
It shall bathe the hills in radiance,
　And crown their brows with light.

It shall flood with golden splendor
　All the huts of Caroline;
And the sun-kissed brow of labor
　With lustre new shall shine.

It shall gild the gloomy prison,
　Darkened by the nation's crime,
Where the dumb and patient millions
　Wait the better-coming time.

By the light that gilds their prison
　They shall see its mouldering key;

And the bolts and bars shall vibrate
With the triumphs of the free.

Though the morning seemed to linger
O'er the hill-tops far away,
Now the shadows bear the promise
Of the quickly coming day.

Soon the mists and murky shadows
Shall be fringed with crimson light,
And the glorious dawn of freedom
Break refulgent on the sight.

NEW-YEAR'S DAY ON THE ISLANDS OF SOUTH CAROLINA, 1863.

BY CHARLOTTE L. FORTEN.

A FEW days before Christmas we were delighted at receiving a beautiful Christmas Hymn from John G. Whittier, written especially for our children. They learned it very easily, and enjoyed singing it. We showed them the writer's picture, and told them he was a very good friend of theirs, who felt the deepest interest in them, and had written this Hymn expressly for them to sing. This made them very proud and happy.

Early Christmas morning we were wakened by the people knocking at the doors and windows, and shouting "Merry Christmas!" After distributing some little presents among them, we went to the church, which had been decorated with holly, pine, cassena, mistletoe, and the

hanging moss, and had a very Christmas-like look. The
children of our school assembled there, and we gave them
the nice comfortable clothing and the picture-books which
had been kindly sent by some Philadelphia ladies. There
were at least a hundred and fifty children present. It
was very pleasant to see their happy, expectant little
faces. To them it was a wonderful Christmas-day, such
as they had never dreamed of before. There was cheerful sunshine without, lighting up the beautiful moss dra-
pery of the oaks, and looking in joyously through the
open windows; and there were bright faces and glad
hearts within.

After the distribution of the gifts, the children were
addressed by some of the gentlemen present. Then they
sang the following Hymn, which their good friend Whittier had written for them : —

> "O, none in all the world before
>   Were ever so glad as we !
> We 're free on Carolina's shore,
>   We 're all at home and free.

> " Thou Friend and Helper of the poor,
>   Who suffered for our sake,
> To open every prison-door,
>   And every yoke to break, —

> " Bend low thy pitying face and mild,
>   And help us sing and pray;
> The hand that blest the little child
>   Upon our foreheads lay.

> " We hear no more the driver's horn,
>   No more the whip we fear;
> This holy day that saw thee born
>   Was never half so dear.

> " The very oaks are greener clad,
>   The waters brighter smile;

O, never shone a day so glad
  On sweet St. Helen's Isle.

"We praise Thee in our songs to-day,
  To Thee in prayer we call;
Make swift the feet and straight the way
  Of freedom unto all.

"Come once again, O blessed Lord!
  Come walking on the sea!
And let the mainlands hear the word
  That sets the islands free!"

Then they sang John Brown's Hallelujah Song, and several of their own hymns.

Christmas night, the children came in and had several grand shouts. They were too happy to keep still. One of them, a cunning, kittenish little creature, named Amaretta, only six years old, has a remarkably sweet voice. "O Miss," said she, "all I want to do is to sing and shout!" And sing and shout she did, to her heart's content. She reads nicely, and is very fond of books. Many of the children already know their letters. The parents are eager to have them learn. They sometimes say to me: "Do, Miss, let de children learn eberyting dey can. *We* neber hab no chance to learn nuttin'; but we wants de chillen to learn." They are willing to make many sacrifices that their children may attend school. One old woman, who had a large family of children and grandchildren, came regularly to school in the winter, and took her seat among the little ones. Another woman, who had one of the best faces I ever saw, came daily, and brought her baby in her arms. It happened to be one of the best babies in the world, and allowed its mother to pursue her studies without interruption.

New-Year's Day, Emancipation Day, was a glorious

one to us. General Saxton and Colonel Higginson had invited us to visit the camp of the First Regiment of South Carolina Volunteers on that day, "the greatest day in the nation's history." We enjoyed perfectly the exciting scene on board the steamboat Flora. There was an eager, wondering crowd of the freed people, in their holiday attire, with the gayest of headkerchiefs, the whitest of aprons, and the happiest of faces. The band was playing, the flags were streaming, and everybody was talking merrily and feeling happy. The sun shone brightly, and the very waves seemed to partake of the universal gayety, for they danced and sparkled more joyously than ever before. Long before we reached Camp Saxton, we could see the beautiful grove and the ruins of the old fort near it. Some companies of the First Regiment were drawn up in line under the trees near the landing, ready to receive us. They were a fine, soldierly looking set of men, and their brilliant dress made a splendid appearance among the trees. It was my good fortune to find an old friend among the officers. He took us over the camp and showed us all the arrangements. Everything looked clean and comfortable; much neater, we were told, than in most of the white camps. An officer told us that he had never seen a regiment in which the men were so honest. "In many other camps," said he, "the Colonel and the rest of us would find it necessary to place a guard before our tents. We never do it here. Our tents are left entirely unguarded, but nothing has ever been touched." We were glad to know that. It is a remarkable fact, when we consider that the men of this regiment have all their lives been slaves; for we all know that Slavery does not tend to make men honest.

The ceremony in honor of Emancipation took place in

the beautiful grove of live-oaks adjoining the camp. I
wish it were possible to describe fitly the scene which
met our eyes, as we sat upon the stand, and looked down
on the crowd before us. There were the black soldiers
in their blue coats and scarlet pantaloons; the officers of
the First Regiment, and of other regiments, in their handsome uniforms; and there were crowds of lookers-on, men,
women, and children, of every complexion, grouped in
various attitudes, under the moss-hung trees. The faces
of all wore a happy, interested look. The exercises com-
menced with a prayer by the chaplain of the regiment.
An ode, written for the occasion, was then read and sung.
President Lincoln's Proclamation of Emancipation was
then read, and enthusiastically cheered. The Rev. Mr.
French presented Colonel Higginson with two very elegant flags, a gift to the First Regiment, from the Church
of the Puritans, in New York. He accompanied them
by an appropriate and enthusiastic speech. As Colonel
Higginson took the flags, before he had time to reply to
the speech, some of the colored people, of their own accord, began to sing, —

> "My country, 't is of thee,
> Sweet land of liberty,
> Of thee we sing!"

It was a touching and beautiful incident, and sent a thrill
through all our hearts. The Colonel was deeply moved
by it. He said that reply was far more effective than
any speech he could make. But he did make one of
those stirring speeches which are "half battles." All
hearts swelled with emotion as we listened to his glorious
words, "stirring the soul like the sound of a trumpet."
His soldiers are warmly attached to him, and he evidently
feels toward them all as if they were his children.

General Saxton spoke also, and was received with great enthusiasm. Throughout the morning, repeated cheers were given for him by the regiment, and joined in heartily by all the people. They know him to be one of the best and noblest men in the world. His unfailing kindness and consideration for them, so different from the treatment they have sometimes received at the hands of United States officers, have caused them to have unbounded confidence in him.

At the close of Colonel Higginson's speech, he presented the flags to the color-bearers, Sergeant Rivers and Sergeant Sutton, with an earnest charge, to which they made appropriate replies.

Mrs. Gage uttered some earnest words, and then the regiment sang John Brown's Hallelujah Song.

After the meeting was over, we saw the dress-parade, which was a brilliant and beautiful sight. An officer told us that the men went through the drill remarkably well, and learned the movements with wonderful ease and rapidity. To us it seemed strange as a miracle to see this regiment of blacks, the first mustered into the service of the United States, thus doing itself honor in the sight of officers of other regiments, many of whom doubtless came to scoff. The men afterward had a great feast; ten oxen having been roasted whole, for their especial benefit.

In the evening there was the softest, loveliest moonlight. We were very unwilling to go home; for, besides the attractive society, we knew that the soldiers were to have grand shouts and a general jubilee that night. But the steamboat was coming, and we were obliged to bid a reluctant farewell to Camp Saxton and the hospitable dwellers therein. We walked the deck of the steamer singing patriotic songs, and we agreed that moonlight and

water had never looked so beautiful as they did that
night. At Beaufort we took the row-boat for St. Helena.
The boatmen as they rowed sang some of their sweetest,
wildest hymns. It was a fitting close to such a day.
Our hearts were filled with an exceeding great gladness;
for although the government had left much undone, we
knew that Freedom was surely born in our land that day.
It seemed too glorious a good to realize, this beginning
of the great work we had so longed for and prayed for.
It was a sight never to be forgotten, that crowd of happy
black faces from which the shadow of Slavery had forever passed. "Forever free! forever free!" — those
magical words in the President's Proclamation were constantly singing themselves in my soul.

SONG OF THE NEGRO BOATMEN AT PORT ROYAL, S. C.

BY JOHN G. WHITTIER.

O PRAISE and tanks! De Lord he come
    To set de people free;
An' massa tink it day ob doom,
    An' we ob jubilee.
De Lord dat heap de Red Sea waves,
    He jus' as 'trong as den;
He say de word: we las' night slaves;
    To-day, de Lord's free men.
        De yam will grow, de cotton blow,
          We 'll hab de rice an' corn:
        O nebber you fear, if nebber you hear
          De driver blow his horn!

Q

Ole massa on he trabbels gone ;
  He leaf de land behind :
De Lord's breff blow him furder on,
  Like corn-shuck in de wind.
We own de hoe, we own de plough,
  We own de hands dat hold ;
We sell de pig, we sell de cow,
  But nebber chile be sold.

We pray de Lord : he gib us signs
  Dat some day we be free ;
De Norf-wind tell it to de pines,
  De wild-duck to de sea ;
We tink it when de church-bell ring,
  We dream it in de dream ;
De rice-bird mean it when he sing,
  De eagle when he scream.

We know de promise nebber fail,
  An' nebber lie de Word ;
So, like de 'postles in de jail,
  We waited for de Lord :
An' now he open ebery door,
  An' trow away de key ;
He tink we lub him so before,
  We lub him better free.
      De yam will grow, de cotton blow,
        He 'll gib de rice an' corn :
      O nebber you fear, if nebber you hear
        De driver blow his horn !

EXTRACT FROM SPEECH BY HON. HENRY
WILSON TO THE COLORED PEOPLE IN
CHARLESTON, S. C., APRIL, 1865.

" FOR twenty-nine years, in private life and in public life, at all times and on all occasions, I have
spoken and voted against Slavery, and in favor of the
freedom of every man that breathes God's air or walks
His earth.   And to-day, standing here in South Carolina,
I feel that the slave-power we have fought so long is
under my heel; and that the men and women held in
bondage so long are free forevermore.

"Understanding this to be your position,—that you are
forever free,—remember, O remember, the sacrifices that
have been made for your freedom, and be worthy of the
blessing that has come to you!   I know you will be.
[Cheers.]   Through these four years of bloody war, you
have always been loyal to the old flag of the country.
You have never betrayed the Union soldiers who were
fighting the battles of the country.   You have guided
them, you have protected them, you have cheered them.
You have proved yourselves worthy the great situation
in which you were placed by the Slaveholders' Rebellion.
Four years ago you saw the flag of your country struck
down from Fort Sumter; yesterday you saw the old flag go
up again.   Its stars now beam with a brighter lustre.   You
know now what the old flag means,—that it means liberty to every man and woman in the country.   [Cheers.]

" You have been patient, you have endured, you have
trusted in God and your country; and the God of our

fathers has blessed our country, and He has blessed you. The long, dreary, chilly night of Slavery has passed away forevermore, and the sun of Liberty casts its broad beams upon you to-day.

"But your duties commence with your liberties. Remember that you are to be obedient, faithful, true, and loyal to the country forevermore. [Cheers, and cries of 'Yes!' 'Yes!' 'Yes!'] Remember that you are to educate your children; that you are to improve their condition; that you are to make a brighter future for *them* than the past has been to *you*. Remember that you are to be industrious. Freedom does not mean that you are not to work. It means that when you do work you shall have pay for it, to carry home to your wives and the children of your love. Liberty means the liberty to work for yourselves, to have the fruits of your labor, to better your own condition, and improve the condition of your children. I want every man and woman to understand that every neglect of duty, every failure to be industrious, to be economical, to support yourselves, to take care of your families, to secure the education of your children, will be put in the faces of your friends as a reproach. Your old masters will point you out and say to us, 'We told you so.' For more than thirty years we have said that you were fit for liberty. We have maintained it amid obloquy and reproach. For maintaining this doctrine in the halls of Congress our names have been made a by-word. The great lesson for you in the future is to prove that we were right; to prove that you were worthy of liberty. We simply ask you, in the name of your friends, in the name of our country, to show by your good conduct, and by efforts to improve your condition, that you were worthy of freedom; to prove to all the world, even to your old

masters and mistresses, that it was a sin against God to
hold you in Slavery, and that you are worthy to have
your names enrolled among the freemen of the United
States of America. [Great cheering.]

"We want you to respect yourselves; to walk erect,
with the consciousness that you are free men. Be humane and kind to each other, always serving each other
when you can. Be courteous and gentlemanly to everybody on earth, black and white, but cringe to nobody.

"You have helped us to fight our battles; you have
stood by the old flag; you have given us your prayers;
and you have had the desire of your hearts fulfilled. The
cause of freedom has triumphed; and in our triumph we
want all to stand up and rejoice together."

EXTRACT FROM A SPEECH BY HON. JUDGE
KELLY TO THE COLORED PEOPLE IN
CHARLESTON, S. C., APRIL, 1865.

"I WILL not, my colored friends, talk to you of the
past. You understand that all too well. I turn to
the hopeful future; not to flatter you for the deeds you
have done during the last four years, but to remind you
that, though you no longer have earthly masters, there is
a Ruler in heaven whom you are bound to obey, — that
Great Being who strengthened and guided your eminent
friend William Lloyd Garrison, who trained Abraham
Lincoln for his great work, in honest poverty and simple-
mindedness; that good God whose stars shine the same
over the slaves' huts and the masters' palaces. His laws

you must obey. You must worship Him not only at the altar, but in every act of your daily life. It will not be enough to observe the Sabbath, to go to Him with your sorrows, and remember Him in your joys. You must remember that He has said to man, 'In the sweat of thy brow shalt thou eat thy bread.' Labor is the law of all. Your friends in the North appeal to you to help them in the great work they undertook to do for you. We want you to work *with* us. We want you to do it by working here in South Carolina, earning wages, taking care of your money, and making profit out of that money. Work on the plantation, if that is all you can do. If you can work in the workshop, do it, and work well. He who does a day's work not so well as he might have done it, cheats himself. Strive that your work on Monday shall be better done than it was on Saturday; and when Saturday comes round again, you will be able to do a still more skilful day's work. We at the North sometimes learn three or four trades. If any one of you feels sure that he can do better for himself and his family by changing his pursuit, he had better change it."

"I like to look at the women assembled here. Remember, my friends, that you are to be mothers and wives in the homes of free men. You must try to make those homes respectable and happy. You are to be the mothers of American citizens. You must give them the best education you can. You must strive to make them intelligent, educated, moral, patriotic, and religious men. Many of you cannot read, but you are not too old yet to learn. A mother who knows how to read can half educate her own child by helping him with his lessons; and the mother who has but little learning will get a great deal more by trying to hear the child's lessons; and so it is with the father.

"You need no longer live in slave huts, now that you are to have your own earnings. I charge you, men, to make your homes comfortable, and you, women, to make them happy. Work industriously. Be faithful to each other; be true and honest with all men. If you respect yourselves, others will respect you. There are Northerners who are prejudiced against you; but you can find the way to their hearts and consciences through their pockets. When they find that there are colored tradesmen who have money to spend, and colored farmers who want to buy goods of them, they will no longer call you Jack and Joe; they will begin to think that you are Mr. John Black and Mr. Joseph Brown." [Great laughter.]

BLACK TOM.

BY A YANKEE SOLDIER.

HUNTED by his Rebel master
    Over many a hill and glade,
Black Tom, with his wife and children,
    Found his way to our brigade.

Tom had sense and truth and courage;
    Often tried where danger rose:
Once our flag his strong arm rescued
    From the grasp of Rebel foes.

One day, Tom was marching with us
    Through the forest as our guide,
When a ball from traitor's rifle
    Broke his arm and pierced his side.

On a litter white men bore him
　　Through the forest drear and damp,
Laid him, dying, where our banners
　　Brightly fluttered o'er our camp.

Pointing to his wife and children,
　　While he suffered racking pain,
Said he to our soldiers round him,
　　" Don't let *them* be slaves again ! "

" No, by Heaven ! " spoke out a soldier, —
　　And *that* oath was not profane, —
" Our brigade will still protect them ;
　　They shall ne'er be slaves again."

Over old Tom's dusky features
　　Came and stayed a joyous ray ;
And with saddened friends around him,
　　His free spirit passed away.

————

At Rodman's Point, in North Carolina, the United States troops were obliged to retreat before Rebels, who outnumbered them ten to one. The scow in which they attempted to escape stuck in the mud, and could not be moved with poles. While the soldiers were lying down they were in some measure protected from Rebel bullets; but whoever jumped into the water to push the boat off would certainly be killed. A vigorous black man who was with them said: " Lie still. I will push off the boat. If they kill me, it is nothing ; but you are soldiers, and are needed to fight for the country." He leaped overboard, pushed off the boat, and sprang back, pierced by seven bullets. He died two days after.

I wish I knew his name ; for it deserves to be recorded with the noblest heroes the world has known.

LETTER FROM A FREEDMAN TO HIS OLD MASTER.

[Written just as he dictated it.]

DAYTON, OHIO, August 7, 1865.

To my old Master, COLONEL P. H. ANDERSON, *Big Spring, Tennessee.*

SIR: I got your letter, and was glad to find that you had not forgotten Jourdon, and that you wanted me to come back and live with you again, promising to do better for me than anybody else can. I have often felt uneasy about you. I thought the Yankees would have hung you long before this, for harboring Rebs they found at your house. I suppose they never heard about your going to Colonel Martin's to kill the Union soldier that was left by his company in their stable. Although you shot at me twice before I left you, I did not want to hear of your being hurt, and am glad you are still living. It would do me good to go back to the dear old home again, and see Miss Mary and Miss Martha and Allen, Esther, Green, and Lee. Give my love to them all, and tell them I hope we will meet in the better world, if not in this. I would have gone back to see you all when I was working in the Nashville Hospital, but one of the neighbors told me that Henry intended to shoot me if he ever got a chance.

I want to know particularly what the good chance is you propose to give me. I am doing tolerably well here. I get twenty-five dollars a month, with victuals and clothing; have a comfortable home for Mandy, —

12

the folks call her Mrs. Anderson, — and the children —
Milly, Jane, and Grundy — go to school and are learning well. The teacher says Grundy has a head for a
preacher. They go to Sunday school, and Mandy and
me attend church regularly. We are kindly treated.
Sometimes we overhear others saying, "Them colored
people were slaves" down in Tennessee.. The children
feel hurt when they hear such remarks; but I tell them
it was no disgrace in Tennessee to belong to Colonel Anderson. Many darkeys would have been proud, as I
used to be, to call you master. Now if you will write
and say what wages you will give me, I will be better
able to decide whether it would be to my advantage to
move back again.

As to my freedom, which you say I can have, there is
nothing to be gained on that score, as I got my free papers
in 1864 from the Provost-Marshal-General of the Department of Nashville. Mandy says she would be afraid
to go back without some proof that you were disposed
to treat us justly and kindly; and we have concluded to
test your sincerity by asking you to send us our wages
for the time we served you. This will make us forget
and forgive old scores, and rely on your justice and friendship in the future. I served you faithfully for thirty-two
years, and Mandy twenty years. At twenty-five dollars
a month for me, and two dollars a week for Mandy, our
earnings would amount to eleven thousand six hundred
and eighty dollars. Add to this the interest for the time
our wages have been kept back, and deduct what you
paid for our clothing, and three doctor's visits to me, and
pulling a tooth for Mandy, and the balance will show
what we are in justice entitled to. Please send the
money by Adams's Express, in care of V. Winters, Esq.,

Dayton, Ohio. If you fail to pay us for faithful labors in the past, we can have little faith in your promises in the future. We trust the good Maker has opened your eyes to the wrongs which you and your fathers have done to me and my fathers, in making us toil for you for generations without recompense. Here I draw my wages every Saturday night; but in Tennessee there was never any pay-day for the negroes any more than for the horses and cows. Surely there will be a day of reckoning for those who defraud the laborer of his hire.

In answering this letter, please state if there would be any safety for my Milly and Jane, who are now grown up, and both good-looking girls. You know how it was with poor Matilda and Catherine. I would rather stay here and starve — and die, if it come to that — than have my girls brought to shame by the violence and wickedness of their young masters. You will also please state if there has been any schools opened for the colored children in your neighborhood. The great desire of my life now is to give my children an education, and have them form virtuous habits.

Say howdy to George Carter, and thank him for taking the pistol from you when you were shooting at me.

From your old servant,

JOURDON ANDERSON.

SERGEANT W. H. CARNEY, of New Bedford, Massachusetts, was very severely wounded when the famous Fifty-Fourth Regiment attacked Fort Wagner; but he resolutely held up the Stars and Stripes, as he dragged his wounded limb along, amid a shower of bullets; and when he reached his comrades he exclaimed exultingly, "The dear old flag has never touched the ground, boys!"

COLONEL ROBERT G. SHAW.

BY ELIZA B. SEDGWICK.

[In the summer of 1863 an attack was made on Fort Wagner, in South Carolina, by the 54th Massachusetts Regiment, composed of colored troops. Their leader, COLONEL SHAW, belonging to one of the best white families in Boston, was killed. When his friends asked for his body, the reply of the Rebels was, " He is buried with his niggers."]

BURIED with a band of brothers,
　Who for him would fain have died;
Buried with the gallant fellows
Who fell fighting by his side.

Buried with the men God gave him, —
Those whom he was sent to save;
Buried with the martyred heroes,
He has found an honored grave.

Buried where his dust so precious
Makes the soil a hallowed spot;
Buried where by Christian patriot
He shall never be forgot.

Buried in the ground accursed,
Which man's fettered feet have trod;
Buried where his voice still speaketh,
Appealing for the slave to God.

Fare thee well, thou noble warrior!
Who in youthful beauty went
On a high and holy mission,
By the God of battles sent.

Chosen of Him, "elect and precious,"
Well didst thou fulfil thy part ;
When thy country "counts her jewels,"
She shall wear thee on her heart.

ADVICE FROM AN OLD FRIEND.

BY L. MARIA CHILD.

FOR many years I have felt great sympathy for you, my brethren and sisters, and I have tried to do what I could to help you to freedom. And now that you have at last received the long-desired blessing, I most earnestly wish that you should make the best possible use of it. I have made this book to encourage you to exertion by examples of what colored people are capable of doing. Such men and women as Toussaint l'Ouverture, Benjamin Banneker, Phillis Wheatley, Frederick Douglass, and William and Ellen Crafts, prove that the power of *character* can overcome all external disadvantages, even that most crushing of all disadvantages, Slavery. Perhaps few of you will be able to stir the hearts of large assemblies by such eloquent appeals as those of Frederick Douglass, or be able to describe what you have seen and heard so gracefully as Charlotte L. Forten does. Probably none of you will be called to govern a state as Toussaint l'Ouverture did ; for such a remarkable career as his does not happen once in hundreds of years. But the Bible says, "He that ruleth his own spirit is greater than he that ruleth a kingdom"; and such a ruler every man and woman can become, by the help and blessing of God.

It is not the *greatness* of the thing a man does which makes him worthy of respect; it is the doing *well* whatsoever he hath to do. In many respects, your opportunities for usefulness are more limited than those of others; but you have one great opportunity peculiar to yourselves. You can do a vast amount of good to people in various parts of the world, and through successive generations, by simply being sober, industrious, and honest. There are still many slaves in Brazil and in the Spanish possessions. If you are vicious, lazy, and careless, their masters will excuse themselves for continuing to hold them in bondage, by saying: "Look at the freedmen of the United States! What idle vagabonds they are! How dirty their cabins are! How slovenly their dress! That proves that negroes cannot take care of themselves, that they are not fit to be free." But if your houses look neat, and your clothes are clean and whole, and your gardens well weeded, and your work faithfully done, whether for yourselves or others, then all the world will cry out, "You see that negroes *can* take care of themselves; and it is a sin and a shame to keep such men in Slavery." Thus, while you are serving your own interests, you will be helping on the emancipation of poor weary slaves in other parts of the world. It is a great privilege to have a chance to do extensive good by such simple means, and your Heavenly Father will hold you responsible for the use you make of your influence.

Your manners will have a great effect in producing an impression to your advantage or disadvantage. Be always respectful and polite toward your associates, and toward those who have been in the habit of considering you an inferior race. It is one of the best ways to prove that you are not inferior. Never allow yourselves to say or do anything in the presence of women of your own color which it would be improper for you to say or do in the presence of the most refined white ladies. Such a course will be an education for them as well as for yourselves. When you appoint committees about your schools and other public affairs, it would be wise to have both men and women on the committees. The habit of thinking and talking about serious and important matters makes women more sensible and discreet. Such consultations together are in fact a practical school both for you and them; and the more modest and intelligent women are, the better will children be brought up.

Personal appearance is another important thing. It is not necessary to be rich in order to dress in a becoming manner. A pretty dress for festival occasions will last a long while, if well taken care of; and a few wild-flowers, or bright berries, will ornament young girls more tastefully than jewels. Working-clothes that are clean and nicely patched always look respectable; and they make a very favorable impression, because they indicate that the wearer is neat and economical. And here let me say, that it is a very great saving to mend garments well, and before the rents get large. We thrifty Yankees have a saying that "a stitch in time saves nine"; and you will find by experience that neglected mending will require more than nine stitches instead of one, and will not look so well when it is done.

The appearance of your villages will do much to produce a favorable opinion concerning your characters and capabilities. Whitewash is not expensive; and it takes but little time to transplant a cherokee rose, a jessamine, or other wild shrubs and vines, that make the poorest cabin look beautiful; and, once planted, they will be growing while you are working or sleeping. It is a public benefit to remove everything dirty or unsightly, and to surround homes with verdure and flowers; for a succession of pretty cottages makes the whole road pleasant, and cheers all passers by; while they are at the same time an advertisement, easily read by all men, that the people who live there are not lazy, slovenly, or vulgar. The rich pay a great deal of money for pictures to ornament their walls, but a whitewashed cabin, with flowering-shrubs and vines clustering round it, is a pretty picture freely exhibited to all men. It is a public benefaction.

But even if you are as yet too poor to have a house and garden of your own, it is still in your power to be a credit and an example to your race: by working for others as faithfully as you would work for yourself; by taking as good care of their tools as you would if they were your own; by always keeping your promises, however inconvenient it may be; by being strictly honest in all your dealings; by being temperate in your habits, and never speaking a profane or indecent word, — by pursuing such a course you will be consoled with an inward consciousness of doing right in the sight of God, and be a public benefactor by your example, while at the same time you will secure respect and prosperity for yourself by establishing a good character. A man whose conduct inspires confidence is in a fair way to have house and land of his own, even if he starts in the world without a single cent.

Be careful of your earnings, and as saving in your expenses as is consistent with health and comfort; but never allow yourselves to be stingy. Avarice is a mean vice, which eats all the heart out of a man. Money is a good thing, and you ought to want to earn it, as a means of improving the condition of yourselves and families. But it will do good to your character, and increase your happiness, if you impart a portion of your earnings to others who are in need. Help as much as you conveniently can in building churches and school-houses for the good of all, and in providing for the sick and the aged. If your former masters and mistresses are in trouble, show them every kindness in your power, whether they have treated you kindly or not. Remember the words of the blessed Jesus: "Do good to them that hate you, and pray for them which despitefully use you and persecute you."

There is one subject on which I wish to guard you against disappointment. Do not be discouraged if freedom brings you more cares and fewer advantages than you expected. Such a great change as it is from Slavery to Freedom cannot be completed all at once. By being brought up as slaves, you have formed some bad habits, which it will take time to correct. Those who were formerly your masters have acquired still worse habits by being brought up as slaveholders; and they cannot be expected to change all at once. Both of you will gradually improve under the teaching of new circumstances. For a good while it will provoke many of them to see those who were once their slaves acting like freemen. They will doubtless do many things to vex and discourage you, just as the slaveholders in Jamaica did after emancipation there. They seemed to want to drive their emancipated bondmen to insurrection, that they might have a pretext for saying: "You see what a bad effect freedom has on negroes! We told you it would be so!" But the colored people of Jamaica behaved better than their former masters wished them to do. They left

12 *   R

the plantations where they were badly treated, or poorly paid, but they worked diligently elsewhere. Their women and children raised vegetables and fowls and carried them to market; and, by their united industry and economy, they soon had comfortable little homes of their own.

I think it would generally be well for you to work for your former masters, if they treat you well, and pay you as much as you could earn elsewhere. But if they show a disposition to oppress you, quit their service, and work for somebody who will treat you like freemen. If they use violent language to you, never use impudent language to them. If they cheat you, scorn to cheat them in return. If they break their promises, never break yours. If they propose to women such connections as used to be common under the bad system of Slavery, teach them that freedwomen not only have the legal power to protect themselves from such degradation, but also that they have pride of character. If in fits of passion, they abuse your children as they formerly did, never revenge it by any injury to them or their property. It is an immense advantage to any man always to keep the right on his side. If you pursue this course you will always be superior, however rich or elegant may be the man or woman who wrongs you.

I do not mean by this that you ought to submit tamely to insult or oppression. Stand up for your rights, but do it in a manly way. Quit working for a man who speaks to you contemptuously, or who tries to take a mean advantage of you, when you are doing your duty faithfully by him. If it becomes necessary, apply to magistrates to protect you and redress your wrongs. If you are so unlucky as to live where the men in authority, whether civil or military, are still disposed to treat the colored people as slaves, let the most intelligent among you draw up a statement of your grievances and send it to some of your firm friends in Congress, such as the Hon. Charles Sumner, the Hon. Henry Wilson, and the Hon. George W. Julian.

A good government seeks to make laws that will equally protect and restrain all men. Heretofore you had no reason to respect the laws of this country, because they punished you for crime, in many cases more severely than white men were punished, while they did nothing to protect your rights. But now that good President Lincoln has made you free, you will be legally protected in your rights and restrained from doing wrong, just as other men are protected and restrained. It is one of the noblest privileges of freemen to be able to respect the law, and to rely upon it always for redress of grievances, instead of revenging one wrong by another wrong.

You will have much to put up with before the new order of things can become settled on a permanent foundation. I am grieved to read in the newspapers how wickedly you are still treated in some places; but I am not surprised, for I knew that Slavery was a powerful snake, that would try to do mischief with its tail after its head was crushed. But, whatever wrongs you may endure, comfort yourselves with two reflections: first, that there is the beginning of a better state of things, from which your children will derive much more benefit than you can; secondly, that a great majority of the American people are sincerely determined that you shall be protected in your rights as freemen. Year by year your condition will improve. Year by year, if you respect yourselves, you will be more and more respected by white

men. Wonderful changes have taken place in your favor
during the last thirty years, and the changes are still
going on. The Abolitionists did a great deal for you, by
their continual writing and preaching against Slavery.
Then this war enabled thousands of people to see for
themselves what a bad institution Slavery was; and the
uniform kindness with which you treated the Yankee soldiers raised you up multitudes of friends. There are
still many pro-slavery people in the Northern States,
who, from aristocratic pride or low vulgarity, still call
colored people "niggers," and treat them as such. But
the good leaven is now fairly worked into public sentiment, and these people, let them do what they will, cannot get it out.

The providence of God has opened for you an upward
path. Walk ye in it, without being discouraged by the
brambles and stones at the outset. Those who come
after you will clear them away, and will place in their
stead strong, smooth rails for the steam-car called Progress of the Colored Race.

DAY OF JUBILEE.

BY A. G. DUNCAN.

ROLL on, thou joyful day,
  When tyranny's proud sway,
    Stern as the grave,
Shall to the ground be hurled,
And Freedom's flag unfurled
Shall wave throughout the world,
    O'er every slave!

Trump of glad jubilee,
Echo o'er land and sea,
    Freedom for all!
Let the glad tidings fly,
And every tribe reply,
Glory to God on high,
    At Slavery's fall!

THE END.

Cambridge : Stereotyped and Printed by Welch, Bigelow, & Co.